MW01612777

Reimagining Rural

Studies in Urban–Rural Dynamics

Series Editors: Gregory M. Fulkerson and Alexander R. Thomas, SUNY Oneonta

This series focuses attention on understanding theoretically and historically the development and maintenance of Urban–Rural Systems through a spatial, demographic, and ecological perspective. It seeks a blending or reintegration of the urban, rural, and environmental research literatures under a comprehensive theoretical paradigm. As such, we further specify Urban–Rural Dynamics as analysis of human population distribution on social variables, including politics, economics, and culture.

Titles in the Series

Reimagining Rural: Urbanormative Portrayals of Rural Life, edited by Gregory M. Fulkerson and Alexander R. Thomas

Reimagining Rural

Urbanormative Portrayals of Rural Life

Edited by Gregory M. Fulkerson
and Alexander R. Thomas

LEXINGTON BOOKS
Lanham • Boulder • New York • London

Published by Lexington Books
An imprint of The Rowman & Littlefield Publishing Group, Inc.
4501 Forbes Boulevard, Suite 200, Lanham, Maryland 20706
www.rowman.com

Unit A, Whitacre Mews, 26-34 Stannary Street, London SE11 4AB

British Library Cataloguing in Publication Information Available

Library of Congress Cataloging-in-Publication Data

Names: Fulkerson, Gregory M., editor. | Thomas, Alexander R., 1969- editor.
Title: Reimagining rural : urbanormative portrayals of rural life / edited by
    Gregory M. Fulkerson and Alexander R. Thomas.
Description: Lanham : Lexington Books, 2016. | Series: Studies in urban-rural
    dynamics | Includes bibliographical references and index.
Identifiers: LCCN 2016013105 (print) | LCCN 2016021939 (ebook) | ISBN
    9781498534062 (cloth : alk. paper) | ISBN 9781498534079 (Electronic)
Subjects: LCSH: City and town life--United States. | Popular culture--United
    States. | Sociology, Rural.
Classification: LCC HT123 .R435 2016 (print) | LCC HT123 (ebook) | DDC
    307.760973--dc23
LC record available at https://lccn.loc.gov/2016013105

∞™ The paper used in this publication meets the minimum requirements of American National Standard for Information Sciences Permanence of Paper for Printed Library Materials, ANSI/NISO Z39.48-1992.

Printed in the United States of America

Contents

Contents

Chapter One

Introduction

The Need to Reimagine Rural

Gregory M. Fulkerson and Alexander R. Thomas

When people think about rural life they tend to envision a range of images from romantic pastoral and agricultural landscapes to the degraded aftermath of a mountaintop removal, the hilarity of backward rural characters on situational comedies, or the grotesque images projected by rural horror films of crazed murders and inbred monsters. The cultural meaning and imagination of rural has become multifaceted and often contradictory. What most of these images have in common is a tendency toward a fictional reality that either no longer exists or else never really existed in the first place. As with most stereotypes, overgeneralized images find a basis in some circumscribed and bounded corner of reality, but the initial limited application becomes transformed with broad brushstrokes into absurd characterizations of entire categories of people. As more and more people are born into an increasingly urbanized world, the direct experiential understanding of rural realities grows scarce. In place of direct encounters, individuals come to rely more heavily upon secondary artifacts of culture to inform their ideas—particularly those supplied by various forms of media, including film, television, music, and literature, as well as by non-fictional sources such as the news media that may inadvertently reinforce stereotypes. Thus informed the urban public grows vulnerable to passive acceptance of overgeneralized ideas that deny the uniqueness, variety, and diversity of rural places and people.

The cultural derogation of rural life is in need of social scientific scrutiny. Just as social scientists have sought to debunk misinformed ideas surrounding gender, sexuality, and race, not to mention issues of social and economic class, so too must they debunk place and space-based stereotypes. This is especially critical as the dominant group of urbanites continues to enjoy

1

spatial privileges and centrality in the world, while rural residents experience the hardships of a weakening rural economy and advanced social and cultural marginalization. The urban cultural response to rural life is not always negative, nor does it always render the rural as irrelevant or unimportant. If rural was unimportant it would be hard to imagine why so many forms of media exist within the rural/country genre. In fact, for many years, this genre commanded television programming during prime time hours, and though it is less central, it continues to be a source of great interest and entertainment on numerous contemporary cable television programs. The cultural treatments are also not entirely negative and derogatory, and range from the educational to the sensational and ridiculous (think Honey Boo Boo). Diving into these various types of media treatments of rural is a valuable activity in the overall process of debunking. That is one of the central goals of this book. At the same time, many treatments of rural do portray the image of inferior, irrelevant, or obsolete communities and ways of life, and this requires the most immediate attention.

THE ESSENTIAL RURAL

There is a tendency to succumb to essentialist thinking when it comes to identifying rural identity, people, or places. The same error has been committed regarding gender, whereby sex was equated with gender; femininity was tied to the state of being woman and masculinity with being male. With regard to rurality, the corollary is to equate living in a census defined rural place and being a rural or "rustic" person, or alternatively, living in an urban space being an urban or "urbane" person (Ching and Creed, 1996). The problem with essentialist thinking is that it downplays the extent to which our concepts are socially constructed. Masculinity and femininity, urbanity and rusticity, are concepts that vary across space and time, whose meaning is constructed by actors and reinforced through narratives. Yet, there are also elements that seem to transcend time and space and have the appearance of being essential to these constructs. This means that we must try to consider what rural means from alternative perspectives.

Defining rural is no easy task, and this may explain why most people in administrative positions prefer to define it by what it is *not* rather than by what it *is*. More specifically the designation of rural is often treated as the residual space that cannot be defined as urban. The US Census, for example, defines very carefully the meaning of urban, designating places as either urban areas or urban clusters based on their level of population density and proximity to other population centers. The Office of Management and Budget refers to places as metropolitan, and while it used to also define places as non-metropolitan—often taken as a proxy for rural—it has recently done away with this terminology by inventing the terms micropolitan and non-core areas. One could easily point out that this pattern of reifying urban and residualizing or erasing rural areas is highly value-laden and that spatial classifications could just as easily adopt the opposite approach of defining urban as the residual of rural. This kind of value bias is part of what we have come to understand as a wider and more pervasive cultural pattern that we refer to as urbanormativity, or the view that urban life is normal and superior, while rural life is aberrant and inferior. Administrative definitions of rural are universally essentialist as they do not involve asking people if they think they personally are rural, instead forcing upon them a classification based on the location of their mailbox.

It is not entirely up to those who hold administrative posts to decide whether or not rural is a label that can be attached to a particular place or person. Everyday people—workers, citizens, and consumers—also hold the power to decide when and how to apply the term rural or urban to a particular place or person. As a matter of personal identity one may identify as a rural or urban person, rustic or urbane, and nobody truly has the power to intervene and object to such self-identification. Issues of authenticity may arise when considering who "deserves" the label of being rural. Is someone who recently migrated to a rural community because they hold an accounting job that they can conduct entirely through the Internet as rural as his or her neighbor who lives on a five generation family farm? Is a coal miner who moves to an elite urban neighborhood as urban as his neighbor that runs a large tech company traded on the stock exchange? These kinds of questions result in different types of responses that range from essentialist to constructivist. One school of thought says you must earn your stripes before you can be called rural, another says you are rural if you say you are, and another says it depends on where you call home.

Resolving the dispute between essentialists and constructivists is not the goal of this volume, and indeed if it were it would almost certainly fail. What we can learn from this is that each has a point. To some degree identity is a personal matter, as is the subjective interpretation of a particular geographic place. However, the essential is always there, rooted in the material world. A personal identification that exists detached entirely from the material may exist only in fantasy. The rural-urban continuum is in some ways similar. We have found a fruitful ground in the middle of these extreme positions by taking a critical approach that attempts to balance the cultural and constructivist with the material and essentialist ways of thinking.

URBAN DEPENDENCY AND URBANORMATIVITY

Although this volume is centrally focused on cultural aspects of the rural life, we should briefly consider more deeply our theoretical understanding of the material interrelationship existing between urban and rural places. Much of the issue in defining each is the subjective nature of the concepts: they emerge not from a dichotomous pairing that exists in nature but rather from a spatial pattern of human settlement that fulfils the requirements of an urban society. Cities are not merely big villages, they are nodes in a complex system of exchange that functions to bring together resources from a wide array of places big and small for the purpose of production. In essence, it is not in the nature of cities to be independent: they arise from the development of the network itself, and it is the development of the network that properly constitutes "urbanization." Reliant on the network of places, what we will term the *urban system*, a city in principle brings together resources from diverse places for production and/or further trade. The production that relies on the urban system is what we have termed *urban production*: production that "is characterized by the fact that the transformation is not the result of an inherently natural process but rather by the exertion of energy by the creator" (Thomas, 2010, p. 34). Urban production relies on an earlier phase of *rural production* in which the required resources are harvested from the environment. In principle, the overall population and geographical extent of a city is determined by its position in the urban system. Cities capable of controlling vast resources, through privileged access to resources or finance, are typically at the top of the urban system and have populations that accord with their relative positions. Population is driven not only through the economic activity generated from such a position but by the mere fact that so many people live locally. A feedback mechanism develops as firms located in large population centers have large markets and ample opportunities to branch out through the city. As noted by Thomas (2005, p. 10):

> Cities have grown not only because of the capitalist need for labor and their potential replacements, but because of the economies of scale produced by bringing ever larger populations into a small geographic area. The population of a large city represents a mass market for an array of goods and services within short proximity of the producer. In addition, access to credit, research, and governmental services give many urban locales a decided advantage over smaller towns that lack many of these attributes. The result is that urban producers in larger cities are able to utilize the economies of scale of their respective cities to produce a greater supply of a given product at a lower cost than possible by companies in smaller towns. The lower production costs and higher profits available to larger producers allow them to undercut the pricing of companies in smaller communities, leading to businesses in smaller towns closing or being bought by larger companies.

Lower level nodes in the urban system often function as regionally important centers for trade as finished goods are exchanged for raw materials from the hinterlands. Without the more global access to resources, products from outside the region are mediated to a degree through the institutions of the global cities, and hence regional centers are smaller both spatially and demographically. Leaving such regional centers, however, are an array of lower-level centers with similar trade functions at levels more basic to the everyday needs of the inhabitants. For example, Boston functions as the global city—a first order city to utilize the terminology in Central Place Theory—for New England. The city is home to much of the region's financial infrastructure, and so, unsurprisingly, an order of magnitude larger than the second order (regional) cities such as Springfield, Providence, and Portland. Each of the regional centers, however, functions as a trade center for their respective region, often selling goods not available in smaller settlements.

As tempting as it is to view the urban system in the manner discussed above, it also reflects an urbanormative assumption: that the countryside is dependent upon the city. In fact, from the dawn of the earliest cities the order of dependency has been the reverse: cities outgrow the carrying capacity of their own immediate hinterlands and thus must extract resources from other places in order to continue to exist; we term this *urban dependency*. The archaeological and literary records of ancient urban systems give testimony to the ramifications of urban dependency. In the Mesopotamian cities of Umma and Lagash during the third millennium BCE, there was a series of conflicts between the rulers of the two cities that required intervention from neighboring cities. Specifically, the agricultural lands between the two cities had all been developed and each city continued to grow, and hence a conflict of a collection of fields arose as the rulers of each city attempted to seize control and not risk the starvation of their respective citizens. Not surprisingly, the earliest evidence of aggressive war and conquest is found during the time period when urban populations grew so large that conquest became necessary, both in Mesopotamia (Ur, 2002) and Mesoamerica (Flannery, 2003). Ultimately, however, the use of coercive means is costly; it is far more efficient to use hegemonic power to gain resources.

It is in this context that we see *urban domination*: the exercise of power over the hinterland by the state for the benefit of urban centers. Driven as it is by objective human needs, an urban population is forced to deal with other populations through either coercive force or through hegemonic means. Coercion tends to be expensive: some form of military is necessary, and members not only must be supplied but their service takes them from other productive pursuits such as farming. Thus, hegemonic means are generally preferable: the population from whom the resources will be acquired are coaxed in some way to *want* to turn over resources. This takes the form of trade, but trade is rarely conducted between two parties with equal power. In the case of trade within the city's hinterland, a system of rural satellites produce and transit resources to the city even though they could potentially be self-sufficient; in such a case the city must provide some incentive to trade. This can be in urban-based finished goods but can also be ideological in nature. In the case of foreign trade, cities typically trade with other cities and so a system of rural extraction or production leads to those resources being transferred to urban interests, the urban interests trading finished materials with other cities, and the products of the trade being distributed back into the countryside. Undergirding this system of exchange is an ideological assumption of the superiority of urban products and culture referred to as *urbanormativity*. Urbanormativity assumes that the conditions and experiences of the city are normal and desirable, often casting the non-urban (i.e., rural) as not normal. For example, various passages of the Hebrew Bible present the temple in Jerusalem as central to religious practice prior to the arrival of the Babylonians even though archaeology has demonstrated considerable diversity of religious practice in the countryside. In the twenty-first century, in a world in which over half the population lives in cities, urban dependency and urbanormativity are important features of everyday life.

CRITICAL RURAL IDEAS AND REIMAGINING RURAL

In recent years there has developed a core of scholars dedicated to developing theoretical ideas and empirical investigations that challenge existing models—both popular and scholarly—of rural life. The work of these last few years has begun to yield a fruit of newly developed ways of understanding rural-urban linkages deserving of greater scholarly attention. It is against this backdrop that we present the current volume, *Reimagining Rural*. Before diving into what this volume will deliver, let's reflect on some of the progress that has occurred thus far.

Our first synthesis of this new scholarly territory began with *Critical Rural Theory (CRT)*, which is a volume that attempted to integrate cultural and material political economic approaches to rural-urban relations in novel ways that drew at least partly on the critical theoretical tradition that is associated with the Frankfurt School and the work of Habermas in particular (Thomas et al., 2011). We also incorporated ideas from Bourdieu and his notion of cultural capital. To some degree we made use of ideas that have a basis in the work of Giddens' notion of structuration, although we extend them to be spatialized (place structuration). The theorizations that have grown out of the study of spatial inequality (Lobao et al., 2007) have also been influential in our work. *CRT* is a volume that attempted to integrate existing theories in novel, prototypical—though admittedly not fully developed—ways of seeing rural. It was meant to provoke thought and discussion around conceptualizing the sociocultural meaning of rural, in contrast to the more conventional political economic or demographic essentialist meanings that are more commonly assigned. The field of rural sociology has not altogether neglected the cultural angle, but scholarship that has focused on rural culture—namely studies of the rural idyll or mystique—have not always taken strides to connect culture to the material world of the political economist, who has reigned supreme in contemporary rural scholarship. We are generally discontent with the odd rift that has formed—in general social science scholarship—between the culturalists and the political economists, and we have sought to at least attempt to bridge the gap. Thus, *CRT* introduced some novel ideas such as urbanormativity, rural representations, and rural simulacra as ways to discuss various cultural phenomena that become infused within the political economic fabric of rural communities. These concepts are used to make the case that rural is yet another social category that is built into a broader system of hierarchy that likewise includes material factors related to social class.

Following the publication of *Critical Rural Theory* was an impressive measure of scholarship that resulted in an edited volume, *Studies in Urbanormativity*, which sought to deepen empirical and conceptual developments that were laid out but as yet somewhat undeveloped (Fulkerson and Thomas, 2013). Out of this emerged a number of impressive studies considering a range of themes that included new approaches to community studies, social problems such as substance abuse and the environmental consequences of urbanization, new approaches to economic development and entrepreneurship, popular culture treatments of rural life found in various media (forerunners to the present volume), analyses of rural tourism, and critical rural studies of food and agriculture. Each of the contributions to that volume provided more energy and momentum toward extending what was begun in *CRT*.

This background of course leads us to the present volume, *Reimagining Rural*. Like its predecessors, this volume seeks to further develop the empirical and theoretical framework of a critical rural lens. This volume is slightly more ambitious in scope and tackles more areas of social life, such as rural education, while delving more deeply into some of the same topics that were broached in *Studies in Urbanormativity*. This volume is divided into two parts. The first provides an empirical examination of media coverage that includes examination of popular television shows (chapters by Fulkerson and Lowe, Jicha, and Lowe) and films (Hayden). The goal of these contributions is to assess the kinds of images and ideas about rural people and life that are being projected to the wider public, and assess the degree to which the images are urbanormative and/or denigrating.

The second part of this volume digs into the sources of rural meaning and knowledge construction. This is done by considering the role of the media, the Land Grant University and higher education (Ching), and rural schools and education (Avery and Sipple) as organizations and institutions operating in an urbanormative society. These selections deal more squarely with the process of knowledge construction that goes beyond the images of media, and point to the power of media in defining who, what, and where the public should direct its attention. The news media, growing increasingly consolidated and regional, threaten to erase from memory the lived experiences of rural communities. The institution of education and learning has immense power when it comes to shaping historical narratives, transmitting cultural values, and developing ideas of what it means to live a normal life. If this is infused with urbanormative bias, then the results will be to reproduce the problems we are attempting to address. These contributions combine to present several forms of evidence that suggest society is organized to privilege the urban experience and urban historical narratives, and ultimately places a higher value on urban people and places.

In the end, we hope this volume provides deeper insight into the cultural problems of urban domination, expands our understanding of the origins of rural stereotypes, and challenges prevailing urbanormative biases to reimagine what it means to be rural. Ultimately the significance of undoing the cultural domination of rural people extends beyond culture and into the material world. In future work we hope to look more closely at the material problems that result from cultural urban domination. Ultimately, we hope that by continuing a back-and-forth exchange of cultural and material analyses we may over time strengthen our theoretical understanding of urban-rural relations and, ideally, help to advance new policies that escape the trap of urbanormativity.

REFERENCES

Ching, B., and Creed, G. W. (1996). Recognizing Rusticity, in Ching, B. and Creed, G. W., *Knowing your place: Rural identity and cultural hierarchy*. New York: Routledge.

Flannery, K. (2003). The origin of war: New ^{14}C dates from ancient Mexico. *Proceedings of the National Academies of Science, 100*, 20, 11801–11805.

Fulkerson, G. M., and Thomas, A. R. (2013). *Studies in urbanormativity: Rural community in urban society*. Lanham, MD: Lexington Books.

Lobao, L, Hooks, G., and Tickamyer, A. R. (Eds.). 2007. *The sociology of spatial inequality*. Albany: State University of New York Press.

Thomas, A. R. (2005). *Gilboa: New York's quest for water and the destruction of a small town*. Lanham, MD: University Press of America.

———. (2010). *The Evolution of the ancient city: Urban theory and the archaeology of the Fertile Crescent*. Lanham, MD: Lexington Books.

Thomas, A. R., Lowe, B. M., Fulkerson, G. M., and Smith, P. S. (2011). *Critical rural theory: Structure*space*culture*. Lanham, MD: Lexington Books.

Ur, J. A. (2002). Settlement and landscape in northern Mesopotamia: The Tell Hamoukar Survey 2000–2001. *Akkadica, 123*, 57–88.

Chapter Two

Representations of Rural in Popular North American Television[1]

Gregory M. Fulkerson and Brian Lowe

Television serves an important socialization function insofar as it helps to inform people about a world in which they may have little direct contact, connection, or experience. In an increasingly urban society the number of people who can claim having any sort of direct experience participating or living in a rural community is diminishing (Fulkerson and Thomas, 2014). In such an urban society, television-produced rural representations may be the only picture of rural life that one ever encounters. This is concerning as fictional representations are often based on stereotypes that promote preju- dice and potentially lead to discriminatory actions against rural people. The goal of this chapter is to provide a basic analysis of rural representations as portrayed in the most popular North American television fictional programs that have a rural theme. Our scope includes the once popular Western genre, as well as evening soap operas, comedies, and the contemporary supernatural and dystopian post-apocalyptic genres. We have decided not to examine the reality television genre here, as this represents a niche and therefore is not consistent with our present focus on mainstream audiences. Jicha provides an analysis of rural reality television in this volume.

Our qualitative content analysis begins in the middle of the twentieth century and proceeds through the present, overviewing patterns that span roughly six decades. Our primary goal is to identify the degree to which television has generated representations that favor one or more of the various themes identified in the scholarly literature on rural representation, outlined below. A secondary goal is to examine each television series considering moral vocabularies, determining whether rural is cast in a dangerous and negative light, and exploring several consistently emerging themes that in-

clude racial exclusivity, adventure and conflict, violence and murder, historical narrative, cultural clash, idyllic small-town life, and rural as wild, simple,
or escape. Before we present our analysis we consider the abovementioned
literature and ideas surrounding the concept of rural representation.

RURAL REPRESENTATION: IMAGES AND MORAL VOCABULARY

The theoretical basis of the sociological concept of representations has origins in the classic works of Durkheim (1915) and his notion of collective
representations as socially shared understanding of how entire groups of
people share ideas about how things work in the world. This concept was
later developed into the notion of social representations by Moscovici
(1984), and more recently elaborated by Hall (2007) in his notion of cultural
representations. Generally speaking, we integrate these ideas to understand
representations as mental models of how things work according to various
social actors, which in turn guides the way they act in response to the object
they are representing. This mental model is the composite picture developed
from images drawn from direct experiences, but is also informed by exposure
to images from secondary sources such as the different types of audiovisual
media. More specifically, we are interested in how social actors come to
generate representations of rural life and people due to their exposure to
popular television imagery.

Scholarly interest in the study of rural representations has been increasing
in recent years, within the European and North American social science
communities. Thomas, Lowe, Fulkerson, and Smith (2011) utilized the concept in their approach to *Critical Rural Theory*, and the concept was featured
more prominently in the follow-up edited volume on urbanormativity (Fulkerson and Thomas 2014). In their preliminary analysis of television and film
media, Thomas et al. (2011) identify the core themes to be rural as simple,
wild, and escape. Rural representations have been dealt with more broadly in
the European scholarly community in the area of rural studies (e.g., Cloke
and Little, 1997). Within this arena, there has been attention to rurality in
mass media (Phillips, Fish, and Agg, 2001), popular magazines (Baylina and
Berg, 2010), and rural reality TV (Jonasson, 2012). Some scholars suggest
that rural representations give rise to rural performances on the part of individuals living in rural communities, resulting in them simulating rural life
(Edensor, 2006; Jonasson, 2012; Wood, 2010). Jonasson (2012) suggests that
rural representations are co-produced while attractive rural living is simultaneously in the process of being co-performed by rural residents. This interesting dynamic leads to an interplay between the reality and the representation, with each informing the other.

Studies of rural representation emphasize the fact that their production is multifaceted and imbued with elements of both external domination and internal resistance (Halfacree, 2007). Rural representations tend to enforce racial exclusivity whereby rural areas are understood to be homogenously white (Agyeman and Spooner, 1997; Holloway, 2007; Neal, 2002). The co-production of attractive rural living is embodied in terms of co-performing an attractive history, a desirable work-life balance, a sense of community inclusion, while maintaining a space for animals, gender, and entrepreneurship (Jonasson, 2012).

In reflecting on the way rural representations play out, Jonasson (2012, p.19) makes an important connection to media:

> Staged performances of rurality are scripted and choreographed events that overtly act out particular representations of rural life (Holloway, 2007; Woods, 2010). These include the portrayal of rural life in film and television programmes, dramatised reconstructions, museums, farm parks, heritage sites and interpretative centres.

Not all studies of rural representations examine the source of those representations—some examine the consequences. For example, Pruitt's (2014) analysis of abortion law examines the legal consequences of misinformed rural representations. She illustrates how embedded urbanormative standards are creating unfair and disproportionate burdens for rural women who must negotiate far longer and more difficult transportation routes than their urban counterparts in order to fulfill their legally mandated visits to medical facilities, as is now required to meet eligibility for an abortion. Similarly, McKinney (2013) has shown how urbanormative standards can translate into unequal environmental burdens for the countryside through her examination of ecological footprints, biocapacity, and entropy of different nations. Finally, Rye (2006) examines the rural representations of teenagers in an attempt to dig into their future plans and desires with regard to living in a rural area, finding that most teenagers held negative views of the rural dull and thus suggests that future migration patterns will support urbanization.

In addition to examining the phenomenon of rural representations, we are interested in the moral claimsmaking that such representations imply. The moral vocabularies approach (Lowe 2006) emphasizes identifying the moral resources—those ideas, symbols, concepts that are deployed as grounds for making claims—utilized in moral claimsmaking and the hierarchy that they inevitably create, with certain resources becoming penultimate and others peripheral. The sociological utility of this approach is that it allows for both the inductive creation of moral resources, claims, and their antecedent behaviors and mapping changes within these constellations over time (Lowe 2010). In the case of rural representations, the moral vocabularies approach allows for the consideration of qualities associated with rural residents (e.g., friendly, self-reliant, unassuming, or, alternatively, wild, dangerous, and rough), and how those images may evolve, especially in light of changing conditions. For example, as we will discuss, *The Andy Griffith Show* depicts residents of small towns as friendly and accommodating, perhaps reflecting their rural surroundings. On the opposite end of the spectrum, *The Walking Dead* reveals a devastated rural America in which strangers must be approached with extreme caution and suspicion, as the desperate conditions lead many people to act in violent and ruthless ways. These contradictory images will have different outcomes for the individual consuming media images, thus informing the rural representations in different manners.

A LATENT INTERPRETIVE CONTENT ANALYSIS OF RURAL-THEMED TELEVISION

The research that we present in this chapter is based on a qualitative content analysis that assumes a 30,000-foot view of the rural television media terrain. We attempt to construct a narrative that maps out the multiple and often contradictory themes associated with rural representations of different popular televisions series. Following established methodological practice, we perform an interpretative qualitative analysis (Berg and Lune, 2011; Miles, Huberman, and Saldaña, 2013). This method interprets human action as a collection of symbols with inherent meaning. We attempt to isolate the essence of meaning rather than condense the data through systematic coding into observable patterns as is the case with a manifest content analysis. While we think there is value in this latter form of coding it would provide a level of depth that would force a sacrifice of breadth that is more important to our current goals. Thus rather than examine the surface structure we are more interested in the deeper underlying structural meanings that can be teased out of a careful review of various television series.

Our unit of analysis is the television series (not individual episodes). Accordingly, we limit our selection to those series that were ranked most highly in terms of popularity and were ostensibly predicated on what we interpret as rural symbols, settings, and characters. We chose this strategy because we reasoned that the most popular rural television series would also have the most influence and impact due to their far-reaching viewership. To determine levels of popularity, we examine three different ranking systems that include the Nielsen ratings, the Internet Movie Database (IMDB), and *TV Guide* ranking. For the Nielsen ratings we note the single most highly rated television series for each given year since the middle of the twentieth century through the present time, and select those with rural themes. For both the IMDB and *TV Guide* rankings, we limit our selection of series to their respective top-100 lists (with the exception of *Dallas* that comes in at 103). The existence of rural symbols was ascertained from series titles and descriptions as well as viewing the shows selectively and reading individual episode descriptions. Detailed information about individual episodes is available through the tv.com website, and these were used selectively in the qualitative content analysis to inform our general understanding and impression of each television series.

Table 2.1.   Top-Rated Rural Programs

Nielsen Ratings. TV shows with the highest average household Nielsen rating for each television season.
- Gunsmoke (1957-58 rating 43.1; 1958-59 rating 39.6; 1959-60 rating 40.3; 1960-61 rating 37.3)
- Wagon Train (1961-62 rating 32.1)
- The Beverly Hillbillies (1962-63 rating 36; 1963-64 rating 39.1)
- Bonanza (1964-65 rating 36.3; 1965-66 rating 31.8; 1966-67 rating 29.1)
- The Andy Griffith Show (1967-68 rating 27.6)
- Dallas (1980-81 rating 34.5; 1981-82 rating 28.4; 1983-84 rating 25.7)

Source: http://en.wikipedia.org/wiki/Nielsen_ratings

TV Guide Ratings. Most Watched Rural TV Shows.
- True Blood (ranked 14th)
- Revolution (ranked 35th)
- Nashville (ranked 39th)
- Parks and Recreation (ranked 45th)
- The Walking Dead (ranked 64th)
- Dallas (ranked 102nd)

Source: http://www.tvguide.com/top-tv-shows.

Internet Movie Database (IMDB) User Ratings. Highest User-Rated Rural TV Shows.
- Fargo (ranked 16th)
- Twin Peaks (ranked 32nd)
- Deadwood (ranked 42nd)

Source: IMDB, http://www.imdb.com/search/title?num_votes=5000,& sort=user_rating,desc&title_type=tv_series.

The primary goal of interpretative latent content analysis is to inductively identify a range of themes. Based on emergent themes, we develop a reflective narrative that attempts to compare contemporary with older imagery of rural representations highlighting their evolution. While our analysis will be inductive, allowing new themes and ideas to emerge from observation, we also take advantage of some existing frameworks in the literature reviewed, such as that offered by *Critical Rural Theory*, that classifies rural as "wild," "simple," and "escape" (Thomas, Lowe, Fulkerson, and Smith, 2010). We approach each television series with the following set of questions:

1. What is the general concept of the television series?

2. What symbols and meanings are associated with rural people and places within the series?
3. What is the moral significance of the rural for each television series? Is it cast as positive and attractive, negative and repulsive, or morally ambivalent?

Table 2.2 found toward the end of the analysis, provides a detailed summary to the answers we found through our research, based on the above set of questions.

According to Nielsen ratings, the most popular television series from 1955 to 1968 shared a common rural focus, beginning with the long running *Gunsmoke*, followed by *Wagon Train, The Beverly Hillbillies, Bonanza*, and *The Andy Griffith Show*. The Western genre reigned supreme for most of this time frame. *Gunsmoke* still maintains the record for the longest running television series of all time, while *Bonanza* and *Wagon Train* each had impressive runs of their own. The other titles from this period are from a different genre. *The Beverly Hillbillies* marks the end of the popular Western genre's dominance, taking instead a comedic approach to rural stereotypes as the title of the show demonstrates. *The Andy Griffith Show* was less ostensibly based on negative rural stereotypes, but the focus was on small town community life, full of characters who are shown to be incompetent, including the archetypical Gomer Pyle—a name that has come to be synonymous with small-minded, bumbling rural folk.

The decade of the 1970s turned to other types of shows that included more general sitcoms such as *All in the Family, Laverne and Shirley*, and *Happy Days*, which did not deal with rural as a core theme and were therefore not analyzed here. In the 1980s there was a return to rural themed shows that included the popular *Dallas* series, which involved another shift into the evening soap genre. In these programs traditional rural themes were less prominent, while the personal relationships of characters were primary, as is typical of the soap opera genre. Following the declining popularity of evening soaps, rural themed televisions shows ceased to command the same level of general mainstream attention, as measured by Nielsen ratings. Thus, early rural representations were embedded in highly popular television series and viewed widely by mainstream audiences from the 1960s through the first part of the 1980s. This may in some way reflect the nature of television watching itself, as most households were limited to only a few networks during this time. Now the main audience for contemporary rural-themed television has shifted into smaller niche markets, partly due to the wider selection of channels, but also due in part to declining general interest in the rural. As Jicha notes in this volume, the networks made a conscious decision to get out of the business of rural television shows, viewing them as outdated and old-fashioned. Thus, they began cancelling one rural show after the next in spite of their resilient popularity, each network fearing it would come to be viewed as out-of-style by the younger demographic.

Recent data on favorite television series show that rural-themed shows are no longer dominant. At the same time, the data suggest that the rural has not been altogether forgotten. According to *TV Guide*, the series *Sleepy Hollow* is ranked as the ninth most popular show at the time of this analysis, followed by 14th place *True Blood*, which though a vampire based show is set in a small town context. In 35th place is *Revolution*, which is a dystopian, post-apocalyptic series that plays out what life would be like if modern society had to revert back to a rural way of life. At 39th, *Nashville* is a show that deals with a southern-country rural theme. *Parks and Recreation* (45th) is based centrally on small town life. *The Walking Dead*, at 64th place, is similar to *Revolution* in terms of being dystopian and post-apocalyptic, but its premise differs in that the decline of modern society is due to being overrun by mindless zombies rather than nanotechnology. The Internet Movie Database (IMDB) has its own ranking of user-rated most popular television shows. Unlike the *TV Guide* ranking, which is limited to shows that are currently being aired, the IMDB ranking includes all shows including those that are not being aired but are still popular with contemporary audiences. The new series, *Fargo*, appears high in this list at 16th, followed by *Twin Peaks* in 32nd place, and *Deadwood* in 42nd place. We therefore base our selection of television series on these ranking systems. We now turn to a more detailed consideration of the series mentioned above, in order to note emergent and recurring themes.

EARLY REPRESENTATIONS OF THE WESTERN FRONTIER

Gunsmoke (1955–1975)

This longest-running television series of all time was based on the "settling" of the Western United States, and takes place in the frontier town, Dodge City, Kansas, in the late 1800s. The main character is U.S. Marshal Matt Dillon, who is responsible for solving a range of social ills that encroach on his town from the surrounding hinterlands. A common theme is the threat of "Indian" raids and related violent encounters, typically portraying the local native population as dangerous and wild. On occasion, representations of natives were more positive, such as an episode when Blue Horse rescues Matt from a prisoner under his arrest that overpowers him. Other problems that arise for Dillon are related to drunkenness, drugs (e.g., opium), gambling, livestock theft (cattle and horses), and violent altercations. Almost every episode includes some form of murder or acts of violence under a variety of circumstances, and many include some form of robbery, theft, or kidnapping. The motives for killings vary from jealousy to revenge against dirty con artists, cheaters, and swindlers. Many of the episodes are based on one-time appearances of unique types of characters passing through town. For example, in the episode "Magnus," Chester receives a visit from an "uncivilized" mountain man, his brother Magnus. Though this episode presents a stereotypical image of an unrefined and awkward rural person, it also shows this person functioning very well in town, thus proving himself worthy of Chester's approval.

The *Gunsmoke* series enjoyed longstanding popularity as it attempted to represent an important part of American history and identity formation—the settling of the West and realization of Manifest Destiny. The challenges facing Dodge City represent the challenges early European settlers encountered during this part of American history. The narrative is of course from the point of view of white European Americans and celebrates their heroism in conquering the dangerous countryside and, indeed, taming it and its (native) inhabitants, while introducing to it civilization, and the establishment of law and order. The main character, Marshal Matt Dillon, represents the cool and rational power of civil society that is at first gentle and understanding, but when required can become as violent as any imposing threat. The city-dwellers in Dodge City are anything but civilized, engaging in a range of pleasure-seeking vices from gambling to drugs and drunkenness. Thus part of the appeal of the show has to do with how European Americans understand themselves as having evolved from the raucous and wild gunslingers of the Old West to the more civilized and peaceful contemporary urbanites of today.

Wagon Train (1957–1965)

This television series spanned 276 episodes and, as the title implies, follows a wagon train that moves across the territory of land bridging Missouri to California in the time period following the Civil War. Major Seth Adams and later Christopher Hale each filled the role of wagon train leaders guiding its travails through the Rocky Mountains, the Plains, and desert country. As with *Gunsmoke*, the concept of this show is tied to the American ideal of Manifest Destiny and taming of the Wild West with each episode devoted to telling a story about a particular character or place. Like *Gunsmoke*, this format is designed to feature a large number of guest appearances with unique characters around whom a new story line could be developed with each episode.

The themes of individual episodes pick up some of the same themes as those found in *Gunsmoke*, in terms of gunfights, gambling, drunkenness, and generally wild behavior. As with *Gunsmoke*, a prominent theme has to do with the taming of the West, encountering and fighting bands of outlaws and its Native American inhabitants. Other stories are about the personal relationships of family members and their lovers. Unlike the *Gunsmoke* series, where Dodge City inhabitants attempt to shelter themselves from the external rural threats, the Wagon Train plunges its characters into direct contact with the rural countryside and all of its associated dangers adding an extra element of adventure. The generally dangerous representation of the countryside is left essentially untouched, and is in fact a defining feature of the Western genre that these shows helped to define.

Bonanza (1959–1973)

The *Bonanza* series enjoyed an impressive fourteen-year run that included 430 episodes. The concept of this show is centered on Ben Cartwright and his three sons (by different wives) who drive livestock across their one-thousand-square-mile Nevada ranch, the Ponderosa. The time period of this series begins in 1859 and continues through the Civil War with each passing season. In keeping with the Western theme of *Gunsmoke* and *Wagon Train*, this series offers many encounters with Native American populations, and features a range of dubious outlaws and swindlers. As with *Gunsmoke*, where the focus remains on Dodge City, the setting is more stationary in terms of its continual focus on the Ponderosa. However, the size of the Ponderosa is so vast that maintaining order on it requires constant movement, allowing the show to resemble the more adventurous character of *Wagon Train*. This show was the last in the Western genre to enjoy widespread mainstream popularity with American audiences, as this genre has now moved into niche status. In most respects, with regard to imagery that informs rural representations, the Bonanza series is largely an extension of the series that came before it, offering little that is novel to the idea of what it means to live in a rural area in the frontier country of late-nineteenth-century North America.

EARLY COMEDIC REPRESENTATIONS OF RURAL SIMPLETONS

The Andy Griffith Show (1960–1968)

This series was based on the daily lives, experiences, and characters of a small community called Mayberry, which is actually based on the real town of Mount Airy, North Carolina. The main character is Sheriff Andy Taylor, who is raising a curious and brash son, Opie, while managing the law enforcement of Mayberry with the help of his deputy, Barney Fife, later replaced by Goober. The show also featured frequent visits from his Aunt Bea, and later in the series we meet the iconic Gomer Pyle, who is the town auto mechanic. Like *The Beverly Hillbillies*, this series was a light and comedic representation of rural people, who are often shown to be low on intelligence and prone to mistakes, as is often the case with Barney Fife and Gomer Pyle. Generally, the show is iconic for its romantic and idyllic view of small town life. The story lines of the episodes are very light including such topics as Aunt Bea opening a Chinese restaurant and then deciding it was more work than it was worth, or Goober's sweetheart flirting with Andy, making him grow jealous. In the opening sequence to the show and at other points, Andy and Opie are seen fishing at a local fishing hole, symbolizing the simplicity of life in an uncomplicated small town where the harmless crimes include such acts as Aunt Bea getting arrested for "gambling" by hosting a Bingo game.

In this series the rural is represented as charming, simple, and safe. The characters are shown to be simpletons with little depth or complexity. The character, Andy Taylor, is a distant analog to *Gunsmoke*'s Matt Dillon, who was constantly battling serious dangers and threats. The ease of policing Mayberry is a fundamental theme of the show—so simple that even a silly and incompetent character like Barney Fife can pull it off. So iconic was the character of Gomer Pyle that modern vernacular continues to invoke the name in reference to small town simpletons. *The Andy Griffith Show* helped to solidify the notion in the American imagination of small town life as a simple care-free life, and has therefore also come to represent the nostalgic yearning many people hold for the simple life that is symbolized by Mayberry.

The Beverly Hillbillies (1962–1971)

With nine seasons, and a total of 274 episodes, *The Beverly Hillbillies* series was by most measures highly popular. It begins with a poor mountain family that strikes it rich through the discovery of oil on their lands, and the family winds up moving into a posh Beverly Hills neighborhood mansion, as if this was necessitated by the fact of becoming wealthy. Most of the episodes involve embarrassing culture clashes with the rustic and unrefined ways of the Clampett family in different situations while mingling with the elites of Southern California. Despite their rough and rowdy ways, the Clampett family—Jed in particular—often introduces moral clarity to the Beverly Hills elite culture who reluctantly accept or at least tolerate the family.

Indeed, *The Beverly Hillbillies* (along with *The Andy Griffith Show*) marks a major shift in the representation of rural. While the Clampett family is unrefined and in many ways wild, they are not shown to be particularly dangerous. In fact, they are represented as naive and harmless as young children. This is demonstrated by Jethro Clampett's continual boasts about his sixth grade education and the pride expressed by the family for his impressive educational accomplishments. This show, like the *Andy Griffith*

Show, offers a shift away from the more dramatic and heroic conquering of the rural countryside as seen in *Gunsmoke* and *Wagon Train*, to the comically embarrassing invasion of the rural Clampett family on the urban elites of Beverly Hills.

RURAL AS STAGE FOR DRAMA

Dallas (1978–1991)

Beginning with a five-part mini-series in 1978, the *Dallas* television series continued for an additional thirteen seasons as a highly successful night-time soap opera. The show is based around the Ewing family headed by patriarch J. R., a successful oil tycoon, his wife Sue Ellen and three sons. The Ewing family lives on a sprawling ranch, Southfork, just outside of Dallas, Texas, reminiscent of the Ponderosa featured on *Bonanza*. However, the story lines of each episode are far removed from the struggles of frontier settlers or ranchers. They revolve instead around the personal relationships of the family members, their romantic and sexual escapades, and their brutal and cold business dealing. There is a constant struggle to maintain control of Ewing Oil in the face of both internal and external threats. Many plots are based on revenge schemes and jealous reactions to affairs and betrayals, making Dallas a rather typical soap opera. On occasion, the episodes include such rural-themed events as cattle drives, poker games, violent brawls, shootings (e.g., the popular "Who Shot J. R." episode), hunting trips, a rodeo, and problems with alcoholism and drunkenness. These aspects of the rural are decidedly less frequent and central in comparison to the focus on the rocky relationships that exist between family members.

The *Dallas* series marks another shift in thinking about rurality that goes further than its predecessors in rendering rural as a background variable. The Western genre was centrally focused on conquering the wild and dangerous countryside in dramatic fashion, the sitcoms of the 1960s focused on the hilarity of rural simpletons and culture clashes between the rustics and urbanites as they sought to assimilate, and by the 1980s rural was reduced to a context, as the *Dallas* series focuses almost exclusively on personal relationship struggles that could play out in almost any setting. The show's main rival, *Dynasty*, was essentially made from the same recipe but takes place in a more urban setting (Denver, Colorado). In the case of *Dallas*, the rural is simply the stage on which the drama of life plays out, providing the costumes, characters, artifacts, and dialogue of an elite rural family, but never itself becoming an object to be conquered, ridiculed, or nostalgically yearned for. At its heart, the story lines of each episode—developed around deceit, jealousy, revenge, and betrayal—could easily be modified to fit an urban setting by changing the names of the characters, their costumes, props, and background scenery. The rival series, *Dynasty*, demonstrates this fact. In other words, for *Dallas*, the rural is simply a background theme and not a fact of existence that presents unique challenges.

NEW REPRESENTATIONS OF WESTERN LIFE

Deadwood (2004–2006)

The HBO series *Deadwood*, created by David Milch, was based on a community of the same name, beginning as a tent camp for gold prospectors and becoming an established community in the Dakota territory (currently Deadwood, South Dakota). While a dramatic series, *Deadwood* depicts several historic figures including Seth Bullock, Al Swearengen, "Wild Bill" Hickok, and Calamity Jane. The program followed the development of Deadwood from a large and lawless tent camp of gold prospectors into a recognizable town that included courts and established businesses. This development also featured the expansion of governmental power despite regional resistance, including Native American military attacks on U.S. Army incursions, and the establishment of legal and economic institutions. The series depicts the emergence of an established town in the wake of gold seeking prospectors and the businesses that emerge around them—primarily saloons and brothels. The series begins in 1876, and follows the efforts of Seth Bullock to establish a hardware store in Deadwood, while brothels and saloons become the hub of activity in Deadwood itself. The killing of "Wild Bill" Hickok and an outbreak of smallpox encourage the creation of municipal government that will also facilitate annexation of Deadwood into the Dakota Territory, and will therefore secure the claims and deeds some in Deadwood have on land and businesses. By the second season, Bullock becomes sheriff of Deadwood and focuses on his ongoing confrontations with Al Swearengen, as well as conflicts within Deadwood over the control of prostitutes. In season three (set in 1877) Deadwood is moving toward annexation, with conflicts over elected offices (Sheriff) and efforts by miners to unionize. Thus, *Deadwood* charts the emergence of a rural community coalescing and manifesting urban institutions (saloons, banks) while its existence is tied to a rural landscape that provides the potential for raw materials. While the characters of *Deadwood* are certainly less encumbered than they might appear in an urban environment, they are not depicted as immune from larger, urban forces. On the contrary, they are propelled by economic and political forces that compel the establishment of institutions.

In many ways *Deadwood* is unique among contemporary shows for clinging to the traditional images, themes, and characters of the Western genre. It is much like *Gunsmoke* in terms of taking place in a single location that must contend with continual external threats and imposing law and order. The series departs in important ways, as *Deadwood* is far more dynamic than Dodge City. Stylistically, *Deadwood* departs by showcasing far more graphic sex scenes and dialogue—so replete with F-bombs that it puts it on par with another popular HBO series, *The Sopranos*. Moreover, *Deadwood* falls short of the moral clarity of the narrative offered by traditional Westerns, adding moral ambiguity that is more typical of contemporary culture. It is in some respects a more "grown up" version of *Gunsmoke*.

NEW REPRESENTATIONS OF RURAL SIMPLETONS

Parks and Recreation (2009–Present)

Beginning in 2009, NBC's *Parks and Recreation* follows several characters involved in the local government of the fictional Pawnee, Indiana. Filmed as a "mockumentary," the program features characters struggling with the apparent absurdities of local government. *Parks* attempts to intersect with current events and trends, such as the anti-government libertarian, Director Ron Swanson, representing the contradictory desires to be free of government while working within it. It also features the difficulties faced by Parks employee Leslie Knope in the wake of the 2008 global financial crisis. As such, *Parks and Recreation* has little that marks it as being exclusively rural, instead relying on general themes of office politics and romantic entanglements. Since its premiere in 2009, the critically-acclaimed series has been included on dozens of television critics' Top-10 lists and was named "TV's Smartest Comedy" in *Entertainment Weekly*'s 2011 cover story, and has received several awards.

As with the 1960s rural sitcoms, *Parks and Recreation* takes a lighthearted and comedic view of small-town life. The central character, Leslie Knope, continually confronts challenges with her job when she must include the community in decision-making processes. The town-hall-style meetings that she holds showcase self-interested simpleminded citizens who care little for Leslie's lofty plans, unable to see past their own immediate self-serving interests. The style of the show is similar to that of the defining series, *The Office*, with emphasis on office politics and character conflicts, only in this case adding the element of government bureaucracy. As with the *Dallas* series, the rural or small town setting could easily be swapped out for a different, even highly urban, context with minor tweaks to the characters and costumes. As a result, the role of rural is similar to that of *Dallas*—it is somewhat arbitrary.

EMERGING REPRESENTATIONS OF THE
RURAL SUPERNATURAL

Twin Peaks (1990–1991)

Created by David Lynch and Mark Frost, the highly popular *Twin Peaks* aired for only two seasons in 1990 and 1991 on ABC, and focused on answering the question "Who killed Laura Palmer?" The series opened with the discovery of the naked dead body of high school student and Homecoming Queen, Laura Palmer, neatly wrapped in plastic in Twin Peaks, Washington. Due to the proximity of the crime to the Canadian border and another apparent victim of the same attack found in Oregon, FBI Special Agent Dale Cooper is dispatched to investigate. The rest of the first season involves a mixture of police procedures and displays of expert knowledge by Cooper and Sheriff Harry S. Truman. There is a gradual revelation that the seeming benign appearance and isolated serenity of Twin Peaks conceals more sinister underlying realities, including romantic infidelities, an underground drug trade and prostitution ring, and ambiguous supernatural forces lurking in the surrounding woods. Sheriff Truman reveals himself to be a member of the "Bookhouse Boys", a secret society devoted to protecting Twin Peaks from malevolent forces that threaten the otherwise peaceful existence that they appreciate about their rural enclave.

The small town atmosphere of *Twin Peaks* features a number of colorful characters and subplots, augmenting the overall hunt for Laura's killer. Eventually, Laura Palmer's killer is discovered to be her father, who is unwittingly possessed by Bob, an evil spirit that emerged from the woods near Twin Peaks. Cooper learns that, according to Native American tradition, the entrances to the White and Black Lodges exist within the woods, and that spirits and humans can move between them. In the final episode of the series, Cooper enters the Black Lodge in the hopes of rescuing Annie Blackburn, but is himself trapped there by Bob, who is shown returning to earth in the body of Dale Cooper.

The images of the rural in *Twin Peaks* are therefore in many respects an amalgamation of images generated by earlier series. The small-town life of *Twin Peaks* is at times shown to be simple, bucolic, and as wholesome as Mayberry. The underlying realities prove to be far more complicated and darker than this surface layer. The wild and dangerous themes of murder and drug trafficking infuse the show with the scary imagery of the Western genre, while the complicated interpersonal relationships add a soap opera-esque quality such as that found in *Dallas*. At the same time, by introducing a place for supernatural forces, the show contributes a hyper-real quality to rural life that is a far cry from any historical narrative that underpins the old Western style. While many of the characters are quirky and comical in the tradition of the 1960s sitcoms, they are also shown to have far more depth and complexity. This is epitomized by Sheriff Harry S. Truman, who like Andy Taylor, is in charge of policing a small town, and like Marshal Matt Dillon is tasked with maintaining order in the face of threats, but exhibits a level of expertise and training that is far more impressive and contemporary than any of his predecessors.

True Blood (2008–Present)

Beginning in 2008, the *True Blood* series on HBO, based on Charlaine Harris' Southern Vampire/Sookie Stackhouse series, depicts the lives of several characters in the village of Bon Temps in rural Louisiana, and centers on Sookie Stackhouse, a reluctant telepathic waitress at Merlotte's Bar and Grill. As the series progresses, Stackhouse and several of the residents of Bon Temps are revealed to be supernatural beings, whose existence is partially revealed in the opening pilot as vampires come out of their coffins globally and reveal themselves to exist. The title of the series refers to a synthetic blood substitute whose commercial availability allows vampires to sustain themselves without consuming human blood. *True Blood* places the residents of Bon Temps, most of whom are white and working-class, in a small bucolic setting that allows for familiarity between characters who are typical small town folk.

The general sense of safety and security that many understand to be endemic of small town life, is slowly eroded by revelations that mythical creatures—vampires, werewolves, and faeries—exist and pose an internal threat to the well-being of Bon Temps. The first five seasons reveal progressively more information about vampire society and politics including the existence of the Authority that coordinated the Great Revelation, by publicly acknowledging the reality of vampires. Season six follows the Louisiana governor's plot to infect vampires with "Hep-V" through deliberately dosing *True Blood* and effectively poisoning vampires that are attempting to assimilate into the larger, human-majority society. Though this plot is eventually discovered and violently terminated, many vampires are left infected, thereby left with a vast appetite for blood before they sicken and experience the True Death.

Season seven begins with an attack on Bon Temps after a meeting led by Mayor Sam Merlott to build alliances between residents and vampires, whereby human residents agree to feed vampires in exchange for these vampires protecting the humans from other infected and ravenous vampires. This season embraces a Hurricane Katrina motif, in that local political leaders and law enforcement discover that urban areas will not be sending assistance and that residents are left to their own devices to support themselves. This motif is emphasized when, following the attack on Bon Temps, several characters travel to neighboring St. Alice, in order to search for residents who were taken captive. St. Alice is found to be completely empty, with "SOS" written on rooftops in a vain effort to summon help from the larger world. The discovery of a mass grave supports Mayor Merlott's assertion that Bon Temps cannot expect assistance from either the state or federal governments, and that it has been left to fend for itself in rural isolation.

The centrality of supernatural beings and forces at work in the *True Blood* series is a continuation of the theme of rural hyper-reality introduced by the *Twin Peaks* series (at least among popular mainstream televisions series). Despite there being supernatural creatures like vampires or shape-shifters, the characters often exhibit qualities of rural people found in earlier characterizations. The law enforcement of Bon Temps is shown in many places to be incompetent simpletons—one sheriff struggling with alcoholism and his predecessor struggling with sanity after being possessed and otherwise burdened with the unknowns of living with supernaturals. The main character, Sookie, is in many regards a typical wholesome southern girl—a virgin, in the beginning, living with her beloved grandmother and unintelligent ex-football jock brother. She is also a faerie and girlfriend to a vampire. The supernatural element allows the show to play with older themes introduced by previous rural representations while adding originality and unexpected twists—much like *Twin Peaks*.

Sleepy Hollow (2013–Present)

Beginning in September 2013, *Sleepy Hollow* is a radical reinterpretation of Irving's *The Legend of Sleepy Hollow*, in which the community becomes the epicenter of supernatural conflict. Ichabod Crane was a loyal British subject who defected to the Patriot cause. When mortally wounded by a masked Hessian cavalryman, who Crane was ordered to kill by General George Washington, he is placed in an enchanted state and buried alive by a coven of witches. Crane rises in the present day as a man outside of history, and discovers that his enemy is in fact the Headless Horseman. Through a mingling of their blood from their initial 1781 battle, Crane and the Headless Horseman are bound to each other and Crane's resurrection has allowed the Horseman to return. Crane is befriended by Lt. Grace Abigale Mills, a local police officer whose mentor, Sheriff August Corbin, was killed by the Horseman. As the season progresses, Crane and Mills learn that Sleepy Hollow is embroiled in supernatural conflict in which secret societies—descendants of the Hessian mercenaries, Freemasons, and covens of good and evil witches—have been awaiting the return of the Headless Horseman as the first of the Four Horsemen of the Apocalypse.

While the woods surrounding Sleepy Hollow are full of danger, the town itself is no sanctuary, as the Horseman and his allies move through and create destruction within it. This point is visually referenced with occasional pano-ramic shots of the actual Sleepy Hollow (with the Tappan Zee bridge visible in the background). The program producers take demographic liberties as the pilot depicts a sign stating that Sleepy Hollow has a population of 144,000 (perhaps a Biblical reference to the Book of Revelations), whereas the actual Sleepy Hollow has a population of under 10,000. *Sleepy Hollow*, along with other contemporary rural-themed series, embraces the supernatural. While it backs away from the future dystopian focus of *The Walking Dead* and *Revolution*, it maintains an apocalyptic element. The rural is clearly represented here as dangerous, providing sanctuary to imposing secret societies and supernatural forces that threaten nearby settlements.

REPRESENTATIONS OF RURAL DYSTOPIA AND APOCALYPSE

The Walking Dead (2010–Present)

The Walking Dead television series (examined more completely in the chapter by Lowe in this volume) is based on the graphic novels of Robert Kirkman, Tony Moore, and Charlie Adlard, and follows the lives of several characters in rural Georgia during a societal collapse precipitated by a plague that causes the dead to become reanimated cannibalistic "walkers." The inclusion of zombies adds a supernatural element, making it fit equally well in the preceding discussion. In terms of rural representations, *The Walking Dead* exemplifies an ambivalence: on the one hand it offers life sustaining resources and lower population density that therefore means that there are fewer threats, from both "walkers" and violent survivors, while conversely the rural does not provide an easy or obvious sanctuary, and its inhabitants are not necessarily more compassionate than their urban counterparts. The characters of the show maintain older ideas of rough and tough cowboy types, like Darryl who was raised in a rural setting and is skilled with his compound bow from years of experience hunting. His brother is far more dangerous and unpredictable, exemplifying the wild and dangerous imagery of Western rustics. At the same time the character Doc, who is the head of the Greene farm and household resembles Ben Cartwright on the Ponderosa, staunchly defending his land against external threats—only in this case, against zombies rather than outlaws.

Whereas traditional Western television series had a preference for the past and the historical reality of westward expansion, what is introduced by the series *The Walking Dead* is a forward looking futuristic perspective that constructs an apocalyptic (or postapocalyptic) narrative. By focusing on the future rather than the past, the show is able to escape the constraints of empirical fact, providing a possibility for the inclusion of supernatural forces.

Revolution (2012–2014)

A science-fiction series set in a near future North America without electricity, *Revolution* parallels some of the future-oriented narrative of *The Walking Dead*, asking how life would change if urban social life were to deteriorate into chaos. Series creator, Erik Kripke, depicts a world in which the Blackout—when all electricity suddenly stops globally—has left 2027 North America divided into several competing centers of power—the Monroe Republic, the Plains Nations, the Georgia Federation, the California Commonwealth, and the Republic of Texas—vying for control of the continent.

The series begins by following the Matheson children, Charlotte, Charlie and Danny as they are thrown into chaos after their father is killed by members of the Monroe Republic militia, under the command of Major Tom Neville, and Danny is taken prisoner. Charlie and her teacher Aaron Pittman, a former technology executive, travel to Chicago to find Charlie's uncle, Miles Matheson. Charlie learns that her uncle was once the co-ruler of the Monroe Republic and that he attempted to assassinate Sebastian Monroe, his former friend from the pre-Blackout Marine Corps. It is later revealed that Rachael Matheson, mother of Charlie and Danny, has been held captive by Monroe as he coerces her to develop a solution to the Blackout that she may be able to accomplish because of her involvement in a military project that weaponized nanotechnology in order to drain an enemy of electricity. The Mathesons then set out across North America in order to find the Tower, a scientific facility that may be able to deactivate the nanotechnology so that "the lights can come back on." The resurgent government of the United States, comprised of the secretive Patriots, is also attempting to temporally deactivate the nanotechnology, allowing for two thermonuclear warheads to be launched at Philadelphia, the capital of the Monroe Republic, and Atlanta, the capital of the Georgia Federation, before the Blackout resumes. As the series proceeds, the Mathesons, joined by Monroe, attempt to prevent the Patriots from taking control over North America. Much of the struggle unfolds in the small town of Willoughby, Texas, that is occupied by the Patriots. The Patriots provide the appearance of being a constructive and securing force while they covertly experiment with biological warfare infecting residents with typhoid, chemical warfare with mustard gas, and a social control program to "reeducate" teenagers to act as unquestioning assassins. This leads to the upending of a Patriot plot to incite war between Texas and California with the penultimate goal of allowing the Patriots to seize control after these dominant forces have weakened, and the nanotechnology responsible for the Blackout is itself planning to build its own powerbase in Bradbury, Idaho.

Much of *Revolution* unfolds in an unfamiliar, neo-rural America that juxtaposes imagery from the older Western genre with a future-oriented focus, in which horses and steam engines are once again used for transportation, and where agriculture becomes widely practiced for food production. While cities are reconstituted after the Blackout, it is clear that urban populations were left without the means to feed themselves and essentially collapsed in the interim. Two of the resurgent cities, Philadelphia and Atlanta, are destroyed by the Patriots so that they can return in force from Cuba. Later we see glimpses of Austin, Texas, and Washington, DC, but most of the series unfolds in unpopulated areas that offer temporary sanctuary. The constant roaming through the countryside is reminiscent of the adventurous spirit of *Wagon Train*, as is the element of survival and threats.

NEW RURAL DRAMA

Nashville (2012–Present)

The serial drama *Nashville* began in October 2012 and, while it takes place in an urban setting, it focuses on one of the quintessential rural cultural products: country and western music. The series follows Rayana James as an established but declining music star and Juliette Barnes as a young ascending performer as they clash over their respective positions within the country music field. The series blurs the distinction between fiction and documentary by hosting several appearances of actual stars such as Bonnie Raitt and Faith Hill. One aspect of the conflict between the main characters is the style of country music—the established and possibly declining country music and the "bubble gum country" that is currently popular but untested and not embraced by older performers. The series highlights actual struggles within Nashville itself over cultural prominence. *Nashville* is about the cultural creation and dissemination of country music, rather than the story of the lived realities of rural America. As such, *Nashville* is distinct from other depictions of country music, such as James Mangold's 2005 *Walk the Line*, about the life and music of Johnny Cash that showcases the dire poverty he endured as a child with his sharecropping family in Arkansas.

In *Nashville*, the focus is largely on the typical soap opera themes such as found in *Dallas*. However, there is greater focus on the setting as the Country genre is centrally defining for the characters. Leaving this aside, it would not be difficult to imagine some of the storylines and characters being essentially maintained but recast in a completely different, even highly urban, setting. To some degree the series *Empire* could be viewed as an urban corollary to *Nashville*. This is always going to be the case when the focus is mostly on interpersonal relationship ups and downs, rather than on engaging in the countryside as its own objective reality—whether cast as bucolic and simple or as dangerous and wild.

EMERGING RURAL VIOLENT CRIME

Fargo (2014–Present)

With the popularity of violent crime series, such as *Law and Order*, *NCIS*, *Criminal Minds*, and *CSI*, it is not surprising to find that at least some include rural themes. The popular FX series *Fargo* is an example. The opening of the 1996 Joel and Ethan Coen film, on which the series is based, claims to be factually based, while in reality it is inspired by a few unrelated crimes in Minneapolis, Minnesota. Interestingly, the city of Fargo, North Dakota, is only mentioned in the film. The story centers around a kidnapping plot, orchestrated by car salesman Jerry Lundegaard, to have two ex-cons kidnap his wife Jean and ransom her to her father and Jerry's boss, asking for one million dollars in ransom. The kidnapping leads to the killing of a Minnesota police officer that is witnessed by a couple, and is subsequently investigated by Police Chief Marge Gunderson. The story follows the investigations of these crimes, which features the unraveling of the kidnapping team and Jerry's eventual arrest. Despite mostly occurring in the Minneapolis area, the film is cited for its depiction of small-town life and for emphasizing the Minnesotan accent.

In 2014, FX aired the first season of *Fargo*. This time it is set in Bemidji, Minnesota, and centers on the murders possibly committed by Lorne Malvo and Lester Nygaard. This series departs from the supernatural theme that became quite popular among rural-themed shows in the contemporary time frame. What is maintained is a representation of rural places as safe havens for brutal and horrific murders (e.g., bodies disposed of in the wood chipper). It also represents an introduction of rural themes to the broader violent crime television genre.

COMPARISON AND REFLECTION

We have focused here on the most popular mainstream television series with rural themes, going back to the mid-1950s and continuing through the present. This long view has allowed us to observe considerable change and evolution, and to draw some conclusions about the general themes and patterns surrounding rural representations. This is significant not only for challenging the baseless ideas held by urbanites, but also for those accepted in rural communities. As Jonasson's (2012) research suggests, television media are influential in shaping rural performances, where everyday life turns into a simulation of an idea.

The earliest rural-themed series engaged in a kind of historical narrative that sought to glorify westward expansion, Manifest Destiny, and the civilizing force of urbanization. Key images include continual conflicts and violent struggles. They often included brushes with Native Americans and bands of outlaws, and therefore, racial exclusion and exclusivity were common. The rural was cast as something raw and dangerous that had to be dominated and overcome, while the process of settlement was equated with the processes of urbanization and civilization. It's not until we move past the Western genre of mid-century that we arrive at the far lighter series that include the hapless comedic dealings of simple, unrefined rural folk and their cultural clashes with (superior) elite and urban people and places. Here the rural ceases to be morally understood as dangerous and wild, and takes on an endearing positive quality, even if it remains demeaning. With the arrival of *Dallas* in the 1980s, focus shifted to the personal ties between the characters and a more ambivalent moral valence became attached to the rural itself, and this coincided with a decision made by the major television networks to back away from rural shows.

What we view as the contemporary period begins after the 1980s, with the show *Twin Peaks* and is characterized by more complex story lines and moral vocabularies. In terms of imagery, the supernatural has played a far greater role in the narratives of the series and was absent in the earlier period. After revisiting the classic Western themes in *Deadwood*—albeit in far more modern terms—the contemporary period of rural-themed series included vampires, zombies, shape-shifters, werewolves, evil spirits, and headless horsemen. Rather than dwell on historical narrative construction as was central to traditional Westerns, contemporary rural series tend to be forward-looking—and the future looks quite bleak. In both *Revolution* and *The Walking Dead* we see apocalyptic dystopian conditions after the collapse of urban society forces a return to rural living (dealt with more completely by Lowe in the volume). The lighter *Parks and Recreation* takes us back to some of the same small-town images as *The Andy Griffith Show* though in modern style.

A look at table 2.2 shows that a majority—about nine out of the fifteen shows we reviewed—cast the rural in a negative light, with a few (three) showing up as ambivalent, and few as positive (three series), built around small town idyllic charm. Most (ten) of the series have a pronounced violent and murderous theme running through them. In terms of the rural, wild, and simple classification scheme, the most prominent is clearly the rural as wild (ten), followed by escape (six), and simple (five).

Table 2.2.   Summary of Popular Rural-Themed Television Series

Show	Premise	Images/Ideas of Representation	Moral Valence
Gunsmoke (1955–1975)	Maintaining law and order in the wild west	Violence and murder Adventure and conflict	Rural is dangerous and negative

Show	Premise	Images/Ideas of Representation	Moral Valence
		Racial exclusion Historical narrative Rural as wild	
Wagon Train (1957–1965)	Negotiating the challenges of the wild west in a wagon train going to California	Adventure and conflict Violence and murder Racial exclusion Historical narrative Rural as wild	Rural is dangerous and negative
Bonanza (1959– 1973)	Maintaining control over a very large ranch while confronting continual external threats	Historical narrative Adventure and conflict Violence and murder Racial exclusion Rural as wild	Rural is dangerous and negative
The Andy Griffith Show (1960–1968)	Poor rural mountain family strikes it rich and moves to elite Beverly Hills	Cultural clash Racial exclusion Rural as simple	Rural is attractive and positive
The Beverly Hillbillies (1962–1971)	Comical story lines set in the iconic and simple small town of Mayberry	Idyllic small-town life Racial exclusion Historical narrative Rural as simple	Rural is attractive and positive
Dallas (1978–1991)	Dramatic series developed around an oil tycoon and his family's rocky relationships	Adventure and conflict Racial exclusion Rural as escape	Rural is ambivalent
Twin Peaks (1990–1991)	A small rural town is turned into a murder scene and sight of investigation	Supernatural forces Violence and murder Idyllic small-town life Rural as wild and simple	Rural is ambivalent
Deadwood (2004–2006)	Frontier gold town is setting for continual conflicts, most violent	Violence and murder Historical narrative Rural as wild	Rural is dangerous and negative
True Blood (2008–Present)	Based on the concept of supernatural beings	Supernatural forces Idyllic small-town life	Rural is dangerous and negative

Show	Premise	Images/Ideas of Representation	Moral Valence
	including vampires that attempt to live together peaceably; focus on Bon Temps, Louisiana	Violence and murder Rural as escape and wild	
Parks and Recreation (2009–Present)	Small town government and community life	Idyllic small-town life Cultural clash Rural as simple	Rural is attractive and positive
The Walking Dead (2010–Present)	Another post-apocalypse survival concept this time based on a zombie takeover	Supernatural forces Violence and murder Adventure and conflict Rural as wild and escape	Rural is dangerous and negative
Revolution (2012–2014)	A story about a post-apocalypse survival when nano-tech robots have hijacked the energy supply	Supernatural forces (technological) Violence and murder Adventure and conflict Rural as wild and escape	Rural is dangerous and negative
Nashville (2012–Present)	Country music scene in Nashville; old versus new styles compete as signified by main characters	Cultural clash (internal) Racial exclusion Rural as escape and simple	Rural is ambivalent
Sleepy Hollow (2013–Present)	Headless horseman returns as a sign of apocalypse	Supernatural forces Violence and murder Historical narrative Rural as wild	Rural is dangerous and negative
Fargo (2014–Present)	Series based on kidnapping turned murder investigation	Violence and murder Rural as wild and escape	Rural is dangerous and negative

In summary, we find that the most popular rural-themed television series are generally cast in a dangerous and negative light, while the most prominent theme is violence and murder. Indeed, the characterization is multifaceted (Halfacree, 2007), but the violent and dangerous image comes through most prominently. The theme of violence and murder generally arises in conjunction with the negative moral valence. Therefore, at best, rural is viewed as a location for a simple life in an idyllic small town, but typically something that should be avoided, overcome, or else dominated.

As the overwhelming characterization of rural is held to be morally dangerous, negative, and implicitly inferior, we find support for the general claim that urbanormativity has a firm grip on popular television (Thomas et al., 2010; Fulkerson and Thomas, 2014). The idea that urbanization is a civilizing force comes through in nearly every case. It is the general narrative—particularly of Westerns—that the settling of the United States and Manifest Destiny are really the first steps toward urbanizing and thus civilizing the nation. In contrast, *The Andy Griffith Show*'s more positive romanticizing of small town life emphasizes the notion that we are now living in a fast paced urban society that longs to get back to a simpler and more rural time—a theme likewise picked up in *The Beverly Hillbillies*. But the incompetent characters and triviality of that life remind the viewer about the inferiority of rural existence. In the dystopian series, the rural is not only inferior but a necessary evil to be negotiated in the wake of a collapsed urban social order.

In terms of couching our findings against the backdrop of research on the rural representations, we find that the dominant description may best be summarized as the rural *scary*. The sheer volume of shootings and murders occurring in rural-themed series underscores this imagery. This image of the rural scary is most pronounced in the rural horror film genre, as reviewed by Hayden in this volume. Next, we find that rural representations often include forms of racial exclusivity, consistent with prior studies (Agyeman and Spooner, 1997; Holloway, 2007; Neal, 2002), and while this theme has diminished over time it has not vanished. Our discovery of the supernatural theme is to our knowledge the first observation of its kind in the rural studies literature on rural representations. The popularity of the supernatural theme in contemporary series highlights that the rural is starting to be considered as part of a hyper-reality to be experienced only in fantasy rather than daily life. In an urbanormative culture, the real rural is understood as deviant and strange, so it only makes sense to couple rural with supernatural themes. With regard to the three-part classification offered by Thomas et al. (2011), we found that the rural as wild theme is most common. When the rural as escape theme emerged it was often in the context of escaping surveillance, social control, and immediate risks in the city, but the rural hinterland was rarely cast as a desirable safe haven or retreat—simply a lesser of two evils. The contemporary series *The Walking Dead* and *Revolution* exemplify these observations.

In closing we would note some limitations of what we have accomplished in our study. This analysis aimed at breadth over depth, and we realize that far closer examination of these individual television series is desirable. Our hope is that this 30,000-foot view may inspire closer examination in future research. We also realize that many would prefer a more systematic coding scheme that is more typical of a manifest content analysis. Again, we think this type of methodology works best when the goal is depth over breadth, and therefore believe future research should consider this approach. Another potential limitation of this study is the sample of television series that were selected, based on popularity. It could be that many of the findings are a function of popularity rather than rurality—as mainstream audiences often enjoy a good violent shoot out, whether in the Old West or in an urban setting. We therefore see value in examining less popular rural-themed series to see if our observations hold up. Similarly, by choosing the television series as the unit of analysis rather than the individual episodes, we are clearly painting with broad brush strokes. A more systematic examination of individual episodes would be a desirable project that could enhance our understanding of popular media-based rural representations. While this study has limitations we think that it has provided some important contributions to our understanding of the television media and its role in propagating various images and ideas that inform the rural representations of society.

NOTE

1. An earlier version of this chapter was presented as a paper at the 2014 meetings of the Rural Sociological Society in New Orleans, Louisiana, at the Waldorf Astoria.

REFERENCES

Agyeman, J., and Spooner, R. (1997). Ethnicity and the rural environment. In P. Cloke, and J. Little, *Contested countryside cultures: Otherness, marginalisation, and rurality* (pp. 197–217). London: Routledge.

Baylina, M., and Berg, N. (2010). Selling the countryside: Representations of rurality in Norway and Spain. *European Urban and Regional Studies, 17*(3), 277–292.

Berg, B. L., and Lune, H. (2011). Qualitative Research Methods for the Social Sciences (8th ed.). New York: Pearson.

Bunce, M. (2003). Reproducing rural idylls. In P. Cloke, *Country visions* (pp. 14–30). Harlow: Pearson.

Cloke, P. (1997). Country backwater to virtual village? Rural studies and 'the cultural turn'. *Journal of rural studies, 13*(4), 367–375.

Cloke, P., and Little, J. (1997). Contested countryside cultures: Otherness, marginalisation and rurality. London: Routledge.

Durkheim, E. (1915). The elementary forms of religious life. (J. W. Swain, Trans.) London: Hollen Streen Press LTD, Geoge Allan and Unwin LTD.

Edensor, T. (2006). Performing rurality. In P. Cloke, T. Marsden, and P. Mooney, *Handbook of rural studies* (pp. 484–495). London: Sage.

Fulkerson, G., and Seale, E. K. (2012). The case of Cooperstown, New York: The makings of a perfect village in an urbanising world. *Sociological Research Online, 17*(4). Retrieved from http://www.socresonline.org.uk/17/4/9.html

Fulkerson, G., and Thomas, A. R. (2013). Studies in urbanormativity: Rural community in urban society. Lanham, MD: Lexington Books.

Halfacree, K. (1993). Locality and social representation: Space, discourse and alternative definitions of the rural. *Journal of Rural Studies, 9*(1), 23–37.

Halfacree, K. (2007). Trial by space for a 'radical rural': Introducing alternative localities, representations and lives. *Journal of Rural Studies, 23*(2), 125–141.

Halfacree, K., and Boyle, P. (1998). Migration, rurality and the post-productivist countryside, migration into rural areas: Theories and issues. London: Routledge.

Halfacree, K., and Rivera, M. J. (2011). Moving to the countryside…and staying: Lives beyond representations. *Sociologia Ruralis, 52*(1), 92–114.

Hall, S. (2007). Representation: Cultural representations and signifying practices. London: Sage.

Holloway, S. (2007). Burning issues: Whiteness, rurality and the politics of difference. *Geoforum, 38*(1), 7–20.

Jonasson, M. (2012). Co-producing and co-performing attractive rural living in popular media. *Rural Society, 22*(1), 17–30.

Lowe, B. (2006). Emerging moral vocabularies: The creation and establishment of new forms of moral and ethical meanings. Lanham, MD: Lexington Books.

Lowe, B. (2010). The creation and establishment of moral vocabularies. In S. Vaisey, and S. Hitlin, *Handbook of the sociology of morality* (pp. 293–312). New York: Springer.

McKinney, L. (2013). A study of sustainability: Entropy and the urban/rural transition. In G. Fulkerson, and A. R. Thomas, *Studies in urbanormativity: Rural community in urban society* (pp. 251–278). Lanham, MD: Lexington Books.

Miles, M. B., Huberman, A. M., and Saldaña, J. (2013). Qualitative data analysis: A methods sourcebook (3rd ed.). Thousand Oaks, CA: Sage.

Miles, M., and Huberman, M. (1994). Qualitative analysis: An expanded sourcebook (2nd Ed.). Thousand Oaks, CA: Sage.

Moscovici, S. (1984). The phenomenon of social representations. In R. Farr, and S. Moscovici, *Social Representations* (pp. 3–69). Cambridge: Cambridge University Press.

Neal, S. (2002). Rural landscapes, representations and racism: Examining multicultural citizenship and policy-making in the English countryside. *Ethnic and Racial Studies, 25*(3), 442–461.

Phillips, M., Fish, R., and Agg, J. (2001). Putting together ruralities: Towards a symbolic analysis of rurality in the British mass media. *Journal of Rural Studies, 17*(1), 1–27.

Pruitt, L. (2014). The rural lawscape: Space tames law tames space. In I. Braverman, N. Blomley, D. Delaney, and A. Kedar, *The Expanding Spaces of Law: A Timely Legal Geography* (pp. 190–214). Stanford, CA: Stanford University Press.

Rye, J. F. (2006). Rural youth's images of the rural. *Journal of Rural Studies, 22*, 409–421.

Thomas, A. R., Lowe, B., Fulkerson, G., and Smith, P. (2010). Critical rural theory: Space*structure*culture. Lanham, MD: Lexington Books.

Woods, M. (2010). Performing rurality and practicing rural geography. *Progress in Human Geography, 34*(6), 835–846.

Chapter Three

Portrayals of Rural People and Places in Reality Television Programming

*How Popular American Cable Series
Misrepresent Rural Realities*

Karl A. Jicha

Since the early 1990s, reality television shows have enjoyed widespread popularity among American audiences. Covering a broad assortment of subject matter and depicting people encountering an even wider variety of "real-life" situations, reality shows have become a proven commodity, generating a windfall for the networks as they are generally low-budget, unscripted (for the most part), and rely on a relatively unknown cast who generally are not professional actors, as noted by Jonsson (2014):

> As a new television season kicks off, series about strange subcultures of survivalists or blue-collar families, many of them with Spanish moss beards and grins that need some dental work, appear at almost every click of the remote.

Enjoying its unexpected rise among the top popular television genres, and firmly embedding itself in American popular culture, reality television has quickly evolved into a number of different subgenres (Haynes, 2014). Among the latest and most popular of these is the growing number of shows with rural-based themes that delve into the occupations, lifestyles, and even life-or-death struggles with the environment of rural Americans. Broadly referred to as part of a "cultural tourism" subgenre that documents the lives and activities of rural Americans, these series are more commonly referred to as "rural reality" television. Despite their popularity, many scholars and television critics have classified this subgenre of reality television as "redneck reality." This negative label is the result of concerns over the substance and legitimacy of a number of series with rural-based themes and critics contend that they unfairly portray the reality of rural people and places and serve to reinforce commonly held rural stereotypes (Buchanan, 2014; Cox, 2011; Hernandez, 2014).

Since the Discovery Channel aired the first episode of *Deadliest Catch* (2005–Present), a show documenting the lives of Alaska crab fishermen on the Bering Sea, the emergence of rural-based reality programs as a form of popular entertainment has been nothing short of extraordinary and unrivaled among other subgenres of reality television. America's obsession with rural reality shows has driven networks to bring countless unusual, and often uncharacteristic, aspects of rural life into mainstream popular culture. However, this *ruralfication* of popular culture has met with mixed reviews. While some shows celebrate rural traditions and values, the content of others has generated serious questions as to their authenticity. As ratings have soared, critics accuse producers and networks of ignoring the rich diversity of rural populations and livelihoods in the pursuit of advertising and marketing profits. There are also valid concerns about the misrepresentation and exploitation of the rural working-class that typically are the focus of the majority of rural reality shows.

This chapter tracks the rise of rural reality television programming over the past decade, provides a 10-category classification system for the 127 rural-themed reality shows that have aired during that time, and examines how rural populations, culture, livelihoods, and places are depicted. The in-depth look into America's obsession with rural reality television presented here is also intended to identify the potential consequences these shows have for a large segment of the population that continues to be misunderstood and, consequently, misrepresented in mainstream American television programming and social media.

The next section of this chapter reviews the factors that led to rural programming's nearly thirty-five-year hiatus from television lineups. Contributing factors included shifting public perceptions of small-town rural America in the 1960s, one of the most socially and politically tumultuous decades in the history of the nation, and networks prioritizing viewer demographics and marketing profitability over ratings. Following this is a detailed discussion of the rise in popularity of reality television and how it generated renewed interest in a new breed of rural programming. The second half of the chapter provides the results of a content analysis of reality television shows designed to identify those with clear rural themes and to trace the rise in popularity of this unique brand of television entertainment. I also ascertain general trends across rural reality shows in order to provide a classification framework. Critics contend that many rural reality shows distort their representations of rural people and places to meet the expectations of their primarily urban audience and this serves to perpetuate long-held stereotypes. In an effort to address this, the chapter closes with a discussion of concerns associated with the "ruralfication" of popular culture when portrayed through an urbanormative (Fulkerson and Thomas, 2013, p. 7) lens.

THE "RURAL PURGE" (1969–1972) AND DECLINE OF EARLY RURAL TELEVISION

In the 1950s and 1960s, Westerns and situational comedies with rural themes enjoyed considerable popularity among American viewers and a number of these series firmly established themselves among the list of top-rated shows, as discussed by Fulkerson and Lowe (this volume). Potentially foreshadowing their eventual decline, many of these rural programs aired at a time when rural populations were experiencing a rapid decline (Kaiser and Bernstein, 2014). The success of these shows may have been partly due to a sense of nostalgia or a reflection of concerns with what was possibly being lost with growing urbanization. Rural people were portrayed as noble yet incredibly naive country folk from deep in the American heartland and the cast of these shows often consisted of well-known actors and actresses with established Hollywood pedigrees (e.g., Andy Griffith, Buddy Ebsen, James, Arness, Lorne Greene, Eddie Albert, and Eva Gabor). This made them comfortable figures that were easy to relate to among viewers. The stories depicted in the shows were typically light and comedic, or action packed and dramatic. The heroes and villains were easy to identify and the shows generally portrayed a picturesque and idealistic side of life in rural America. Many of the 1960s rural-themed television series experienced long runs and achieved high viewer ratings. Among the more popular shows were *The Andy Griffith Show* (1960–1968), *The Beverly Hillbillies* (1962–1971), and to a lesser extent, *Green Acres* (1965–1971), *Petticoat Junction* (1963–1970), and *Hee Haw* (1969–1971). However, the popularity of these shows was not enough to save them as network executives were concerned that they primarily appealed to an older rural demographic and were not worthy of advertising dollars in the long-term (Kaiser and Bernstein, 2014). Contributing to the growing concerns over the viability of rural-themed television programs was the fact that the Columbia Broadcasting System (CBS) had grown particularly sensitive to its own image due to its growing reputation as the "Country Broadcasting System" that catered to older, rural, and less affluent viewers (Kaiser and Bernstein, 2014). At the time CBS was the leader in popular rural-themed shows. Eventually, the belief that rural programming was no longer relevant to the times and unpopular with the 18 to 49-year-old urban demographic led the networks to take drastic measures. What ensued was what was referred to in media circles as the *rural purge*, a three-season period (1969–1972) during which American television networks—CBS in particular— cancelled nearly all of their rural-themed shows. This move was surprising to many as a number of these shows were among the ratings leaders at the time they were not renewed. Despite this, four shows were dropped at the conclusion of the 1969–1970 television season, another seventeen the following year, and six more between 1971–1975, including two long-running westerns, *Gunsmoke* (twenty years) and *Bonanza* (fourteen years). Many of the shows that were not renewed continued to enjoy popularity as reruns in syndication, but an era had drawn to a conclusion.

The fact that the major networks were more concerned with the demographics of their viewers than with ratings demonstrated the strength of the voice of younger urban viewers who were more interested in dramas, sitcoms, crime and action series, and family shows that were centered in urban and suburban locales and that represented what they believed to be contemporary urban dwellers and issues and that were considered to be progressive and socially relevant given the times. This led to the popularity of shows such as the *Brady Bunch* (1969–1974), *All in the Family* (1971–1979), *M*A*S*H* (1972–1983), the *Bob Newhart Show* (1972–1978), and *Emergency!* (1972–1977).

It is important to note that a small number of new rural-themed drama programs such as *The Waltons* (1972–1981) and *Little House on the Prairie* (1974–1983) did experience some success throughout the 1970s and into the early 1980s. *The Dukes of Hazzard* (1979–85) was the lone exception to the rule about the ban on rural-themed comedies. Aside from this limited slate of programs (see Fulkerson and Lowe, this volume), rural life was rarely ever depicted in network television outside of nature and hunting and fishing shows until the turn of the twenty-first century when cable channels embraced the popularity of reality television. Even then, rural-themed shows have rarely resurfaced in programming among the major networks.

THE RISE OF REALITY TELEVISION AND THE RURAL RESURGENCE

The genre of reality television owes much of its evolution to the assortment of talk shows and niche programming featuring live studio audiences and colorful casts in their everyday settings (e.g., cooking and outdoors shows) that broke from traditional pre-filmed shows with trained actors. Some television scholars argue that MTV's *The Real World* (1992–Present), provided the initial model for what most have come to identify as contemporary reality television (Ouellette and Murray, 2004). The gradual rise in popularity of *Real World*, which followed the experiences of groups of young adults living together under one roof in a new city, "trained a generation of young viewers in the language of reality TV" (Ouellette and Murray, 2004, p. 5). According to Ouellette and Murray (2004), *Real World* paved the way for the *Survivor* franchise (2000–Present) and *Big Brother* (2000–Present), reality game shows that first aired internationally in the late 1990s before breaking into the American market,. The popularity of these shows marked the full emergence of this genre which has withstood the test of time as both are still currently in production.

Most viewers could probably identify what constitutes reality television. However the industry itself has not provided a clear definition of the genre (Nabi, 2007). As a result, this task has been left in the hands of television scholars. Nabi and colleagues (2003, p. 304) provide perhaps the most inclusive description of reality television which they define as "programs that film real people as they live out events in their lives, contrived or otherwise, as they occur." Identifying characteristics are that they: (a) involve "real people" playing themselves; (b) are filmed to some degree in actual living or working conditions of the cast; (c) involve both the ordinary and extraordinary aspects of their lives; (d) are largely unscripted; (e) typically have a distinctively well-spoken narrator who provides an introduction to each show and who announces the transition from one scene to the next; and (f) are produced for the primary purpose of viewer entertainment (Nabi, 2007; Ouellette and Murray, 2004).

Since its beginnings in the early 1990s, the genre of reality television has evolved into a number of different subgenres (Haynes, 2014). Series have commonly revolved around the divergent themes of game shows (e.g., *Survivor*, *Big Brother*, *The Apprentice*), dating programs (e.g., *The Bachelor*, *The Bachelorette*), talent contests (e.g., *Americas Got Talent*, *American Idol*), makeovers (*Queer Eye for the Straight Guy*, *Extreme Makeover*, *Pimp My Ride*), legal and courtroom television (e.g., *Cops*, *Judge Judy*, *The Peoples' Court*), celebrity series that make past-their-prime pop culture stars appear more like "regular" people (e.g., *The Surreal Life*, *Celebrity Rehab with Dr. Drew*), reality sitcoms (e.g., *The Simple Life*, *The Osbournes*), and docusoaps (e.g., *The Real World*, *The Real Housewives of Orange County*) (Ouellette and Murray, 2004).

One can add the subgenre of docu-series to those listed above. These shows examine the occupations and lifestyles of hard-working American men and women and rural reality shows began as a spin-off to this subgenre. Perhaps the most popular series from this subgenre was the Discovery Channel's *Dirty Jobs* (2005–2012) whose host always began each show with the statement that "My name's Mike Rowe, and this is my job. I explore the country looking for people who aren't afraid to get dirty — hard-working men and women who earn an honest living doing the kinds of jobs that make civilized life possible for the rest of us. Now, get ready to get dirty." Mike

Rowe, who is also a voice artist, also serves as the narrator of *Deadliest Catch*, the series this chapter identifies as the show that sparked the popularity of rural reality television.

The decade following the series premier of *Deadliest Catch* witnessed the gradual rise of rural reality television as arguably the most diverse and expansive of all reality show subgenres. As the number of shows and channels carrying them have grown, rural reality television has certainly attracted a wide viewership while capturing a substantial share of the ratings as described by Jonsson (2014).

Despite the massive viewership of the World Cup this summer, *Duck Dynasty*, about the Robertson family of Louisiana and its successful duck-call business, hovered at the top of the rankings after becoming one of the biggest cable hits in history in 2013. *Swamp People, Mountain Men*, and a handful of other rural reality TV shows competed for slots in the Top 25, and others garnered significant viewership. This included *American River Renegades*, which chronicles the lives of fishermen from the Great Pee Dee River in South Carolina to the northern reaches of the Mississippi.

The Appeal of Rural Reality Television for American Viewers

The degree to which viewers have embraced rural reality television over the past decade has been nothing short of surprising given the nearly complete exclusion of rural-themed shows from the major networks since the 1970s. The steady wave of new shows depicting rural occupations, colorful, and often bizarre, characters behaving well outside the boundaries of conventional social norms, natural and often remote settings in the farthest reaches of the United States, rural people living off the land, and rags-to-riches stories have drawn viewers from every age demographic. Reality TV's simple formula has provided viewers with a dramatic break from traditional programming as it provides unpredictable plot lines and the opportunity to watch real people put into situations that viewers normally would never consider. It has become an addiction for many viewers and fits perfectly with the current era of social media where viewers can write about shows online and converse with other fans in real time. It seems that a new rural-themed show is introduced every few weeks and there appears to be no end in sight as there is a limitless pool of material to draw from.

Much of the appeal for rural reality television relates to the fact that shows are not nearly as scripted as mainstream reality shows (Ouellette and Murray, 2004). While many cast members in other subgenres of reality TV are overly concerned with the trappings of popular culture, those on rural reality shows are generally portrayed as being down-to-earth and extraordinarily ordinary. In a 2011 *Los Angeles Times* editorial, television critic Robert Lloyd (2011) alluded to this in his comment that:

Some (cast members) smoke cigarettes, and not to look sophisticated. They dress in their own clothes, for comfort or for work. Many could stand to lose a few pounds, to start. With some exceptions—the female characters tend to be conventionally hot, conventionally—they are not like people Hollywood casts for lead roles. Some are even old—the men of "Gold Rush," out of work and prospecting for gold, are almost all in their 40s, 50s and 60s, and that is part of the story. As TV, there is something refreshing about it.

If viewers were seeking a break from normal programming fair, this subgenre of reality television has certainly delivered. New shows reveal a side of America that most urban viewers, who comprise the majority of the audience, are completely unaccustomed to and they have the opportunity to watch rural residents doing seemingly unreal things in a modern world (Lloyd, 2011). Jonsson (2014) further explains that rural reality television shows could not have picked a better time to emerge and to gradually dominate cable ratings:

> The rise of redneck TV has paralleled one of the toughest economic stretches for the American worker since the Great Depression, a time of polarized politics and economic data that shows the middle-class dream is slipping away. Some experts believe this malaise has pushed Americans toward the visual equivalent of escapism and comfort food: shows about family, adventure, danger, elemental nature, and colloquial wisdom, such as "Swamp People" star Jeromy Pruitt complaining about a tough day on the bayou: "It's hard as Chinese arithmetic out here, boy."

Perhaps it is largely the belief that there is something better out there, a more preferable way of life that is simpler and more rewarding than the normal eight to five day job that draws many viewers to rural reality shows. Among those amassing the highest ratings are series about industrious Americans working the land, carving out a living in often uninhabitable places using their own hands. Far removed from the crowds and hustle and bustle of urban areas, these shows provide viewers with a backstage pass to indulge themselves in the often life-or-death struggles of hardworking rural people hunting hogs, grappling with alligators, catching fish with their hands or contraptions derived from the resources around them, and living off the land, all the while feeling content with their way of life. Many of these shows offer a viewer discretion advisory at the beginning, one of the most popular of which is from *Swamp People*, the number one rated cable show during its time-slot: "The way of life depicted in this program dates back 300 years. Hunting, especially alligator hunting, lies at its core. Some images may be disturbing . . . viewer discretion is advised."

Further contributing to the rise in popularity of rural reality television is that producers can create a seemingly limitless number of series since filming is less expensive as it does not require highly paid and trained professional actors and actresses, relies on an abundance of natural sets, and props are often whatever is on hand at the time. Coupled with the largely unscripted nature of rural reality series, this means shows can be produced quickly, cheaply, and without many of the complication associated with costly traditional television series. With advertisers always seeking ways to reach the prized demographic category of 18–49 year-old urban viewers, rural reality television provides an attractive opportunity as should one show fail, there is always another that can quickly replace it (Streisand, 2001). The flexibility of rural reality shows allows producers to match the viewer's demands. If they like shows that focus on dangerous occupations, there is a limitless array of jobs, no matter how obscure, in rural areas to choose from. If they want drama and conflict between cast members, they create tension by pitting competing groups against one another in search of riches (e.g., *Gold Rush* and *Bering Sea Gold*) or by creating a wrap up show that airs after each episode and provides cast members with a chance to air their opinions of one another and to answer viewer questions live.

Rural reality television offers armchair adventurers of all ages the opportunity to experience a completely different way of life that often takes them well outside of their comfort zone. At the same time, the down home cast and natural settings are not typically portrayed as dirty, ignorant, menacing, or, in some cases, highly sexualized as the rural men and women stereotyped in the popular "rural slasher" movies *Texas Chainsaw Massacre* (1974) and *The Hills Have Eyes* (1977) (DeKeseredy, Muzzatti, and Donnermeyer, 2014, p. 180) or the inbred (see Hayden, this volume) and sinister mountain men and ruthless Bayou swamp trappers in dramatic thrillers such as *Deliverance* (1972) and *Southern Comfort* (1981). Rural reality shows have softened the image of rural Americans to some degree. This makes them less scary and mysterious. However, the topics covered and the depictions of rural people are still carefully crafted by the producers of these shows and are intended to provide some measure of familiarity that meets the preconceived expectations of the viewers who are largely based in urban areas.

The remainder of this chapter presents the results of a content analysis of reality television programming that provide a more precise picture of the evolution of the subgenre of rural reality shows by tracing its growth over the last decade and identifying the networks and channels that have served as its primary champions. From the results of the content analysis, I provide a 10-category classification system for rural reality shows based on shared themes or formats. The chapter concludes with a critical assessment of the extent to which rural reality television distorts the reality of twenty-first century rural America.

RESEARCH METHODS

Holsti (1969, p. 14) defines content analysis as, "any technique for making inferences by objectively and systematically identifying specified character-istics of messages." For this study, I adopted a systematic approach towards identifying the prevalence of rural reality shows in television programming by conducting an exhaustive content analysis of all reality shows aired on the major networks and cable channels. In keeping with Krippendorff's (2004) criteria for conducting content analyses, I used the reality television show as my unit of analysis and defined this broad genre of television programming based on the identifying characteristics provided by Nabi and colleagues (2003) and Ouellette and Murray (2004) that set it apart from traditional television shows. Accordingly, a reality television show is any program that films purportedly real people living out events in their lives as they occur in a largely unscripted manner.

I limited my search criteria to the traditional major networks (ABC, CBS, NBC, PBS, and FOX) and cable channels that air weekly series. I further restricted the number of shows in my analysis to those that aired between 2005 and 2015, as I make a case for *Deadliest Catch* being the pioneering show that sparked America's current love affair with rural-themed reality programs. Following the exploits of crews aboard Bering Sea fishing vessels based out of Dutch Harbor, Alaska, during the Alaskan king crab, snow crab, and bairdi crab seasons, *Deadliest Catch* quickly became a worldwide phe-nomenon and currently airs in over 200 countries. Arguably the Discovery Channel's biggest hit program, the show has garnered numerous television awards and is one of the highest rated reality shows of all time. Americans fell in love with the ship captains and crew members as they braved the treacherous waters of the Bering Sea and put their lives on the line every week. Within a few short years of the first season of *Deadliest Catch*, a host of other shows featuring dangerous occupations in rural locations appeared on other cable channels.

In order to identify reality shows that focused on rural people and places, I looked for decisively identifiable rural symbols in show titles and descrip-tions that were provided on the channel websites. I further explored the presence of identifying markers of rural-themed shows by viewing episodes of any that remained ambiguous. Rural symbols included any clear reference to rural Americans, places, occupations, or lifeways as the focus of the pro-gram, derogatory and stereotypical slang or names in the show title, and other indicators that the focus of the show was on rural people and their lived experiences in the United States. A simple reference to country was not sufficient as shows had to specifically involve people and places that were by definition rural. After an exhaustive search to identify rural-themed pro-grams, I verified that all locations depicted in the shows met the U.S. Census

Bureau's definition of rural. I also kept any shows that were slightly above the population threshold if the show clearly referred to the cast or setting as rural.

One category of shows that made reference to or depicted rural regions of the United States was excluded on the basis that episodes were filmed in largely uninhabited areas and frequently traveled to locations in other countries. These shows included the more than half-dozen survivalist expert programs such as the extremely popular *Survivorman* (2004–Present) with Les Stroud, *Man vs. Wild* (2006–2011) with Bear Grylls, *Dual Survival* (2010–Present), and a number of others that pit former military and primitive survival experts against rugged and inhospitable environments.

Purpose of Analysis

This study marks the first attempt in the literature to compile a comprehensive list of rural reality shows and I formulated the selection criteria as there was no preexisting context for analyzing this data. Establishing a detailed summary of rural reality shows makes it possible to track the growth of this subgenre of reality television and identify which channels and networks air the largest number of shows. In addition, it provides a basis from which to categorize rural reality series based on shared themes and other common characteristics. The ultimate purpose of which is to discern how network and cable channels depict rural people and places and characterize them through a popular medium that is found in virtually every American household, over 80 percent of which are located in urban areas.

THE EVOLUTION OF RURAL REALITY
TELEVISION (2005–2015)

After a meticulous content analysis, I identified 127 television series that had rural-based themes (see Appendix for complete listing), were filmed in the United States, and that aired between 2005 and 2015. The findings of the content analysis are presented in figure 3.1 which depicts the dramatic rise of what has become a considerably large, yet relatively unexplored, subgenre of reality television. As anticipated, *Deadliest Catch* provides a fitting starting point for tracking the transformation of rural reality television from obscure and unnoticed to a widely popular phenomenon.

After its premiere in 2005, *Deadliest Catch* stood alone among the ranks of American rural-based reality shows until 2007 when History (originally the History Channel) released *Ice Road Truckers*. Following the experiences of truck drivers hauling cargo on seasonal routes across frozen lakes and rivers in remote Arctic territories in Canada and Alaska, *Ice Road Truckers*

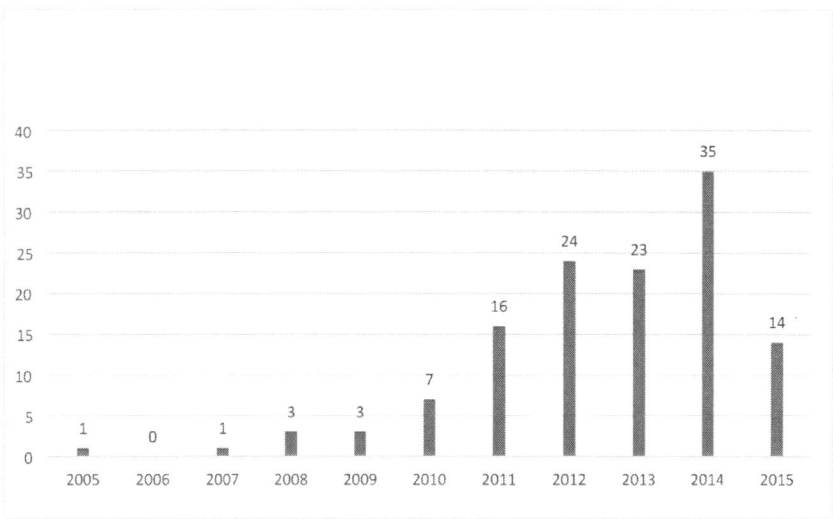

Figure 3.1.

became the second in a long line of series depicting dangerous occupations in rural and remote regions of the United States.

Following the popularity of *Ice Road Truckers*, three more rural reality shows aired in 2008 representing a seemingly insignificant increase. History produced another successful series titled *Ax Men* that followed in line with the early trend towards shows about dangerous rural occupations. TruTV followed suit with *Black Gold*, a series chronicling workers on oil drilling rigs in Andrews County, Texas. However, Country Music Television took things in a decisively different direction with *My Big Redneck Wedding*, a show hosted by comedian Tom Arnold that featured over-the-top weddings between "country couples" and served to reinforce some of the worst stereotypes of rural Americans. Seemingly insignificant at the time, this brand of rural reality show served as a sign of things to come.

The 2009 television season witnessed only three additional rural reality series. Two of these, *Billy the Exterminator* on A&E and History's *Swamp Loggers* followed the increasingly common theme of out-of-the-ordinary and dangerous occupations. The third series that aired that year introduced a third new category of rural reality shows that documents the experiences of law enforcement in rural areas. The National Geographic Channel's *Alaska State Troopers* featured the exploits of officers from all over the state and most of the episodes focused on crime in some of the most remote territories.

There was a slight uptick in new series in 2010 and several new shows branched out from previous formats. A few shows continued to focus on dangerous occupations and law enforcement, but two extremely popular new shows, the Discovery Channel's *Gold Rush* and History's *Swamp People* broke ground for another wave of rural subject matter, the rags-to-riches story and depictions of the traditional livelihoods of rural people. *Gold Rush* follows the trials and tribulations of several groups of families and friends trying to strike it rich in the gold fields of the Yukon Territory of Alaska. These groups of men and women experience immense struggles at times but eventually they hit pay dirt and reap the rewards of their hard work and sacrifices. *Swamp People* follows families from the swamps of the Atchafalaya River basin in Louisiana who hunt alligators for a living just as their ancestors had before them. In addition to these shows, RFD-TV, owned by Rural Media Group, aired the first episode of *Rural Heritage* in 2010, which offers how-to pointers on preserving traditional skills and technology that our grandparents use.

Over the next four years (2011–2014) rural reality programming experienced unprecedented growth with the introduction of ninety-eight new shows. Sixteen new shows aired in 2011, followed by twenty-four in 2012, and twenty-three in 2013. As the numbers climbed, new themes emerged and additional cable channels began to embrace this popular formula for reality show success. The recent rise of rural reality shows peaked when a record thirty-five new shows aired in 2014.

This past year, rural reality television experienced a substantial drop in the production of new shows in comparison to each of the previous three years as only fourteen new shows emerged. This, however, does not necessarily indicate a decline in the popularity of rural reality. Instead, it may be the result of market saturation where many of the shows that aired since 2010 are still airing new episodes. The production of so many new shows ensures that there will be something for nearly every viewer. An interesting aspect of rural reality shows is the channels that serve as the primary supporters and benefactors of this popular form of entertainment (see figure 3.2). Somewhat surprisingly, all of the shows identified in the content analysis appear on cable and not the traditional networks.

As the figure shows, rural reality television series are primarily the property of the "flagships" of educational television, the Discovery Channel, A& E, the National Geographic Channel, History, and Animal Planet. These "defenders" of quality educational programming appear to have latched onto this proven commodity and, between them, the five major cable channels have accounted for seventy-nine of the 127 series (62.2 percent) identified in the content analysis and have remained the primary producers of rural reality series throughout the last decade. While they already air some of the most popular series in this subgenre, they have still managed to produce nearly two-thirds (65.3 percent) of the forty-nine new shows from 2014 and 2015. While the educational value of the shows aired on these channels is some-

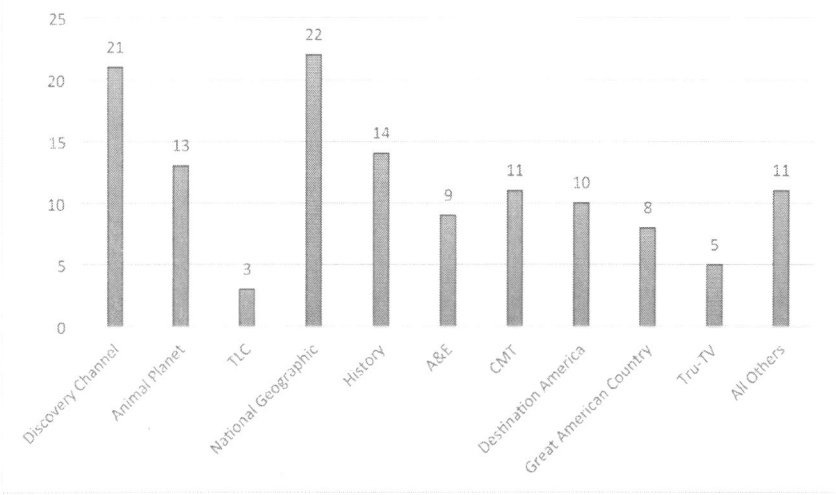

Figure 3.2.

times questionable and they fail to capture the rich diversity of rural people and places, they have largely managed to avoid content that is blatantly disrespectful. The titles of their shows also tend to avoid the use of derogatory labels such as redneck, hillbilly, hick, and hayseed, with the exception of National Geographic's *Rocket City Rednecks* and Animal Planet's *Hillbilly Handfishin'*. At the same time many of the titles of their shows reflect antiquated or obscure lifestyles and activities that are atypical of populations residing in twenty-first century rural America.

SHARED THEMES ACROSS RURAL REALITY SERIES

As rural reality series have become a fixture on cable television, general themes have emerged, several of which were mentioned in the previous section. Early shows focused on unusual and extremely dangerous jobs in the remote reaches of the United States. Often filmed in visually stunning locations, shows such as *Deadliest Catch* portray rural people as hard-working, determined, and extraordinarily courageous men, and in rare cases women, whose primary goal is to provide for their families or to maintain a family legacy. The series that followed over the next ten years often broke from this mold and established popular, yet widely divergent subgroups of rural reality shows. This section provides a 10-category classification system for all 127 shows based on shared themes interpreted through a review of program titles and content descriptions. While some shows could arguably fit into multiple categories, most follow a singular theme.

Dangerous and Dirty Jobs

This subset includes a large number of shows that depict rural occupations that pose considerable risk of injury, and even death, to rural workers. These include jobs in the fishing (e.g., *Deadliest Catch* and *Swamp People*), timber (e.g., *Ax Men* and *American Loggers*), and mining industries (e.g., *Coal* and *Black Gold*), as well as transportation (e.g., *Ice Road Truckers* and *Flying Wild Alaska*), and a number that directly involve wildlife (e.g., *Billy the Exterminator* and *Call of the Wildman*), and other often unfamiliar professions that put workers at risk. Most of these shows feature fields dominated by men, with women playing lesser supportive roles. The casts of shows in this subgroup of rural reality television are usually portrayed in a very favorable light and reflect many core American values as they are hardworking and put family first. They are usually well-spoken and most break out of the stereotyped mold of the ignorant and backwards hillbilly.

Rural Law Enforcement

This subset of rural reality shows follows wildlife (e.g., *Alaska Wildlife Troopers* and *Wild Justice*) and police (e.g., *Alaska State Troopers* and *Southern Justice*) officers as they patrol the backwoods and remote corners of the United States, battling wild animals, criminals, and inhospitable environments. They test their wits and training as they intercede between residents and wild animals, break up drug rings, track fugitives in small isolated towns and villages, and work to protect wildlife and natural areas. Series include the experiences of both male and female officers and are one of the few categories of rural reality television that include minorities among their primary cast members.

Rags to Riches

This subset includes a range of scenarios where people living in rural areas give up their jobs in pursuit of their dreams to strike it rich mining (e.g., *Gold Rush* and *Bering Sea Gold*), rise from humble beginning to become multimillionaires (e.g., *Duck Dynasty* and *Billy Bob's Gags to Riches*), or make a living by selling whatever valuable natural resources they can find (e.g., *Filthy Riches* and *Smoky Mountain Money*). Other series in this grouping share the common theme of making money fast in unconventional ways that most Americans would never consider or, in some cases, lower themselves to. The casts of these shows are often depicted as desperate, greedy, competitive, and scoundrels who are down on their luck. There is a sense of excitement in what they do, but their livelihoods involve a considerable degree of risk that most people are not cut out for.

Family Values

A small number of shows follow families that are not what most viewers would consider to be the typical American domestic unit. Some focus on the outlandish and often disturbing behavior of working-class rural families. Shows such as *Here Comes Honey Boo Boo* cause a considerable stir in both the popular press and on social media sites. The portrayal of rural American families as dysfunctional, loud, and socially inept does little more than perpetuate "redneck" stereotypes (Cavalcante, 2014). In contrast to this brand of entertainment, others popular shows such as the multi-dimensional *Duck Dynasty* promote strong family values and *Country Bucks* and *Boss Hog* depict rural families that work and play together.

Backwoods Survivalist

A close connection to the land has always been a hallmark of traditional rural life. Included in the "Backwoods Survivalist" category of rural reality shows are a large number of series that follow individuals and families as they leave behind the trappings of the modern world to make a living off the land. Subsistence living is the common theme of these shows as is an extreme dissatisfaction with urban life. Traumatic circumstances may lead some to make this life-altering decision (e.g., *Alaska Bush People*) while others simply decide that the modern world no longer holds anything for them (e.g., *The Legend of Mick Dodge*). Other cast members simply view living off the land as part of their heritage and do not know any other way of life (e.g., *Mountain Men*, *Yukon Men*, *The Woodsmen*). In keeping with most other rural reality shows, these series tend to have few female leads among the cast members. While their stories are somewhat easy for viewers to relate to, their appearance and behavior is often outlandish and always atypical. They are depicted as the most unusual of American heroes.

Traditional Lifeways

This grouping of shows depicts rural people struggling to preserve traditional cultural practices at all costs. Some (e.g., *The Pioneers* and *Frontier House*) literally step back in time as cast members attempt to reconstruct a way of life from generations past. Others follow rural entrepreneurs trying to make a living off traditional means, engaging in often illegal practices such as making moonshine. In the show *Moonshiners*, colorful characters with names like "Tickle" and "Jim Tom" try to preserve a way of life and age-old mountain moonshine recipes before they are lost forever. Perpetually at odds with law enforcement, male and female moonshiners also struggle with the elements, fellow moonshiners, angry landowners, and the difficult decision of going legit or keeping a storied piece of mountain heritage alive. There are also a number of shows that claim to break through cultural barriers by providing viewers with an inside look at the lives of groups that adhere to strict traditional religious practices (e.g., *American Colony: Meet the Hutterites* and *Amish: Out of Order*) as they struggle with the pressures and vices of the modern world.

Buying Rural

This distinctive subset of rural reality television follows couples who are generally from urban areas as they search for their dream home in out-of-the-way rural towns and scenic isolated areas with sparse populations (e.g., *Moving Country*, *Buying Alaska*, *Buying the Bayou*, and *Buying Hawaii*). These shows promote the beauty and splendor of rural America while real estate agents attempt to sell cabins and land that offer perspective buyers the opportunity to own their very own piece of heaven. For those that want to escape the hustle and bustle of the city, these shows provide viewers with a glimpse of what they could have, for the right price.

Mystery Hunters

For those who are bored with traditional science fiction shows or who grew up dreaming of catching a glimpse of Bigfoot, this category follows casts of typically scruffy ghost and monster hunters as they trek through heavily wooded rural regions of the country and interview rarely believable witnesses about mythical creatures (e.g., *Alaska Monsters* and *Mountain Monsters*). Bobo and other cast members from the popular Animal Planet series *Finding Bigfoot* humorously make supposed Bigfoot calls in attempts to draw one of these illusive beings out of the woods. Claiming to have made multiple sightings in the past, this group of professional mystery hunters has yet to acquire visual evidence. Still, the hunt continues. These series are very entertaining, but tend to portray rural people as uneducated, gullible, slow-witted, and eager to promote themselves and their hometowns through first-hand accounts of mythical creature sightings. The male cast members usually have long unkempt beards, a disheveled appearance, are quick to shoot first and ask questions later, and their dialogue is often accompanied by subtitles. These shows play off our fascination with rural folklore and the supernatural—a theme also noted by Fulkerson and Lowe (this volume) in their review of fictional rural television.

How-to Guides

Another small number of rural reality series provide viewers with step-by-step instructions on home repairs, restoration projects, preservation tips, and other useful do-it-yourself pointers (e.g., *Rural Heritage*, *Barn Hunters*, and *Barnwood Builders*). Typically airing on channels such as Great American Country and other rural networks, these shows provide tips on how to be more self-reliant and some are intended primarily for rural audiences.

Pure Redneck Reality

The final subset of rural reality shows plays off the all too familiar "fish-out-of-water" formula reminiscent of earlier popular rural-themed shows such as *The Beverly Hillbillies*. The titles of these shows often include derogatory terms for rural people and are the most obvious purveyors of stereotypical images of rural America. Among them are such shows as *Hollywood Hillbillies*, *Hillbillies for Hire*, *R U Faster than a Redneck*, *My Big Redneck Family*, and *My Big Redneck Vacation*, to name a few. Some of these shows clearly poke fun at rural people and treat them in accordance with many long-held urban beliefs about people from the South or mountain regions of the United States. Older male leads frequently appear shirtless (e.g., Porter Ridge) and require subtitles in order for viewers to understand them, while depictions of rural women are highly sexualized with female cast members usually appearing in tight-fitting cut-off shorts ("Daisy Dukes") and flannel shirts unbuttoned far enough so that they leave little to the viewer's imagination. Others shows follow cast members from rural towns as they make the uncomfortable transition to living in urban areas. In this case, rural and urban are treated as a strict dichotomy where residents from one are completely out of place in the other.

DISTORTING THE REALITY OF TWENTY-FIRST CENTURY RURAL AMERICA

As Lichter and Brown (2011, p. 566) point out, there is an "increasing interdependence of rural and urban life" and drawing "sharp rural-urban distinctions seems increasingly obsolete or even problematic." Rural and urban America have become increasingly interconnected economically, socially, and culturally and even those rural populations traditionally left behind are much less isolated from mainstream influences. As a result, the social and spatial boundaries between rural and urban have become blurred (Lichter and Brown, 2011). Despite this growing interdependence, the diverse experiences and characteristics of rural people and places remain largely misunderstood by much, if not the majority, of the nation's population. Popular culture, largely informed by broadcast media, helps to create and reinforce popular misconceptions that are legitimated by an urbanormative ideology that anything urban is normal and anything outside of that is marginalized (Fulkerson and Thomas, 2013).

Television and the film industry have long played a key role in stereotyping people in rural areas of the United States as "ignorant and uncouth hillbillies" (DeKeseredy, Muzzatti, and Donnermeyer, 2014, p. 179). Similarly, they tend to portray rural areas as far removed from the urban world and scenic, yet forbidding places fraught with danger. Rural reality shows still depict the landscape as wild and full of potential natural threats around every corner. One notable change is that rural reality series do not focus exclusively on the rural South. Shows cover a wide range of geographic regions spanning seemingly every state.

With regards to rural people, the steady stream of rural reality shows on cable television over the past decade appears to have done little to alleviate persistent stereotypes. One critical change is that most shows have, for the most part, steered clear of vilifying rural residents who live in the swamps and mountains as demented and in-bred murderers and rapists. In cases where bizarre and unpredictable characters do emerge, they are usually pitted against the more mild-mannered and slightly less unpredictable main cast members (e.g., Shelby Stanga from *Ax Men* and *Legend of Shelby the Swampman*). The people are not as frightening as they have been portrayed in the past, but rarely is any mention made of their receiving an education beyond high school. In cases where educational attainment is brought up, it is usually in the "Rags to Riches" subset of shows and treated as an anomaly among people from rural areas (e.g., the family members from *Duck Dynasty* who all have college or, in some cases, graduate degrees).

While rural reality shows depict their rural cast members as personable, ingenious, and even lovable, they continue to reinforce long-standing stereotypes by ignoring the rich diversity of people, places, occupations, and lifestyles that are characteristic of twenty-first century rural America. Furthermore, they continue to promote the idea that there is a sharp rural-urban dichotomy and that most rural Americans live as they did in the distant past. These misrepresentations are not obvious to most, but are damaging nonetheless as they are viewed by critics as exploitative and damaging to rural communities.

To be fair, a good number of rural reality shows do provide favorable images of rural people. These typically are from among the large pool of "Dangerous and Dirty Jobs" and "Rural Law Enforcement" subgroups. The focus of many of these series is on the nature of the occupation and the experiences of the brave men, and occasionally women, who engage in them. However, most rural reality shows still project images and portrayals of people and places that fit predictable and stereotypical molds. This is particularly problematic as television is an extremely powerful source of information and agent of socialization found in virtually every household (Buchanan, 2014; DeKeseredy, Muzzatti, and Donnermeyer, 2014). It serves as one of society's primary modes of disseminating mainstream cultural values and norms. Any misrepresentations of people and their way of life will undoubtedly leave a lasting image in the minds of most viewers that will shape how they regard others that are different from themselves. Critics contend that mass media and entertainment companies based in metropolitan areas outside of the South are particularly influential in Southern, and rural, popular culture, even more so than are people who actually reside in those locations (Cox, 2011; Hernandez, 2014). It does not help that the majority of viewers are also from urban settings.

Aside from the concern that rural reality shows reinforce rural stereotypes, there are other issues that have gone largely unaddressed in the literature. These include the extremely narrow depictions of occupations, gender roles, and the increasing racial and ethnic diversity in rural America. The subgroup of series that focuses specifically on rural occupations portrays them as dangerous, stressful, and adrenaline-pumping jobs that can only be done by the very brave few who have the grit and determination to perform them. They typically require people working together as a team and are most commonly associated with natural resource extraction, public safety, or involve interactions with wildlife. All of the jobs are filmed outdoors and in rugged environments that often involve extreme weather conditions. This representation of rural occupations, while exciting and entertaining to watch, is anything but the norm in most rural locations. Similarly to urban America, rural economies have become increasingly diverse, with a decreased dependence on agriculture, mining, and manufacturing and an increased dependence on service-related occupations (Brown and Schafft, 2011; Flora and Flora, 2013). In fact, over three-quarters of jobs in rural areas today are in services and a substantial number of these are low-skill low-wage positions (Brown and Schafft, 2011). While most service jobs may not make for exciting reality television, they are overlooked and even frequently downplayed in rural reality shows. Why would you work in an office if you could be outdoors making a living off the land?

Women in twenty-first century rural America continue to face substantial challenges closely related to those they confronted throughout the past (Tickamyer and Henderson, 2003). While women's roles have changed substantially, they continue to face considerable adversity in terms of gaining entry into occupations in nontraditional fields (Lobao and Meyer, 2001) and being underrepresented in stable high-paying occupations (Tickamyer and Henderson, 2003). Female-headed households with children in nonmetropolitan areas also experience a higher poverty rate in comparison to their metropolitan counterparts (48.42 percent to 39.4 percent in 2014) (USDA-ERS, 2015).

Many rural reality shows reflect the challenges rural women face today in that the gender roles of female cast members tend to be very narrowly defined. Most wives on these shows do not work outside of the home and, while they may occasionally assist their husbands on hunts, their primary role is to support their spouses and to serve as the family caregivers. Those that attempt to break from traditional gender roles, such as the female loggers in *Ax Men*, have to work extra hard to earn the respect of the men they work with. At the same time, they are typically scantily clad and serve minor roles in comparison to the men. While some shows (e.g., *Swamp People*) do have key female cast members who more than hold their own against men, these are the exception rather than the norm.

In addition to the misrepresentations of rural occupations and women, racial and ethnic minorities are nearly completely overlooked in rural reality television. In fact, this segment of the population of rural America is rarely even seen on the screen and their experiences in twenty-first century rural America are all but ignored. A few shows such as *Swamp People* and those that film in Alaska frequently cover the difficult circumstances faced by American Indian and Alaskan Native cultures. However, in other series, racial and ethnic minorities are practically nonexistent. Given the current social and political climate related to racial inequality, this is a particularly concerning trend.

As of the 2010 census, rural areas remain less racially and ethnically diverse than urban areas, as approximately 78 percent of the population are non-Hispanic white, compared to 64 percent of the population in the United States as a whole (HAC, 2012). Despite the fact that rural areas are less racially diverse than urban areas, Brown and Schafft (2011, p. 122) point out that "the minority experience has deep roots in rural America, from the largely rural Black Belt of the Southeast, to the Latino border areas of the Southwest, to the rural American Indian reservation lands." It is important to note that while the total number of rural African Americans has dropped over the past two decades, Hispanics and Latinos represent the fastest growing segment of the rural population (Lichter and Brown, 2011). The argument here is that the diverse lived experiences of minority populations in rural America deserve more attention and rural reality shows have, by and large, neglected their stories. Perhaps this is a reflection of the fact that the majority of those who view rural reality shows are non-Hispanic whites and the cable networks are simply meeting the demands of their audience. At the same time, given the number and wide assortment of series, there has to be a place for more coverage of the experiences of minority populations.

CONCLUSION

The current popularity of rural television shows in the United States has been nothing short of surprising given the major networks' mentality towards rural-themed programs during the rural purge of the late 1960s and early 1970s. This chapter outlined the various social, cultural, and economic factors that paved the way for rural reality shows. The content analysis of reality shows that aired from 2005–2015 indicated that the number of shows with rural-based themes has steady increased on cable television to the point that they have literally saturated the weekly lineups of the channels with the largest viewership. They have become a proven commodity and appear set to remain so for the present time.

As popular as this subgenre of reality television is, many of the shows raise concern among viewers, critics, and scholars with regard to their representation of rural people and places. While some shows provide a positive characterization, others merely provide entertainment value for viewers while reinforcing age-old stereotypes. As mentioned at the end of this chapter, the true reality of rural America is rarely depicted in rural reality television. The lived experiences of groups such as rural women and racial and ethnic minorities often go unnoticed or shows actually go so far as to reinforce popular misconceptions surrounding them.

As an emerging force in American popular culture, rural reality television deserves the attention of scholars across a variety of disciplines, as this chapter and other recent contributions to the literature have just scratched the surface. Some of the limitations of this chapter that could be addressed in the future include the need for a more rigorous quantitative content analysis of rural reality shows that would either provide support for the author's classification system or that would offer new insights that could lead to the construction of a more refined number of subgroups. With 127 shows and counting, more rigorous methods are required for a more valid interpretation of the words, messages, and symbols that are characteristics of these shows.

Another important step would be to precisely identify what it is about rural reality shows that intrigues viewers. Is it the casts themselves, the sets where the action or drama take place, or the actual topics that are presented that are so unfamiliar and appealing to most viewers? Extensive survey research could help identify the factors that have contributed to the widespread acceptance of these shows and to determine which demographic groups are most likely to watch them. In turn, another important task to undertake would be to examine how these shows shape viewer impressions of rural people and places. This could inform scholars of the potential consequences of the messages and images that are conveyed.

REFERENCES

A&E Shows. (2015, December 20). Retrieved from http://aetv.com/shows/.

Animal Planet TV Shows. (2015, December 20). Retrieved from http://animalplanet.com/CMT TV. (2015, December 22). Retrieved from http://cmt.com/shows/.

Brown, D. L., and Schafft, K. A. (2011). *Rural people and communities in the 21st century.* Malden, MA: Polity Press.

Buchanan, B. (2014). Portrayals of masculinity in the Discovery Channel's Deadliest Catch. In A. Slad, A. Narro, and B. Buchanan, *Reality television: Oddities of culture* (pp. 1-20). Lanham, MD: Lexington.

Cavalcante, A. (2014). You better "redneckognize"!: Deploying the discourses of realness, social defiance, and happiness to defend here comes Honey Boo Boo on Facebook. In A. Slade, A. Narro, and B. Buchanan, *Reality television: Oddities of culture* (pp. 39-66). Lanham, MD: Lexington.

Cox, K. (2011). *Dreaming of Dixie: How the south was created in american popular culture.* Chapel Hill: University of North Carolina Press.

DeKeseredy, W. S., Muzzatti, S. L., and Donnermeyer, J. F. (2014). Mad men in bib overalls: Media's horrifcation and pornification of rural culture. *Critical Criminology, 22*, 179-197.

Destination America TV Schedule. (2015, December 21). Retrieved from http://destination-america.com/tv-shows/tv-schedule/.

Discovery Shows. (2015, December 20). Retrieved from http://discovery.com/tv-shows/.

Flora, C. B., and Flora, J. L. (2013). *Rural communities: Legacy and change (4th Edition).* Boulder, CO: Westview Press.

Fulkerson, G., and Thomas, A. R. (2013). *Studies in Urbanormativity: Rural Community in Urban Society.* Lanham, MD: Lexington.

GAC Shows. (2015, December 22). Retrieved from http://greatamericancountry.com/shows.

HAC. (2012). *Rural research brief: Race and ethnicity in rural America.* Housing Assistance Council. Retrieved from http://www.ruralhome.org/storage/research_notes/rrn-race-and-ethnicity-web.pdf

Haynes, J. (2014). "I See Swamp People": Swamp people, southern horrors, and reality television. In A. Slade, A. Narro, and B. Buchanan, *Reality television: Oddities of culture* (pp. 245-257). Lanham, MD: Lexington.

Hernandez, L. H. (2014). "I Was Born This Way": The performance and production of Southern masculinity in A&E's Duck Dynasty. In A. Slade, A. Narro, and B. Buchanan, *Reality television: Oddities of culture* (pp. 21-36). Lanham, MD: Lexington.

History Shows. (2015, December 20). Retrieved from http://history.com/shows.

Holsti, O. R. (1969). *Content analysis for the social sciences and humanities.* Reading, MA: Addison-Wesley.

Jonsson, P. (2014). *The Rise of 'Redneck TV': Why TV's plunge into backwoods family, danger, and colloquial wisdom transfixes America (and the world). Do the shows depict caricatures or gritty authenticity?* Retrieved from The Christian Science Monitor: http://www.csmonitor.com/USA/Society/2014/1005/The-rise-of-redneck-TV.

Kaiser, S. B., and Bernstein, S. T. (2014). Rural representations in fashion and television: Co-optation and cancellation. *Fashion, Style, and Popular Culture, 1*(1), 97-117.

Krippendorf, K. (2004). *Content analysis: An introduction to its methodology (2nd edition).* Thousand Oaks, CA: Sage.

Lichter, D. T., and Brown, D. L. (2011). Rural America in an urban society: Changing spatial and social boundaries. *Annual Review of Sociology, 37*, 565-592.

Lloyd, R. (2011). *TV's Rugged, Rural Breed.* Retrieved from Los Angeles Times: http://articles.latimes.com/2011/dec/01/entertainment/la-et-1130-redneck-tv-20111201.

Lobao, L., and Meyer, K. (2001). The Great Agricultural Transition: Crisis, Change, and Social Consequences of Twentieth Century U.S. Farming. *Annual Review of Sociology, 27*, 103-124.

MAV TV Automotive Reality. (2015, December 22). Retrieved from http://mavtv.com/automotive-reality.html/.

MTV Shows. (2015, December 22). Retrieved from http://mtv.com/shows.

Nabi, R. L. (2007). Determining dimensions of reality: A concept mapping of the reality TV landscape. *Journal of Broadcasting and Electronic Media, 51*(2), 371-390.

Nabi, R. L., Biely, E., Morgan, S. J., and Stitt, C. R. (2003). Reality-based Television Programming and the Psychology of Its Appeal. *Media Psychology, 5,* 303-340.

National Geographic Shows. (2015, December 20). Retrieved from http://channel.nationalgeographic.com/shows/.

Ouellette, L., and Murray, S. (2004). *Reality television: Remaking television culture (2nd edition).* New York: New York University Press.

REELZ Channel Shows. (2015, December 22). Retrieved from http://reelz.com/watch/.

RFD-TV Shows. (2015, December 22). Retrieved from https://rfdtv.com/category/267410/shows.

Streisand, B. (2001). Did You Say Reality TV? Or Surreal TV? *U.S. News and World Report, 130*(3), 36-37.

Tickamyer, A. R., and Henderson, D. A. (2003). Rural women: New roles for the new century? In D. Brown, and L. Swanson, *Challenges for Rural America in the Twenty-First Century* (109-131). University Park: Pennsylvania State University Press.

USDA-ERS. (2015). *Poverty rates by family type and metro/nonmetro residence.* United States Department of Agriculture, Economic Research Service. Retrieved from http://www.ers.usda.gov/topics/rural-economy-population/rural-poverty-well-being/poverty-demographics.aspx

Chapter Four

Inbred Horror Revisited

The Fear of the Rural in Twenty-First Century Backwoods Horror Films

Karen Hayden

In previous work on images of rural communities in popular culture in the United States, I explored what I call "inbred horror"—the fear of the rural community as monstrous, insular, and dangerous due to isolation and presumed inbreeding, or sexual relations and procreation among closely related people (Hayden, 2014a and 2014b). I looked at popular cultural examples of depictions of rural, close-knit communities as the degenerate, deviant other to an urbanormative standard (cf. Hayden, 2014a, p. 181; Fulkerson and Thomas, 2014; Cloke and Little, 1997). I also considered the messages that these inbred horror stories relay to their audiences. I argued that small, rural, tight-knit communities in which "everyone is related" and "everyone knows everyone" came to signify, for those on the outside, a cautionary tale. Rural communities are constructed as backwards; they are degenerate, anti-modern and anti-urban (cf. Fulkerson and Thomas, 2014). In the urban/rural divide and cultural ideal of urbanormativity (cf. Fulkerson and Thomas, 2014; Thomas, Lowe, Fulkerson, and Smith, 2011) the message of the tight-knit community is clear: primitivism, savagery, regression, degeneracy, and an overall devolution will result if groups are allowed to become too close, too insular, too familiar (cf. Hayden, 2014a, p. 181–182; Hayden, 2014b; Fulkerson and Thomas, 2014).

In this chapter, I extend my analysis of these widely held misrepresentations of rural life and show how they allow urban or suburban dwellers to distance themselves from these supposedly inbred and grotesque rural others. By closely examining and interrogating this rural cultural bogeyman—and

they are almost always men—my goal is to provide a more nuanced understanding of how social representations of the rural have become increasingly
skewed and distant from reality while reinforcing urban life as a normal state
of affairs (Fulkerson and Thomas, this volume). I also consider structural and
spatial issues of inequality that both cause and result from rural misrepresentations (Fulkerson and Thomas, this volume). How does this particular form
of rural othering operate to reproduce inequalities and allow for the real
social ills that affect people in rural areas to go unnoticed? No direct line can
be drawn from stereotypes of rural people as inbred, degenerate monsters to,
for instance, the relative lack of media coverage of the 2010 West Virginia
coal mine explosion that killed twenty-nine miners. Because the stereotypes
and caricatures of rural people as monstrous others have become hegemonic,
however, these images play into what DeKeseredy, Muzzati and Donnermeyer call a "masking or 'conscious disguise' of real issues about crime, violence, and gender relations in rural contexts" (2014, p. 19). If popular culture
imagery constantly reminds us that rural folk are scary monsters, why should
we care if they die in mine explosions deep in the mines of West Virginia?

In this chapter I will continue to explore inbred horror themes, focusing
specifically on the film genre known as backwoods horror movies. The stock
image of scary, inbred rural folk has become such an identifiable characterization in movies that backwoods horror films, also known as "hillbilly hor-
ror/slasher" and even "inbred movies," are now recognized as a genre unto
themselves, as exemplified by film critics' lists, such as "The Top 25 Backwoods Horror and Suspense Movies" compiled by Mark H. Harris for
About.com and "The Top 10 Inbred Movies of All Time" on the *Bloody
Disgusting* website (Hayden, 2014b, p. 194; see also DeKeseredy, Muzzatti,
and Donnermeyer, 2014; and Murphy, 2013). In their recent article about the
horrification and pornification of rural culture, DeKeseredy et al. state that,
"in-depth content analysis of rural horror movies and pornographic media are
required to provide better answers to questions" about gender, race, and
violence (among other issues) and "many critical criminologists are well-
suited to take on these tasks . . ." (2014, p. 192). In this chapter I take up this
task, conducting a content analysis of a purposive sample from the backwoods horror movie genre. I conduct an in-depth analysis of one archetypal
inbred horror film franchise: the *Wrong Turn* movies, of which there are six.

WHY THE *WRONG TURN* MOVIES?

The *Wrong Turn* movies may seem, at first glance, to be unworthy of any
serious academic time or thought. These are not good cinematic works by
any measure. The final two movies in the series are bad beyond words. There
are, however, several reasons to pay close attention to these films if we are to

understand the making and remaking of the inbred horror mythology in the twenty-first century.

This collection of films was selected for a detailed analysis for three reasons: (1) the movies traffic in the types of exaggerated, grotesque, monstrous rural imagery that I am studying. It's really all they have to offer the viewers and the films just keep churning up these images and making them more and more horrific as the franchise goes on. (2) The timespan in which the films emerged and the longevity of the franchise is important. And (3) the movies have been profitable; people are watching them.

First and foremost, the theme of rural, isolated people inbreeding and degenerating into subhuman, cannibalistic monsters runs throughout the collection of films and grows more and more grotesque and outlandish over the course of the franchise. While the filmmakers try to add some new twist or element to each installment, the basic conceit remains throughout: A small group (usually about six to eight) of young, attractive, middle-class, mostly white adults is detoured or lost in the Appalachian hills of West Virginia. While they try to make their way through the woods, they are attacked by three grossly malformed men whose ages are hard to estimate given their horrific countenances. The viewers come to know these three brothers as the Hillickers: Three Fingers; One Eye, and Saw Tooth. The brothers appear, in one form or another, in each of the films. That they are the result of inbreeding is established as the opening credits roll in the original *Wrong Turn* film when printed pages with the words "genetic mutations" and "facial deformities due to inbreeding" flash on the screen. In later films, the "inbrededness" of the people is hinted at through references to "inbred hillbillies"; "hillbilly freaks"; and "banjo-playing rednecks." These terms are already embossed with meaning and are enough to signify the inbred monsters to come.

Second is the timespan in which the films emerged: 2003 through 2014. There has been scant academic attention paid to backwoods horror films, but much of the small body of literature that exists tends to focus on rural-themed horror films of the 1960s and 1970s, most notably *Two Thousand Maniacs!* (1964), *Deliverance* (1972), better characterized as a backwoods suspense/thriller film, *The Texas Chainsaw Massacre* (1974), and *The Hills Have Eyes* (1977)—progenitors of all subsequent backwoods horror films (cf. Clover, 1992; Bell, 1997; Sharrett, 1984; Rodowick, 1984). There are some excellent newer additions to the literature on backwoods horror films, but these works do not focus specifically on the long-running *Wrong Turn* film franchise (see DeKeseredy, Muzzatti, and Donnermeyer, 2014; Murphy, 2013). I focus here on the *Wrong Turn* films because they bring the inbred horror mythology into the new century and inculcate it, over and over again, to legions of (mostly) young viewers.

The original *Wrong Turn* movie was released in theaters in 2003 by Summit Entertainment. After the original all of the subsequent films were released by Twentieth Century Fox Home Entertainment and went straight to DVD or on-demand formats. The sequel, *Wrong Turn 2: Dead End* came out in 2007 and then a *Wrong Turn* film was released almost every two years, give or take, until the last installment, *Wrong Turn 6: Last Resort*, in 2014 (See Table 4.1). There is some talk in online forums of a *Wrong Turn 7* coming in 2017, but these rumors are unconfirmed (see *MGDSQUAN*, May 7, 2015, on http://www.horrorsociety.com and Todd Rigney, May 30, 2015, on http://www.dreadcentral.com).

Table 4.1.   *Wrong Turn* Films and Year Released

Film	Year Released
Wrong Turn	2003
Wrong Turn 2: Dead End	2007
Wrong Turn 3: Left for Dead	2009
Wrong Turn 4: Bloody Beginnings	2011
Wrong Turn 5: Bloodlines	2012
Wrong Turn 6: Last Resort	2014

Since the *Wrong Turn* movies emerged around the turn of the millennium and continued well into the first decade and a half of the new millennium, we can look closely at how and why the themes of inbred horror are reconstructed and recreated in current American popular culture. Why do these images still tap into the imagination of the horror-viewing public? The *Wrong Turn* movies rely heavily on the inbred rural tropes established in earlier rural horror films, especially *The Texas Chainsaw Massacre*, and exploit them over and over again for all they are worth. They recycle centuries-old misconceptions about inbreeding in rural areas and shore up very damaging notions about rural people. I look at these films to see if their messages have stayed true to the original backwoods horror films of the 1970s, if and how they have changed, and what new themes are explored.

Finally, I focus on these movies because they have been, at least until the final installment, profitable. While details on the exact amount of money earned by the films are hard to ascertain, since there are six of them, they must have brought in some returns or Twentieth Century Fox would have put an end to them.

According to three movie data websites: TMDb: The Movie Database (https://www.themoviedb.org/), IMDb: The Internet Movie Database (http://www.imdb.com/), and The Numbers: Where Data and the Movie Business Meet (http://www.the-numbers.com/), the *Wrong Turn* franchise did indeed turn a profit. The data are incomplete since only the first film made it to the box office. Further, there are no data available on *Wrong Turn 5: Bloodlines.* It is difficult to ascertain profits from streaming and other straight-to-DVD or on-demand forums. But after totaling up the available earnings minus the production budgets, I estimated the net earnings for all six films to be anywhere from around $25,000,000 to $32,000,000 (See table 4.2). I also was not able to find any data on marketing and other expenses, so this is a rough estimate (see also *MGDSQUAN*, May 7, 2015 on http://www.horrorsociety. com/).

Table 4.2. Estimated Profits for Wrong Turn Franchise

Film	Year & Format	Est. Production Costs	Est. Sales	Est. Profits
Wrong Turn	2003, Theater	$10,000,000	$28,649,556	$18,649,556
WT2: Dead End	2007, DVD	$4,000,000	$9,009,641	$5,009,651
WT3: Left for Dead	2009, DVD	$2,000,000	$5,689,328	$3,689,328
WT4: Bloody Beginnings	2011, DVD	$2,000,000	$3,148,521	$1,148,521
WT5: Bloodlines	2012, DVD	No Data	No Data	No Data
WT6: Last Resort	2014, DVD	$1,200,000	$1,008,317	$–191,683
TOTALS		$19,200,000	$47,505,363	$28,305,373

While the law of diminishing returns clearly operates for the *Wrong Turn* franchise, overall the films sold, and the horror-viewing public bought their messages of rural people as inbred, degenerate, grotesque, violent, cannibalistic, insular monsters who will attack any interlopers who dare enter their home. These themes have been profitable enough that the online discussions of a seventh installment seem plausible (see https://www.facebook.com/ WrongTurn7Movie/ and *MGDSQUAN*, May 7, 2015, on http:// www.horrorsociety.com/).

I will turn to an examination of the themes and messages conveyed in the films. Horror films, even bad ones, are allegories. What lessons are learned from these films and are they the same lessons conveyed over and over again? Do these films offer any new cautionary tales? What is warded off in these monster stories?

INCEST AND INBRED IMAGERY

The fact that the Hillickers are the products of, and ostensibly engage in, inbreeding is established early in the first *Wrong Turn*. The opening scene flashes the words that clearly convey the message in black and white print. The opening also presents the severe physical deformities of the three brothers—appearances so grotesque that there is no question that they are inbred and inbreeding has caused them to devolve, to degenerate and to become less than human. It is closeness to a fault. They share genetic material like hand-me-downs; their chromosomes have become frayed and defective.

They are animal-like, making only grunting and snorting noises that the three brothers seem to understand. While these are heightened, exaggerated stereotypes of inbred rural folk; they are not new. These images were the stock-in-trade of earlier backwoods horror films such as *The Texas Chainsaw Massacre* and *The Hills Have Eyes*. A new twist on the inbreeding leading to degeneracy theme emerges when the viewers learn that the Hillickers' inbredness also seems to allow them to *regenerate*. Especially in films two through six, the Hillicker brothers are indestructible.

The theme of the monster that cannot be killed runs throughout horror movies and especially horror film franchises. But in this collection, the filmmakers attribute their *inability* to feel pain and their *ability* to regenerate to congenital abnormalities due to inbreeding. This idea is made obvious in the prequel segment of *Wrong Turn 4: Bloody Beginnings* when the young Hillicker boys are behind bars in the "Glenville Sanatorium" in West Virginia. A doctor describes the boys as having a congenital disease that results in their inability to feel physical pain; he also says they are "extremely smart and dangerous." This asylum scene is borrowed from another horror franchise, the *Halloween* films, and thus not new to the horror genre. What is new, though, is that the inbred, rural, hillbilly monsters are described as extremely smart and as possessing almost superhuman abilities—they can withstand physical pain. This assertion that they are smart, or cunning, is reinforced when the boys use a bobby pin to break out of their cell and release all the other patients in the sanatorium. The boys proceed to cannibalize the nearest orderly.

CANNIBALISM

Cannibalism in rural horror films is also nothing new—it was firmly established in the 1960s with *Two Thousand Maniacs!* and then reified in the films of the 1970s. The *Wrong Turn* movies are nothing if not derivative of these earlier films. Cannibalism runs throughout the *Wrong Turn* movies and grows more gruesome and outlandish with each, for example, people being skinned and eaten alive; people's brains being eaten while their blood is still pumping; and the Hillickers drinking the blood of live victims as they hang upside down from trees. As with earlier rural horror movies, the root cause or reason for the cannibalism is never revealed—it's simply part and parcel to their degeneracy. Perhaps once you have broken the incest taboo, all taboos are fair game, so why not eat people?

In two of the *Wrong Turn* sequels, the reason for the Hillickers' cannibalism is suggested, however. In *Wrong Turn 2: Dead End* and *Wrong Turn 5: Bloodlines*, we learn that there has also been an environmental spill or disaster of some sort related to the paper mill that used to operate in the region. The chemicals from the old mill have killed off all of the wildlife in the region, so naturally they must eat any strangers who wander into the vicinity. In homage to *The Hills Have Eyes*, the chemicals also appear to have had a hand in the genetic abnormalities suffered by the inbred locals, as two victims in *Wrong Turn 2: Dead End* stumble upon the abandoned paper mill and find large barrels of chemicals labeled "Causes Birth Defects." This environmental storyline is dropped by the final installment, *Wrong Turn 6: Last Resort*, which features a deer hunting scene, so the wildlife seems to have returned to the area. In the end, the Hillickers are back to eating people because that is what inbred monsters do.

ROOTEDNESS IN PLACE AND TIME

A central theme in the mythology of inbreeding is rootedness to the region, to the very soil from which these horrific creatures spring (Hayden, 2014a). This theme is illustrated in the *Wrong Turn* films through camera angles and cinematography making the brothers appear as part of the woods themselves. They peer, unseen by their prey, from behind trees; they move undetected through the wilderness; they are part of the land. They have animal-like senses of smell and hearing. They are territorial and protect their home through elaborate and barbaric booby traps, always involving barbed wire, which the films establish as a rustic, backwoods signifier.

The notion of a people that time forgot, like the theme of rootedness to ancestral home, also constructs the Hillickers as rooted, mired, bogged down. It is an anti-modern, anti-urban image. In a post-modern world where geographical and upward mobility is the norm and stands for progress and advancement, these territorial people stay tied to the land in a chosen state of decline. And they turn truly degenerate when their land is intruded upon by outsiders from the modern world who often barge right into their cabin in the woods (Murphy, 2013). The tension between progress and regress, rise and decline, movement forward versus deep-rooted immobility is reinforced in these images of people hunkered into their rustic cabin (Hayden, 2014a, p. 200).

In some of the later films in the series, this theme of rootedness in place and time is betrayed, however, when the locations of the films change. While all the films take place in West Virginia, in some installments the Hillicker brothers leave their den and the woods. It is hard to know if this change is a statement about newfound mobility among this inbred group or if it is the result of sloppy screenwriting and writers running out of story lines in the woods.

In *Wrong Turn 4: Bloody Beginnings* the setting changes. We learn that as youngsters in 1974, the three brothers were rounded up and put in a sanatorium because they were found standing over the dead bodies of their parents. No further explanation is given on this matter. When the film flashes forward to 2003, we find that the three brothers, now adults, live in the since abandoned sanatorium, even though in earlier films they resided deep in the West Virginia woods.

In *Wrong Turn 5: Bloodlines*, the rootedness motif is dropped again. In this film, the Hillickers are on the move in a town called Fairlake, West Virginia, to free a relative (father or grandfather, this is not fully explained) from jail. The population of Fairlake, the viewers learn, disappeared in 1817. The locals and college kids that flock to the town once a year for a music festival, the "Mountain Man Festival," believe the 1817 townsfolk were eaten by mountain cannibals. This film has more inconsistencies than I can count, but in an interesting turn of events, the brothers are not only mobile, they also figure out how to disable the entire town's cell towers and power sources, thus enabling them to free their captive relative and slaughter many concertgoers. The film series is fraught with temporal and storyline inconsistencies, so it is likely that these two departures from the rootedness theme are not significant, but the brothers' ability to disable an entire region's power sources marks a major leap ahead for people who have been portrayed as atavistic throwbacks to an earlier time and place.

GENDER AMONG THE INBRED

The fate of female victims in slasher films has been considered in the academic literature on horror films (see Clover, 1992; DeKeseredy et al., 2014; Murphy, 2013). Females as inbred monsters in horror films, however, have received little to no academic attention. This is most likely because inbred monsters in backwoods horror films are almost solely represented by men— brothers. In all but two of the *Wrong Turn* films, inbred girls or women are absent. Inbreeding seems to result in predominantly male offspring who possess hyper-masculine strength and brutality. In *Wrong Turn 2: Dead End*, grossly malformed females appear. In one scene, a younger female is shown giving birth in a filthy cabin in the woods. She squats briefly and a monster child is born. The same female appears in a later scene wherein she and her mate are having sex in the woods—they rut like animals. This same character is also shown perpetrating some violence, but her role centers mainly around sex and breeding. Also in *Wrong Turn 2*, an older couple, male and female, seem to represent the matriarch and patriarch of the inbred family, but the female elder does not take part in a lot of the action in the film.

Wrong Turn 6: Last Resort features a key female figure. In this film an outsider learns that he has inherited an inn, the Hot Springs Hotel, in the remote woods of West Virginia. He and a small group of his friends set off from New York to find the place and when they come upon it, there is a male and female couple working at the reception desk. The two are not "inbred looking." They suffer from no noticeable facial abnormalities. Yet the male calls the female "sister" as they kiss romantically. As the film develops, or devolves, we learn that the "normal looking" brother and sister are related to the Hillickers who work at the inn, butchering and serving human flesh to unsuspecting guests. Here again we find the Hillickers are uprooted from the cabin in the woods.

We learn that the sister, Sally, is barren, unable to conceive due to years of inbreeding. She needs Danny, the newcomer, the outsider who inherited the inn. Danny is a family member, but not so closely related. She hopes that mating with him will produce a child. Sally is portrayed as hypersexual—she even uses an almost dead male victim as a sex toy. She is driven by her desire to breed. As she pursues Danny, she tells him "your blood, our blood beats inside us." Later, Danny is brought to meet his "extended family" deep in the woods beyond the inn. Sally tells Danny that these are all his kin, explaining that there are three original families in the woods: the Creightons, the Bogles, and the Hillickers. Danny is surrounded by inbred monsters, males and females, each more deformed than the last. Sally asks Danny, "How do we preserve our family strength? We keep to our own." She goes on to explain that the genetic abnormalities are the "price of purity." That night, Danny has sex with Sally. In the final scene of the film, Danny is the lone survivor from the group of outsiders with whom he arrived. He has chosen his kin over his friends, all of whom have died gruesome deaths at the hands of Three Fingers, One Eye, and Sawtooth. Danny stays at the hotel with Sally, presumably to carry on the inbred family lineage.

In this final scene of the final *Wrong Turn* movie (to date), we see a women introduced as a key inbred protagonist. She is oversexed, forceful in her singular pursuit of procreation, and her mission is tightly bound to the inbreeding and degeneracy themes that run through all the films. She is presented as a female rural stereotype—a hyper-sexualized breeder, but she is given some agency as she acts to procure a suitable related partner with whom to continue the inbred bloodline.

DISCUSSION

As I found in my earlier exploration into the mythology of inbrededness, several powerful, and powerfully modern, notions are called upon to assemble the rural, insular, isolated community as inherently degenerate, regressive, and horrific (Hayden, 2014a). Misconceptions and partial understandings about heredity and genetic transmission in isolated groups are entwined and shored up with age-old notions of inbreeding leading to genetically malformed offspring. The belief that the children of inbreeding would inevitably be of a lesser stock and somehow physically and/or mentally malformed has been challenged scientifically, yet it became unquestioned common knowledge in eighteenth century America (Hayden, 2014a). In the *Wrong Turn* film franchise, this conventional wisdom is reborn, recycled, and reinvigorated in the new millennium with inbred horror tales that work to teach this notion to a new generation of horror fans, thus guaranteeing that these stereotypes permeate the popular culture and imagination.

In the imagery of the inbred community, sexuality is front and center. Inbred, rural people are circumscribed by the perception that they practice a form of degenerate sexuality. Inbreeding connotes loveless sex and procreation among too closely related people (Hayden, 2014a). They are said to breed like animals in the barnyard, or to rut like wildlife in the forest, as in *Wrong Turn 2: Dead End.*

Another damning perception of supposedly inbred people is that they are tribal, clannish, closed off to others. Their bodies are not fully individuated; their minds not properly civilized (Hayden, 2014a). They are too familiar, sharing flesh and blood among the group, like communal property. And as we see so graphically illustrated throughout the *Wrong Turn* films, if you intrude upon them, they will descend upon you *en masse*. They are a collectivity that chooses to not mix with others. This is clearly a problem in a postmodern, individuated, geographically mobile, and technological society. The result of this extreme urbanormativity is that rural people are simply and profoundly *not like us*. The mythology of inbrededness taps into the larger mythology of degeneration—it glimpses the dark underbelly of progress (Hayden, 2014a, p. 200). Inbreeding is a corruption by blood, an irreversible decline. And it is the opposite of a cosmopolitan, urbane norm. At the turn of the new millennium, the *Wrong Turn* films remind us again and again of the frailty of progress. We must continue to push forward or we tempt a fate like that of the Hillickers: degenerate, malformed, and grossly disfigured.

Conclusions and Future Directions

In Kathleen Stewart's groundbreaking ethnography of abandoned West Virginia coal camps and "hollers," the author explores the social imagery of a space that resists capitalism, modernism, and urbanormative standards. She acknowledges that these "trashy" pockets can be found across the American cultural landscape, from backwoods New England to rural California. As she puts it:

> In the two political imaginaries of center and margin there is a telltale contrast: the one, relatively self-assured and oblivious to its privilege, delimits clean lines of will and action to leave its mark on the world, while the "Other" raids and poaches, stays at the ready to take advantage of opportunities that come along . . . and sifts through signs of its own otherness . . . for something of lasting value. The one might come to imagine itself as structure and order while the "Other," with no power to keep the surrounding other at a distance sees itself in moments of engagement and encounter and the sheer nervous movement of contingency and indeterminacy (Stewart, 1996, p. 42).

Inbred horror themes in popular culture serve to reify the rural "Other" and maintain their lack of power and their distance from the urbanormative center. The theme of 2015's Rural Sociological Society's Annual Meetings in Madison, Wisconsin, was "Knowing Rural." Conference attendees were reminded that:

> Making sense of rural experiences requires understanding the diverse geographies, economies, and communities that make up rural places. After all, rural landscapes include sites of high-amenity recreation, industrialized agriculture production, chemical processing plants, prisons and pocket-size organic farms. And these sites are undergoing significant change. As rural population's age and rural communities confront the emergent complexities of contemporary life, the lived experience of rurality is undergoing rapid transformation (Annual Meeting Program 2015).

This type of knowledge and understanding is hindered by stereotypes of rural people perpetuated in popular culture as inbred, monstrous, homicidal, and cannibalistic maniacs. This form of othering allows outsiders to disregard rural people and to view them as not fully human. Their exploitation by the coal industry, paper mills, or the fishing or logging industries is not an issue; their lack of health care is not a concern. They only appear in the media as curiosities or monstrosities, so why should we be concerned about their severe intergenerational poverty?

Similarly, in Donnermeyer and DeKeseredy's recent book *Rural Criminology* (2014) the authors call for a critical criminological perspective within studies of rural crime. If we continue to see rural people as homicidal maniacs, we will not recognize the real, lived experiences of the diverse inhabitants of rural places, including both victims and perpetrators of real rural crimes—domestic violence, arson, burglaries of farm equipment, drug abuse, such as oxycodone, which started as a rural drug problem and spread into cities and suburbs and is now linked to the heroin abuse plaguing the United States.

Can We Talk about the Rural in Popular Culture without Talking about Monsters?

There are a few newer movies that critique or even parody the stereotypes of the backwoods horror film genre. *Tucker and Dale vs. Evil* (2012) is a great example of a film that turns these "backwoods folks as inbred monsters" tropes on their heads. Set in the Appalachian Mountains in West Virginia, the film follows two harmless, kind-hearted rural young men—locals—who buy an old shack in the middle of the woods to fix up as a retreat for fishing. The men, Tucker and Dale, are happened upon by a group of college students who tell scary stories of college students who, while on a Memorial Day outing twenty years earlier were murdered by the locals. In the Dale and Tucker plot, though, the college students are so hapless that they seem to be throwing themselves into harm's way while in the vicinity of Dale and Tucker. The two locals try to help these accident-prone youths; for example, they come to the aid of a young co-ed, Allison, who fell into the water near their fishing boat. They bring her to their cabin so she can recuperate. Her friends of course think the protagonists have brought her there to eat her, just like the locals do in all of the backwoods horror films. As the story unfolds, more and more of the college students get killed off by their own haplessness and reliance on stereotypes. For instance, one college guy runs into a tree, impaling himself with a branch because he sees Tucker gestating with a chainsaw. What the victim does *not* see is that Tucker had run into a bees nest with his chainsaw, and is waving it around, looking very much like Leatherface from *The Texas Chainsaw Massacre* in an attempt to get the bees away from him. The entire movie follows this narrative of Tucker and Dale trying to help the helpless city-folk, but still appearing as though they are out to get them.

A similar parody is presented in the *Harold and Kumar Go to White Castle* sequel, titled *Harold and Kumar Escape from Guantanamo Bay* (2008). The film features a sequence in which the protagonists stumble upon a backwoods scene that inverts many hillbilly horror stereotypes. The backwoods people are helpful and hospitable; their trailer is neat as a pin; the man of the house is a fastidious clean freak. The inbred stereotype rears its ugly head, however, when Harold and Kumar stumble upon the couple's cycloptic son who was hidden in the basement. Basement of a trailer you ask? It's a stoner movie. Here the inbred boy, the cyclops, serves to illustrate how ridiculous the inbred monster stereotypes are, and he is certainly a step forward in the popular imagery of the rural. These parodies also further illustrate just how taken-for-granted the rural stereotypes in horror films have become.

A more serious example of rural people in cinema being depicted in a much more nuanced way is *Winter's Bone* (2010). The film is not a horror film although it does include one scene that could be perceived as gory; it is a drama/suspense film set in a rural place. This critically acclaimed film focuses on Ree, played by Jennifer Lawrence, a teenaged girl trying to keep her family together in the face of extreme poverty in the very rural Ozarks. The movie paints an unromantic, realistic portrait of a strong female protagonist who is not the victim or perpetrator of a bloody crime; she does not wear cut-off jean shorts; and she and her family survive through her strength and grit. Jennifer Lawrence starred in the movie before she was cast as Catniss Everdeen in *The Hunger Games* series and there are some interesting parallels to be drawn between these two strong female characters from rural settings.

In future work on images of rurality in U.S. popular culture, I hope to explore more antidotes to the rural stereotypes offered in backwoods horror films. Scholars of rural people and places must continue to ask, "Can we talk about rural people, places, and culture without talking about inbred monsters?" I will examine new rural imagery of the late twentieth to early twenty-first centuries such as those presented in *Tucker and Dale vs. Evil* and *Winter's Bone*. I will look for other areas within popular culture that present more nuanced examples of rural imagery and explore new messages that are starting to appear.

REFERENCES

Annual Meeting Program. (2015). Madison, WI: Rural Sociological Society.

Bell, D. (1997). Anti-Idyll: Rural Horror. In P. Cloke, and J. Little, *Contested countryside cultures: Otherness, marginality, and rurality* (pp. 94-108). New York: Routledge.

Boorman, J. (Director). (1972). *Deliverance*. United States: Warner Brothers Studio.

Cloke, P., and Little, J. (1997). *Contested countryside cultures: Otherness, marginality, and rurality*. New York: Routledge.

Clover, C. J. (1992). *Men, women, and chainsaws: Gender in the modern horror film*. Princeton, NJ: Princeton University Press.

Craig, E. (Director). (2010). *Tucker and Dale vs. Evil*. United States: Reliance Big Pictures.

Craven, W. (Director). (1977). *The Hills Have Eyes*. United States: Blood Relations Co.

DeKeseredy, W. S., Muzzatti, S. L., and Donnermeyer, J. F. (2014). Mad men in bib overalls: Media's horrification and pornification of rural culture. *Critical Criminology, 22*, 179-197.

Donnermeyer, J., and DeKeseredy, W. (2014). *Rural Criminology*. New York: Routledge.

Fulkerson, G. M., and Thomas, A. R. (2014). *Studies in urbanormativity: Rural community in urban society*. Lanham, MD: Lexington.

Gordon Lewis, H. (Director). (1964). *Two Thousand Maniacs!* United States: Jacqueline Kay, Inc. and Friedman-Lewis Productions.

Granik, D. (Director). (2010). *Winter's Bone*. United States: Anonymous Content.

Hayden, K. (2014a). Stigma, reputation, and place structuration in a coastal New England town. In G. Fulkerson and A. Thomas, *Studies in urbanormativity: Rural community in urban society* (pp. 67-85). Lanham, MD: Lexington.

Hayden, K. (2014b). Inbred horror: Degeneracy, revulsion, and the fear of the rural community. In G. Fulkerson and A. Thomas, *Studies in urbanormativity: Rural community in urban society* (pp. 181-205). Lanham, MD: Lexington.

Hooper, T. (Director). (1974). *The Texas Chainsaw Massacre*. United States: Vortex.

Hurwitz, J., and Schlossberg, H. (2008). *Harold and Kumar Escape from Guantanamo Bay*. United States: Mandate Pictures

Lynch, J. (Director). (2007). *Wrong Turn 2: Dead End*. United States: 20th Century Fox Film Corporation.

MGDSQUAN. (2015, May 7). What are the chances of Wrong Turn 7 in 2016. Retrieved from *Horror Society*: http://www.horrorsociety.com.

Milev, V. (Director). (2014). *Wrong Turn 6: Last Resort*. United States: 20th Century Fox Home Entertainment.

Murphy, B. (2013). *The rural gothic in American popular culture: Backwoods horror and terror in the wilderness*. New York: Palgrave.

O'Brien, D. (Director). (2009). *Wrong Turn 3: Left for Dead*. United States: 20th Century Fox Home Entertainment.

———. (Director). (2011). *Wrong Turn 4: Bloody Beginnings (A Prequel)*. United States: 20th Century Fox Home Entertainment.

———. (Director). (2012). *Wrong Turn 5: Bloodlines*. United States: 20th Century Fox Home Entertainment.

Rigney, T. (2015, May 30). Wrong Turn 7 launches Facebook page, promises 2017 release. Retrieved from *Dread Central*: http://www.dreadcentral.com.

Rodowick, D. N. (1984). The enemy within: The economy of violence in The Hills Have Eyes. In B. Grant, and C. Sharrett, *Planks of reason: Essays on the horror film* (pp. 438-449). Princeton, NJ: Princeton University Press.

Schmidt, R. (Director). (2003). *Wrong Turn*. United States: Summit Entertainment.

Sharrett, C. (1984). The idea of apocalypse in The Texas Chainsaw Massacre. In B. Grant and C. Sharrett, *Planks of reason: Essays on the horror film* (pp. 382-404). Princeton, NJ: Princeton University Press.

Stewart, K. (1996). *A space on the side of the road: Cultural poetics in an "other" America*. Princeton, NJ: Princeton University Press.

Thomas, A., Lowe, B., Fulkerson, G., and Smith, P. (2011). *Critical rural theory: Structure*space*culture*. Lanham, MD: Lexington.

Chapter Five

Reconsidering the Rural in the End

Rural Representations in Post-Apocalyptic Settings

Brian M. Lowe

This chapter considers the rising popularity within popular cultural media of the apocalypse and post-apocalyptic narrative, emphasizing a tendency to reimagine rural as a safe haven or sanctuary from the dangers of a collapsing urban social order. The premise that threads through many of these works is that the urban environment not only collapses in the face of cataclysmic forces, but must be abandoned by survivors in the wake of these forces making the rural a zone for retreat and survival, as articulated by Sheridan (2013, p. 50):

> Los Angeles is an immense, fragile, vulnerable city. The vulnerabilities are in plain sight. Fifteen million souls, balanced like a dew drop on a spider web. How fragile are these systems? Have we waited too long? The climate change science is right there, whether you believe it or not. The earthquake warnings are out there. Like the song says, "just because you're paranoid doesn't mean they're not out to get you."

This phenomenon of viewing the rural as sanctuary has been dubbed the rural reversal. This chapter begins by reviewing the meaning of urbanization, the general rise of the apocalypse and post-apocalyptic narrative through a range of examples, and then turns more directly to cases that emphasize the rural reversal. The chapter concludes with a consideration of how the social imaginary is reimagining rural through popular culture.

URBANIZATION AND THE
POST-APOCALYPTIC NARRATIVE

Ferdinand Tönnies's famous typology of gemeinschaft (community) and gesellschaft (society) is often drawn upon[1] to describe the profound changes
experienced by the Western world evolving from rural agrarian economies,
dominated by tradition and extended kinship systems, into economically differentiated urban and rationally-oriented societies with which people are
most familiar today. The patterns described by Tönnies have also been observed in the non-Western world, as Diamond's (2012, pp. 4–5) observations
of New Guinea from 1931 to 2006 provide supporting evidence of Tönnies's
ideas:

> Still another distinction of the 2006 crowd compared to the 1931 crowds was a
> feature that we take for granted in the modern world: most of the people
> crammed into that airport were strangers who had never seen each other be-
> fore, but there was no fighting going on among them. That would have been
> unimaginable in 1931, when encounters with strangers were rare, dangerous,
> and likely to turn violent. Yes, there were those two policemen in the airport
> hall, supposedly to maintain order, but in fact the crowd maintained order by
> itself, merely because the passengers *realized [sic]* that none of the strangers
> was about to attack them, and that they lived in a society with more policemen
> and soldiers to call on in case a quarrel should get out of hand. In 1931 police
> and government authority didn't exist. The passengers in the airport hall en-
> joyed the right to fly or travel by other means to Wapenamanda or elsewhere
> in Papua New Guinea without requiring permission. In the modern Western
> world we have come to take the freedom to travel for granted, but previously it
> was exceptional. In 1931 no New Guinean born in Goroka had ever visited
> Wapenamanda a mere 107 miles to the west; the idea of traveling from Goroka
> to Wapenamanda, without being killed as an unknown stranger within the first
> 10 miles from Goroka, would have been unthinkable. (italics not in original)

The past several decades have seen sweeping urbanization continue in both
developed and developing nations—the growth of cities and international
markets, the proliferation of information technology, and other components
of the juggernaut of modernity (Giddens, 1984). The process of urbanization
is broadly understood to be irreversible, unidirectional, or even inevitable
(Fulkerson and Thomas, 2014), but there has arisen in popular media an
emerging post-apocalyptic counter-narrative that tells another story. These
narratives appear in a range of popular cultural media, including television
series, as well as in a host of novels and film media. These narratives explore
the possibility that the structures that support the familiar urban gesellschaft
life may quickly be eviscerated and experience collapse in the face of crisis.

Gross and Gilles (2012) assert that some sort of narrative about great
catastrophes and destructive transformations of the world go back to ancient

times, transcending geographic and cultural boundaries. What is new is how deeply the expansion of the catastrophic narrative has permeated the social imaginary (discussed later):[2]

> Yet to dismiss our contemporary apocalyptic beliefs with an imagined histori-cal relativism ("People have always thought this way.") is to miss the larger story. We have reached a sort of mocking détente in America—with the left scoffing at the Rapture, and the Right rejecting the science behind global warming—at the expense of understanding the common lens through which most Americans are now looking at the world. The apocalyptic ideal has vaulted from religious esoterica to pop culture headline; yesterday's dishev-eled whackos are today's middle class. . . .
>
> Yet Americans increasingly have turned to apocalyptic metaphors to explain and justify a world and nation that look radically different from just a decade ago. In the absence of any other explanatory narrative—which our media, failing spectacularly at placing the news it reports into a larger context, rarely offers—the apocalypse serves as a way of coping with "unpreceded" events, offering the promise that the chaos of our times will eventually prove to have some kind of redemptive meaning (Gross and Gilles, 2012, pp. 12–13).

A casual survey of popular culture supports the thesis set forth by Gross and Gilles (2012) that the post-apocalyptic narrative has indeed taken root within popular culture.

Examples include the *Mad Max* film series, directed by George Miller. Beginning as a low budget Australian film released in 1979, *Mad Max* found widespread popularity with two subsequent films—*Mad Max 2: The Road Warrior* (1981) and *Mad Max Beyond Thunderdome* (1985). The films center on an Australian police officer, Max Rockatansky (played by Mel Gibson), who is cast into the post-apocalyptic future of the desolate Australian out-back where individuals fend for survival by fighting over gasoline and spare parts for motorized vehicles. The franchise was revived in 2015 with *Mad Max: Fury Road*, and proved to be a critical success.[3]

An examination of online booksellers also evidences this trend in the expanding popularity of the apocalyptic narrative. A search of Barnes and Noble yields 3,217 items for "apocalyptic and post-apocalyptic science fic-tion"; searching for "post-apocalyptic" through "science fiction and fantasy" yields 14,946 titles. A search for "post-apocalyptic fiction" on the widely popular Amazon.com website yields 19,025 results. These searches include subcategories within them that include "teen and young adult" books that feature the *Divergent* series, by Veronica Roth, as well as the *Hunger Games* trilogy, by Suzanne Collins.[4] The post-apocalyptic theme has entered secon-dary school curricula through the teaching of works of Huxley's *Brave New World* and, more recently, of Lois Lowry's *The Giver*.[5] Both of these works imagine future societies that have been engineered as corrective responses to the conditions that resulted in catastrophes of the past.

In a survey of "Apocalyptic, Post-Apocalyptic, and Dystopian Books and Media," Danner (2012) identifies possible causes of apocalypse in narratives aimed at high school audiences, including zombies, war, a virus outbreak, a natural disaster, and technology. In recent science fiction and fantasy, examples such as S. M. Stirling's *The Change* series, begin with a global and inexplicable sudden termination of all electrical devices, internal combustion engines, and even the efficacy of gunpowder, driving populations back into the Middle Ages. Other works consider the possibility of environmental disasters, or those that simply allow the apocalypse to rest in an unexplained past.

As another example, Tim LaHaye and Jerry B. Jenkins authored a sixteen-book series, *Left Behind*, that has collectively sold over fifty million copies, with the goal to communicate the Christian vision of the Rapture—an event whereby believing Christians instantly disappear and the world enters into a period of Tribulation with seven years of war and disaster. The book series altered the perception of large publishing houses of Christian literature, as discovered by National Public Radio's Karen Grigsby Bates in her interview with Mr. Lance Fensterman, director of Book Expo America:

> Before *Left Behind*, if you wanted a novel with a Christian theme, the easiest place to find it would have been one of the thousands of Christian bookstores that dot the country—fiction that had religious faith as a central part of the storyline was usually hard to find in mainstream bookstores. Then, Tim La-Haye and Jerry Jenkins published a novel called *Left Behind*. It's a thriller based on the book of Revelation. Suddenly, Christian literature became very visible, very quickly.
>
> Mr. LANCE FENSTERMAN (Director, "Book Expo America"): I think that probably, this *Left Behind* series brought into the fore and was accessible enough that someone who maybe wasn't a very ardent Christian or wasn't a very evangelical Christian—it made it relevant to them as well as they were just kind of passive Christians, because that is a good story at the core. I mean, there's—you know—it's one of the greatest stories ever told.
>
> GRIGSBY BATES: Lance Fensterman is the director of Book Expo America, the largest bookseller's convention in the U.S. He says that while there had been Christian books before *Left Behind*, this novel with its modern-day apocalyptic scenario caught the interest not only of Christian readers, but of secular readers as well—which, he says, caught publishers' attention.
>
> Mr. FENSTERMAN: Money talks, and it forced publishers to—and bookstores for that matter—to really look at the genre as legitimate. Not a boutique, per se, but as a legitimate mainstream seller (Fensterman, 2007).

While some of the popularity of the *Left Behind* series might be attributable to the growing visibility of conservative Christians who espouse the theology echoed in these books, Fensterman cited the ecumenical appeal of the modern day apocalyptic narrative. We now turn to a narrower focus on those apocalyptic narratives that emphasize the rural reversal.

THE RURAL REVERSAL

Examples abound of recent films depicting variation of the rural reversal, such as the disease-based apocalypse of *28 Days Later* (2002) and its sequel *28 Weeks Later* (2007), where the United Kingdom becomes decimated by a virulent disease, the Rage Virus, that almost instantly transforms humans into violent, homicidal, and cannibalistic creatures. In the original film, survivors must flee London, as it is comprised almost solely of the infected, and look for possible sanctuary in the rural. In *28 Weeks Later* a NATO-occupied London is devoid of the infected and is being rebuilt after a quarantine period. However, pockets still exist, and once again spread rapidly in the city. The film concludes with the beginning of a global apocalypse: images of the infected running rampant under the Eiffel Tower in Paris.

The theme of rural reversal is similarly portrayed in the 2013 film, *World War Z*, directed by Marc Forster, and based on the Max Brooks novel of the same name. Here the infected first appear on camera in downtown Philadelphia, where Gerry Lane (played by Brad Pitt) and his family attempt to flee, as vehicles are trapped in traffic with frightened pedestrians. Escaping Philadelphia, they flee to Newark, New Jersey, in a stolen camper and are rescued from a temporary refuge in an apartment building by military helicopter, so that Lane's skills as a former United Nations investor may be put to use in investigating the cause of the pandemic. While Lane's family lives aboard an impromptu flotilla in the Atlantic, Lane is sent first to South Korea and then to Jerusalem in seeking the plague's origin. While the Israelis believe that they can survive because of an enormous wall that has been built around the perimeter of the city, it is soon scaled by a massive attack of the infected, and Lane and an Israeli soldier escape by forcing their way onto a commercial aircraft. They manage to fly to rural Wales, outside of Cardiff, where they crash near a World Health Organization laboratory. With the assistance of scientists, Lane discovers that the infected will not attack a person infected with a dangerous (but curable) disease, thereby offering survivors at least a temporary camouflage. Lane is eventually reunited with his family, now housed in a military base in rural Nova Scotia, while global images depict the same pattern of cities occupied by the infected. Like the *28 Days* films, in *World War Z*, the urban becomes an apocalyptic trap, where survivors must flee to the rural for sanctuary and subsistence. Even one of the world's oldest cities, Jerusalem, is unable to withstand the infected onslaught.

This theme of the rural as sanctuary has appeared in variations of postapocalyptic television. The Glen A. Larson and Ronald D. Moore reimagined version of *Battle Star Galactica* (2004–2009)[6] begins with a similar premise to the 1978–1979 original series with the backdrop of a cataclysmic conflict between humanity and the Cylons. In the 2004 series, the Cylons were robots that had labored on the twelve colony planets that comprised humanity's domain. The series opens with a devastating attack by the Cylons, who have returned to the human worlds forty years after the initial conflict, with weapon systems and technologies far superior to the human military—and they have evolved into human simulacra, initially indistinguishable from humanity. As in the original series, the narrative follows humanity being devastated in the initial Cylon attack, with the twenty-first century innovation of the Cylons deploying thermonuclear weapons against major cities. While the vestiges of cities flee to an improvised fleet of spacecraft equipped with Faster-than-Light technology, other human survivors remain in rural and wilderness areas to avert the attack and join the human fleet. Eventually Karl Agathon (played by Tahmoh Penikett), a Colonial military officer, is reunited with the fleet and reveals that he observed the Cylons in rural areas capturing human women for an experiment to breed a human/Cylon hybrid. Later in the series, others whose survival depended on being distant from cities in the initial attack, are able to make their way to the fleet. The rest of the series features the human fleet attempting both to evade the Cylons, including those in their own midst, while seeking the location of the legendary Earth, as foretold in the polytheistic Sacred Scrolls. In essence, the strategic objective for the remaining human leadership is to follow myths from a pre-modern civilization, eventually discovering salvation in the form of an undeveloped planet which will allow for human colonization.

As examined in another chapter in this volume (by Fulkerson and Lowe), *Revolution* (2012–2014) featured a post-apocalyptic scenario in which all electrical devices mysteriously ceased functioning due to nano-technology. With the resultant loss of electricity, American society rapidly unravels as governmental and economic structures are unable to function without electricity. When the nano-technology is briefly deactivated, this allows for a nuclear launch against two cities, Philadelphia (capital of the new Monroe Republic) and Atlanta (capital of the Georgia Federation), allowing for an invasion of the former United States by the former United States government that has been in exile in Cuba. In the world of *Revolution*, the urban can no longer exist on the scale that it did, and is threatened by savage attacks from isolated areas.

The pattern of rural or small towns as relatively safe havens is visited in the science-fiction series *Defiance*, where earth has been partially colonized by seven different species (and an eighth in the third season) in an effort to survive an impending supernova in their home solar systems. The series focuses on the community *Defiance* (2012–2014), built on the ruins of St. Louis, as they attempt to negotiate life in a world with alien beings, animals, mutants, and a balance of political powers that exist in New York City and Brazil. Even this fragile order is upended when the urban capitals of the Earth Alliance and the Votan Collective are destroyed by an ancient, alien technology. Once again Defiance is isolated, but its isolation has prevented its ultimate destruction, while the cosmopolitan cities are laid to waste.

Sam Sheridan's (2013), *The Disaster Diaries*, provides important reflections on the rural reversal along with general guidance and preparation strategies for the apocalypse, drawing on his own experiences in learning wilderness emergency medicine, combat gun fighting, evasive/stunt driving, and adopting a demanding physical training regimen. Sheridan (2013) emphasizes a common theme in survival scenarios: the vulnerability of urban life and the coming rural reversal. Sheridan (2011, pp. 111–113) recounts a conversation had with Matthew Beaumont, author of *The Spectre of Utopia*, and the revealing chapter, "The City of the Absent":

> "I was watching *28 Days Later*," he told me over the phone in his soft, cultured accent, and I wondered, "Why do I take such pleasure in this empty city?" The movie is about a character who wakes up in an empty London and gradually realizes it's filled with zombies. The most poignant moments come from the incredible views of major city landmarks—famous bridges, Piccadilly Circus—all empty and littered with trash.
> Dr. Beaumont coined the term socially empty space. He writes, "Socially empty space is a species of space in which, because one expects it to be filled, densely populated, like the emblematic spaces of metropolitan modernity, the absence of people is perceived almost as a presence. It is urban space that vibrates with a sense of absence. . . .
> "The destruction of the city is associated with a new beginning," he says. "The sense is, the city is the problem, and if it can be cleansed, we can start again. . . .
> "Being alone in a city, I can go anywhere," said Dr. Beaumont. "We live in these cities with such strict rules, existence is utterly routine and defined by regulations. In a postapocalypse, the city becomes a game, a playful space. We can go into any forbidden area. It's thrilling."
> In his book, he writes, "In a metropolitan society dominated by the routine experience of a mass of people, in all its positive and negative aspects, and of a spatial regime that is once anarchic and elaborately regimented, the city of the absent is simultaneously a dream of being freed from the constraints of capitalist modernity and a nightmare of being cut loose from its consolations."

Sheridan (2013) summarizes by arguing that TEOTWAWKI ("The end of the world as we know it") moment ". . . means that nothing you know in the world—your job, your car, your shitty apartment—matters anymore. The world is over. The boss you hate and your suffocating mortgage payments—none of that is important. You can start over and build a new society. The dystopian is actually utopian" (p. 112). Perhaps this is the appeal—for both purveyors of the post-apocalyptic and those actively preparing for it—beyond the satisfaction that comes from correctly predicting the cause of the apocalypse (Gross and Gilles 2012), is the promise that if we survive, we get to reshape the world.

LIVING THE POST-APOCALYPTIC:
THE CASE OF *DOOMSDAY PREPPERS*

The specter of apocalypse is reflected in the reality television genre. Beginning in 2012, the National Geographic Channel began airing *Doomsday Preppers*, a series that features individuals, families, or small groups that are "prepping" for one or more catastrophes that will herald "the end of the world as we know it." Each episode features either an individual or a representative of a larger group, who would directly face the camera and explain what catastrophe was anticipated and how that person or group was "prepping" in anticipation. The sources of apocalypse ran from the natural—earthquakes or solar flares that would generate destructive electro-magnetic pulses—to varieties of social and economic collapse, or governmental takeovers. The majority of "preppers" formed a consensus that escaping the urban was a necessary precondition for surviving in the post-apocalyptic world.

In season 1, individual "preppers" were introduced by name, geographic location, and profession, followed by a one sentence explanation of what they were "prepping" for and how they were doing it. In general, their activities included stockpiling survival items that would sustain them after conventional infrastructures failed, making sources of food and water unavailable. These plans were then critiqued by the unseen organization called Practical Preppers, whose evaluation was read by the series narrator. A central component of the preparations involved the strategic decision to "bug out"— to leave one's primary residence for a location that would provide both material necessities and protections from anticipated attacks—or to "bug in"—to remain in one's residence because it provided both material necessities and insulation from attack. In most cases, "preppers" anticipated that their locations would be attacked, either by "looters" or other unprepared individuals that were desperate for survival items or possibly from governmental agents. In this analysis of Doomsday Preppers, participant(s) were coded in terms of their initial location (rural, suburban, or urban), what was the perceived primary threat that would initiate the apocalypse, and what their primary survival strategy location was—to "bug out" to an alternative location that was later recorded, or to entrench and "bug in." Season 1 featured ten episodes and a total of thirty-five "preppers" set in predominantly rural survival locations, while another nineteen were located in a completely rural setting, in part because they offered better access to food and water and were more isolated from larger populations presumed to become threatening in the wake of collapse, regardless of the initial source. Several of these rural "preppers," including a couple in the premier episode, had specifically relocated to a rural location because it provided space and/or resources in order to "prep." Conversely, only five "preppers" were located in urban areas, and four of those "preppers" made preparations to "bug out" to a rural location. Only one "prepper," a New York City firefighter who feared the consequences of a possible volcanic eruption in Yellowstone National Park, planned to "bug in" to the family apartment. This decision was critiqued by Practical Preppers and the need for multiple locations was stressed. Eight of the ten suburban "preppers" planned to "bug in" into homes, the majority of which had been augmented by some sort of fortification, in addition to large stores of food and water, as well as the capabilities to produce both. One family, fearing the collapse of the Greenland polar ice and the subsequent flooding caused by rapid sea level rises, left suburban Jacksonville, Florida, for the elevation of the mountains of rural Tennessee.

Season 2 continued the familiar pattern from season 1, with the addition of a 100-point scale based on five measures—food, water, shelter, security, and the "x-factor"—in order for the evaluators from Practical Preppers to offer a more quantitative evaluation of the subjects of each program. Season 2 featured forty-two different Preppers over the course of seventeen episodes and featured more suburban participants (twelve), eight urban participants, and twenty-two rural participants. The majority of suburbanites had taken significant steps to prepare their homes to "bug in," including in some cases explicitly constructed bunkers that could endure whatever calamity unfolded. Bunkers were a preparation not limited to suburbanites, as one resident of Nashville planned to travel 1,800 miles to an underground bunker, and another planned to travel from Wisconsin to central Kansas where he was transforming a decommissioned Atlas F Intercontinental Ballistic Missile (ICBM) into a bunker. A new development in this season involved residents—one each from a rural, suburban, and urban location—to initiate larger preparations in the community. This trend reflects an aspect of the subculture in which preppers describe themselves as "coming out" to non-preppers as they discuss their fears and efforts to prepare for apocalyptic events. This season also emphasized the general lack of confidence that macro-scale structures will be able to perform as normal or to endure some sort of "black swan" event, like a terrorist attack, solar flare, or economic crisis. It is noteworthy that in season 2, only two urban residents planned to "bug in," as all other urbanites saw the urban as a hostile environment during a time of crisis. A National Geographic mini-series that involved one participant was *Doomsday Castle* (2013), based on "Brent Sr.," who involved most of his ten adult children in his effort to build a Neo-Medieval castle in rural North Carolina where his family could retreat in case an EMP burst—either from a solar flare or from an enemy attack—destroyed the electrical grid. As with the majority of participants, these preparations rested on the premises that attack from the outside was inevitable and therefore needed to be prepared against, and that the rural environment with its lower population density and greater proximity to natural resources made it a logical sanctuary. In sum, the participants of these programs, despite their differences in what events might precipitate the "shit hitting the fan" (an often repeated phrase); there was a significant consensus that survival entails leaving the fragile and potentially dangerous urban environment.

RURAL REVERSAL AND THE *PLANET OF THE APES*

The centrality of the urban in the post-apocalyptic holds as well for other species. In Franklin J. Schaffner's (1968) *Planet of the Apes*, three surviving astronauts travel through space to arrive on an apparently desolate world in the year 3978 (having departed Earth in 1972). After a landing that submerges their ship the three astronauts leave the crash site in search of desperately needed provisions, led by Taylor (played by Charlton Heston). They eventually find a lush region and an adjacent cultivated field that is guarded by scarecrow-like figures. In the field they encounter mute humans in animal skins who are madly snatching fruit from the fields. Suddenly, a horn blast signals a coordinated attack by bipedal gorillas that both shoot some of the mute humans, and capture others through the use of nets deployed by gorilla cavalry. Taylor is captured and separated from fellow astronauts Landon and Dodge, and is taken to Ape City. There, Taylor comes to grasp the enormity of the reversal from Earth: here primates, including Gorillas, Chimpanzees, and Orangutans, have developed an urban civilization that includes science, law, a military, and religion. While initially unable to speak due to a throat wound, Taylor is eventually able to communicate with two veterinarians, Zira (played by Kim Hunter) and Cornelius (played by Roddy McDowall), who marvel at his capacity for abstract thought speech. Taylor's life is threatened by Dr. Zaius (played by Maurice Evans), who is both Minister of Science and Chief Defender of the Faith. To escape the possible fate of vivisection, Taylor is aided by Zira and Cornelius to flee to the Forbidden Zone, a desolate area where Cornelius had led an archeological dig a year earlier in a cave that appears to have once been a living structure. In the site, Taylor identifies ancient objects, including dentures and a talking doll that suggest that human civilization had existed on this planet long ago, and that humans had once been able to speak. Pursued by Dr. Zaius and gorilla soldiers, Taylor and Nova (played by Linda Harrison), another mute human rescued from Ape City, ride along the shore line deeper into the Forbidden Zone, ignoring the caution of Dr. Zaius that "you may not like what you see."

The film ends with Taylor's anguished realization made in front of the half-buried Statue of Liberty that the mission had not taken the astronauts to some distant planet, but to Earth in a future in which humanity had destroyed itself and the apes had emerged as the new dominant species. The cities had been wiped out, and with that, even the capacity for speech had been lost.

The 1970 sequel, *Beneath the Planet of the Apes*, continues this urban theme through a war between the gorillas of Ape City and human mutants endowed with mental powers including telepathy and the capacity to generate compelling illusions. Astronaut Taylor and mute human Nova are joined by another astronaut, Brent (played by James Franciscus), who has embarked on a rescue mission for the first expedition. After being captured and fleeing Ape City, Brent flees into the Forbidden Zone and discovers the ruined remains of the Queensboro subway station, thereby revealing to him that he has returned to a future, post-apocalyptic Earth. Brent also discovers the human mutants, who are residing in the ruins of the New York Public Library and have a massive missile in the ruins of St. Patrick's Cathedral that they worship as a divinity, and that Taylor identifies as a "doomsday bomb" based on the alpha and omega letters on the tails. The film concludes with the gorillas invading the New York City underground, leading Taylor to detonate the missile and ensure the apparent destruction of all life on Earth. In this narrative, the ruined city is proof of the grand but doomed past, and the resurgent cities of apes and mutants lay the foundation for the final destruction of sentient species and the biosphere.

This narrative is subsequently transformed and gives the rural reversal a central thematic role, beginning in the Rupert Wyatt version of *Rise of the Planet of the Apes* (2011). In this reimagining of the fall of humanity and the rise of fully sentient primates, scientist Dr. Will Rodman (played by James Franco) works for Gen-Sys in the development of a drug intended to reverse Alzheimer's disease. In the course of his work, he finds an infant chimpanzee who had been exposed to the drug in utero. Rodman spirits the chimpanzee home, and notes his precocious intelligence as well as the success of the experimental drug in healing Rodman's father (played by John Lithgow). After several years, the chimpanzee, named Caesar by Rodman's Shakespeare-loving father, develops an awareness of the place of primates in North American society, and loses his place in Rodman's home and is forced into an animal sanctuary with other primates. Eventually, Caesar (now played by Andy Serkis) obtains aerosol canisters of ALZ-113, the next generation of the anti-Alzheimer's drug that is discovered to have the effect of elevating the intelligence of chimpanzees, orangutans, and gorillas, while simultaneously developing a highly contagious virus amongst humans. After Caesar and his companions escape from the animal sanctuary, they attack the Gen-sys laboratory and expose all the captive test primates contained there, thus creating a huge group of intelligent and belligerent primates. After a running battle through San Francisco and across the Golden Gate Bridge, Caesar and the surviving primates escape into the canopy of Muir Woods National Park. The closing credits feature a global map with links between urban airports, depicting the spread of the lethal virus through air travel, in a motif reminiscent of Terry Gilliam's 1995 *Twelve Monkeys* and the deliberate spread of a lethal contagion through airports.

Dawn of the Planet of the Apes (2014) is set ten years after the plague and subsequent societal collapse, a period during which Caesar and his followers have developed their own settlement in the woods and an apparently thriving social order. This bucolic existence is threatened when this community meets a small group of human survivors, led by Malcolm (played by Jason Clarke), who have come into the forest from a slowly rebuilding and fragile San Francisco in the hopes of resuscitating a hydroelectric dam. This peaceful coexistence is short-lived, as many of the primates are deeply suspicious of the humans because of their experiences at the hands of biomedical researchers, and soon the apes attack and briefly occupy San Francisco, led by the usurper, Koba (played by Terry Kebbell). The film culminates with a battle between the apes and humans, with the fragile alliance of humans and apes apparently destroyed, especially in the wake of news that the San Francisco survivors have used hydroelectric power to contact other humans via radio, and these humans are bringing military assistance to bear. In short, in this latest iteration of the *Planet of the Apes* themed-work, the rural is where new life and civilization may take hold and it is the attempt to revive the urban that revisits destruction on humanity, first aided by experimental science and systems of international air travel.

RURAL REVERSAL AND *THE WALKING DEAD*

The Walking Dead series exemplifies the rural reversal through repeated iterations of three dominant themes of the reversal: *the urban is deadly*; *the urban is a resource to be scavenged*; and *the rural periphery is a sanctuary.* The landscape of the highly popular series is littered with the structures and equipment of contemporary society, where all of the actual institutions themselves have been eviscerated by the rise of the "walkers."

The introductory episode to *The Walking Dead* ("Days Gone By"), establishes the themes of institutional collapse and dislocation through the experience of Deputy Rick Grimes (played by Andrew Lincoln). Grimes is shot during a roadside altercation and awakens weeks later in a hospital devoid of medical staff or patients. Unable to find any medical personnel, Rick flees the hospital wearing his medical garb and heads to his family home, only to discover that his wife Lori (played by Sarah Wayne Callies) and son Carl (played by Chandler Riggs) have fled this unexplained catastrophe. From the beginning of the series, the theme is of densely populated areas that in the pre- apocalyptic period were powerful and affluent becomes deadly in the post-apocalypse. Season 1 of *The Walking Dead* featured Rick being rescued by a group of scavengers in Atlanta, who live on the edge of the city in their camp in order to venture into the city, claim supplies, and flee. The subsequent return to Atlanta in order to seek sanctuary from the CDC only results in the realizations that the capacity for governments to contain this disaster have failed, and that "we are all infected." In season 2, survivors from eastern cities report that they are also filled with walkers, and must be avoided. In season 5, the return to Atlanta results in violent death and the perception that those who survive in Grady Hospital are immediately surrounded by walkers and their likely overwhelming of the hospital. Conversely, areas that had once been relegated to the rural—farms, prisons, and stockyard terminals—become valuable resources in the post-apocalyptic world because they offer supplies, some defense (primarily fences and walls) and isolation. The prison is the focus of much of seasons 3 and 4, and the site of two battles over who will control the buildings that in the pre-apocalyptic world were relegated to isolated areas because affluent urban centers rejected them. Similarly, the small town of Woodbury became a simulacrum of normalcy for survivors, offering the veneer of stability while keeping the devastation of the post-apocalyptic world at bay. The safety of Woodbury is proven to be illusory, as apparently is the normalcy of the Alexandria Safe Zone. While the world of *The Walking Dead* does not preset the rural as being devoid of dangers from the living or the dead, it does appear to be significantly safer than the urban.

The dangers inherent in urban settings as a theme found in *The Walking Dead* are continued in the 2015 six-episode spinoff series, *Fear the Walking Dead*, set in Los Angeles. The series follows two blended families as the "walkers" begin to appear. Their existence is at first dismissed as Internet rumor and the visions of drug addicts, as the premier episode opens with a heroin addict awakening in an abandoned church used by other addicts that sees a woman whose face is saturated with blood after eating another person. High school counselor Madison Clark (played by Kim Dickens) is told by Tobias, a bright, but socially isolated, student, that he fears these rumors and that "when civilization ends, it ends fast," presaging the societal disruptions that emerge. The school population dwindles as students are either withheld by their parents or have simply disappeared. Police are seen loading water and food into their cruisers in apparent preparation to abandon their duties and flee the city. Los Angeles quickly erupts in riots, and the Clark family retreats to their suburban home, accompanied by another family that was forced to abandon the urban core. The suburban enclave is occupied by the army under martial law, while plumes of smoke are seen floating over the downtown. The first season ends with the Clark family escaping the military enclosure of their neighborhood with a stranger whose home overlooks the ocean, where a ship can be seen that can help them escape the coming catastrophe. In *Fear the Walking Dead*, the urban and suburban must be abandoned for the possible frontiers of ocean or desert. The same year AMC has also aired *Into the Badlands*, set in an indeterminate future that unfolds "after the wars," when the majority of the population is confined to regions controlled by one of seven warlord Barons whose armies of "clippers" use martial arts and weapons to defend their territory. In *Badlands* the post-apocalyptic world is devoid entirely of urban life.

THE POST-APOCALYPTIC AND THE SOCIAL IMAGINARY

The significance of the *rural reversal* lies in what Charles Taylor (2004) identifies as the social imaginary: "the ways people imagine their social existence, how they fit together with others, how things go on between them and their fellows, the expectations that are normally met, and the deeper normative notions and images that underlie these expectations" (p. 23). Taylor's conception of the social imaginary implies that vehicles for expressing how the world is perceived to behave (or to have behaved in the past) is instructive in understanding how those that share a social imaginary may act in the future. For example, Stout (2006) argues that the American Civil War was both propelled into existence and sustained in part through the support given from clergy through sermons in both the Union and Confederacy.[7] Conant (2008) argues that the British Security Coordination (BSC) operated an ongoing propaganda campaign to encourage American participation in the Second World War in the United States partially by producing literary contributions to popular magazines that emphasized the war effort as heroic and righteous. Rodgers (2011, pp. 15–16) notes that the domestic political "war of ideas" that began in the 1970s saw a massive increase in the creation and delivery of presidential speeches in support of particular agendas. Polletta (2006) argues that much of the discourse within social movements—both internal and directed externally—are driven by such narratives or stories.

Questions of perceptions and representations of persons, subjects, phenomena, and the like have long been a part of the sociological agenda in several different paradigms including Symbolic Interactionism, Constructivism (for example, see Best, 2012) and the *Social Construction of Reality* (Berger and Luckmann, 1966). What these and other theoretical orientations suggest is that perceptions, informed by some form of representations—visual, symbolic, narratives, and so on—are significant variables within explanations of the creation and maintenance of social orders. For example, Altheide (2002, 2006) and Glassner (1999) argue that public perceptions of crime and terrorism are largely derived from popular cultural and other mass mediated sources, rather than from closely scrutinized factual research, contributing to the increased fear of criminal victimization in the 1990s despite the decline in measurable victimization by the FBI. Bob (2005) argues that specific international problems—such as a specific human rights crisis—rise or fall within the international community based on how it fares within the global morality market. Such multi-vocalic and often contradictory sources of information contribute to Manjoo's (2008) assertion that contemporary American social life is becoming impervious to solely factual persuasive methods. De Zengotita (2005) and Gabler (1998) likewise contend that social life in postindustrial societies is increasingly influenced by mediated appearances (see also Baudrillard, 1994). In sum, these works suggest that how the world is imagined or perceived—even if these perceptions are not empirically supported—may serve to inform future actions and plans created in anticipation of such trends. While imagining factors that may cause future difficulties or threats and then acting accordingly (for example, see Giddens, 1984), such exercises are necessarily fraught with limited information or difficulties in imagining how future events may pose degrees of risk.

In the case of the social imaginary and the perception of potential risk, those events that are evocative, especially in the case of how information is presented, may become more influential than information that is presented in more analytical terms. For example, journalist Terry Gross on National Public Radio's *Fresh Air* pressed author David E. Hoffman on his account in *Dead Hand: The Untold Story of the Cold War Arms Race and Its Dangerous Legacy* on how President Reagan was propelled towards nuclear disarmament by the 1983 television mini-series, *The Day After*—a dramatization of the days preceding and following a thermonuclear exchange between the United States and Soviet Union in Lawrence, Kansas:

> GROSS: I still want to get back to the movie "The Day After" a second. This is the movie that, you know, made-for-TV movie that depicted a nuclear attack on the United States and how horrible it would be. I'm always a little confounded and disturbed when I hear how moved President Reagan was about that. And here's why: Everything that was in that movie about what would happen, I'd already heard that from so many experts, from doctors, from physicists, from, you know, political experts. Journalists were writing about it. And to think that Reagan didn't know this, that he hadn't thought about the extent of that devastation until seeing a made-for-TV movie, when the information was already out there. What does that say?
>
> Mr. HOFFMAN: Terry, he was a Hollywood man through and through and to him, a made-for-TV movie was much more powerful than all of those briefing books . . .
>
> GROSS: I don't know. Okay . . .
>
> Mr. HOFFMAN: Look, in his diary Reagan wrote: Columbus Day, in the morning at Camp David I ran the tape of the movie ABC is running on the air

November 20. It's called "The Day After." It has Lawrence, Kansas, wiped out
in a nuclear war with Russia. It's powerfully done—all $7 million worth. It's
very effective. It left me greatly depressed. So far, they haven't sold any of the
25 spot ads scheduled and I can see why.
(Soundbite of laughter)

Mr. HOFFMAN: My own reaction was one of our having to do all we can to
have a deterrent and see there is never a nuclear war.
Those were Reagan's words written in his own diary at the time. That's not a
press release. That's the man speaking.

GROSS: Right.

Mr. HOFFMAN: And Edmund Morris, his official biographer said that Reagan was dazed by this film and four days later was still fighting off the
depression caused by "The Day After" (Hoffman, 2009).

Clearly, Gross is incredulous that Reagan's position on arms control is transformed not by access to classified data on scenarios about the possible consequences of thermonuclear war, but instead is moved by the theatrical depiction of the likely consequences of such an event on individual Americans.

SOCIAL IMAGINARY, THE SUBCULTURE OF TREPIDATION, AND THE RELIGION OF FEAR

In *The Religion of Fear: The Politics of Horror in Conservative Evangelicalism* (2008), Jason Bivins contends that "political cultures are narrated and
taught" partially through books, films, and other mediated representations
that contain rhetoric or imagery drawn from a "common symbolic pool"
(Bivins, 2008, p. 4). Bivins investigates "conservative religion" (not simply
conservative American Protestantism, in terms of its "position of social and
political conservatism" partially through popular cultural representations that
both reflect and reinforce these socially and culturally conservative perceptions through generating a religion of fear:

> The religion of fear is a mode of social criticism and a political sensibility
> (which I often refer to as a "discourse," emphasizing its pedagogic and repre-
> sentational aims). Its creators are politically motivated and engaged, drawing
> on and influencing broader cultural transformations through a social critique
> expressed in popular entertainments. These pop expressions do representation-
> al and rhetorical work for readers and audiences, linking fears of damnations
> to a carefully identified range of sociopolitical practices and beliefs (Bivins,
> 2008, p. 5).

This religion of fear therefore encourages "fear talk" about identified issues
and as an expression of political religion is " . . . located in multiple spaces
outside of those commonly recognized: in stories, in habits of consumption,

in perception, in forming habits of thought and bodily habits" (Bivins, 2008, p. 8). Bivins cites as one example of the religion of fear the "hell houses" that are sponsored by conservative evangelical churches, in which guests see scenarios depicting the grisly deaths of teenagers due to immoderate behaviors, such as drunk driving accidents or AIDS, and conclude with an opportunity for the audience to be "saved" and avoid these potential fates and the purported demonic punishments awaiting the unsaved. These representations both intersect with realistic potentials for the audience members, such as the hazards of teen driving, and the existing individualistic and pietistic theology of conservative evangelism that includes blaming the alcohol companies for drunk driving. The religion of fear contributes to a self-perpetuating "fear regime", " . . . similar to what Michel Foucault called an 'episteme,' a culturally or politically produced conception of 'truth,' which ties together and grounds other social discourses" (Bivins, 2008, p. 15). These "fear regimes" therefore encourage and reinforce particular perceptions within the mediated representations that believers consume. For example, the *Left Behind* series that provides a thriller genre account of the Rapture in which believers are raptured into heaven, while the rest of humanity undergoes trials and tribulations that culminate in a global military conflict. These earlier discussed novels provide a "fear regime" that reinforces central tenants of conservative evangelicalism—that the end of the world is rapidly approaching, that adherence to biblical principles is urgent, and that a conflict in Israel is inevitable and desirable. Consequently, conservative evangelicals like Pastor John Hagee have created Christians United for Israel that actively promotes the imperative of preserving Israel.[8] The significance here is that this narrative promoted through novels is supplemented through handbooks and reference guides, theological apologetics denouncing the dozens of books that critique the series, daily calendars, greeting cards, CD-ROMs, DVDs . . . and the *Left Behind: Eternal Consequences* video game—a strategy-game that involves battling Global Community peacekeepers or demons with the power of prayer, while searching for Tribulation clues that unlock different areas of the game (Bivins, 2008). The importance here is that these religious claims are circulated through portions of the popular cultural milieu and have consequences well outside of the believers' communities, such as political support for "Pro-Israel" policies and hostility towards comprehensive sex education in secondary schools. These mediated representations may also contribute to an emotional regime—a "set of normative emotions and the official rituals, practices, and emotions that express and inculcate them" (William Reddy, cited in Bivins, 2008, p. 15). The religion of fear is significant as it provides a template for considering *how* a comprehension of an imminent "black swan" event (Taleb, 2007) might be promoted through mediated representations that are not driven by a single source such as government sponsored propaganda, and how the resulting anxiety of such a subculture could palpably influence perceptions and a variety of actions, including attitudes towards abortion, homosexuality, American military involvement in the Middle East, or the preparatory actions that individuals must take before these destructive events unfold—such as leaving the urban for the rural life.

CONCLUSIONS: FICTION AND PERCEPTION FEED THE SOCIAL IMAGINARY

The above has suggested two interconnected trends: the growth in popularity of the post-apocalyptic narrative within North American popular culture and the emergent theme of the rural reversal. From recent films, television programs, and novels like *Station Eleven* (2014) and *California* (2014), the appeal of the end of the world has grown considerably, transcending any subcultures, such as science fiction enthusiasts or evangelicals embracing the *Left Behind* series. Many of these works have demonstrated recognition that the urban environment is fragile and increasingly vulnerable to a host of possible threats—a trend paralleled by the subjects of the *Doomsday Preppers* series. While some of the concerns of the "preppers" may be partially driven by businesses such as Wise Foods, a company that produces food intended for long-term storage and a sponsor of *Doomsday Preppers*, such actors cannot explain the numerous sources from whence these same concerns (re)emerge. While some social scientists might be tempted to relegate the significance of fictional representations to cultural analyses, this project suggests that the border between fictional narrative and potential or counterfactual worldview is far more permeable.

For example, Griffin (2001) notes that *The Turner Diaries*, a fictional account of the destruction of the American Federal Government and its ultimate usurpation by white nationalists (written by William Pierce, a leader of the National Alliance) was a favored book of Timothy McVeigh. McVeigh purportedly took copies of *The Turner Diaries* to gun shows and other events and sold them at cost, apparently eager to disseminate its messages. One key event in the novel is the destruction of the J. Edgar Hoover Building in Washington, D.C., by a fertilizer and fuel truck bomb: a method nearly identical to the destruction of the Federal Office Building in Oklahoma City, Oklahoma, that McVeigh was convicted of and executed for. This connection between McVeigh and *The Turner Diaries* was not simply made by a few observers, but rather was entered into evidence by Federal prosecutors. This is not to say, of course, that those who consume post-apocalyptic popular culture and/or prepare for some potential disaster are moving towards violent confrontations with their host societies. The McVeigh case does highlight how popular culture may mirror and influence concerns that are taken outside of the realm of entertainment, and possibly vice versa.

This project does suggest that the groundswell of perceptions that the urban is fragile and potentially deadly does suggest that the confidence of older forms of modernity and stability of the urban has declined, and that perhaps we have entered what Giddens (1984) termed the high modern with its relentless reflexivity and risk assessment, highlighting those flaws that were once concealed. Williams (2011) argues that apocalyptic narratives may be understood both in the early Christian "lifting of the veil" (including the revelation of that which has been previously concealed) and alternately " . . . is the end of a *totality*, here meaning not the sum of all things but the ordering of those things in a particular historical shape. This end, therefore, is the collapse of a system of "real abstractions" and their real effects, of the intersections and stresses between ideas about the world and how the world is shaped into accordance with those ideas" (Williams, 2011, p. 5).

While Williams writes about the "films and cultural legacies" as they intersect with the collapse of capitalism, a parallel case may be made with the rural reversal: a growing realization that expectations of ceaseless urbanormativity is both unsustainable and increasingly problematic in light of the numerous vulnerabilities that urban dwellers are subjected to, and an increasing loss of legitimacy in dominant social and political institutions to sustain these systems in the event of a natural or social (or combined) disrupting effect. As Williams writes about various apocalyptic narratives, " . . . this doesn't mean *total destruction* but rather a destruction of *totalizing* structures, of those universal notions that do not just describe "how things are" but serve to prescribe and insist that "this is how things must be" (Williams, 2011, p. 5). In the cases of a trend in both fictional narratives and earnest undertakings in the face of ambiguous threats, the rural reversal suggests that perhaps the expectations of ceaseless, unbounded urbanization are being challenged, while a countervailing narrative of the rural as a desirable locale is being proffered. Perhaps part of the appeal of these narratives is that, as Sheridan (2013) suggests, the thought that the rules and structures that both constrain and enable (post)moderns are also restrictive, and that the subversive thoughts of life without them could be invigorating and liberating—at least until the antibiotics and toilet paper run out.

NOTES

1. Often used in introductory social sciences courses that address urbanization.
2. Especially in the United States.
3. The film received a *New York Times* Critic's Pick from A. O. Scott and a 97 percent "fresh" rating from metadata website Rotten Tomatoes (15 May 2015), and as of September 2015 earned over $153 million in the United States (IMDb). In December 2015, *Mad Max Fury Road* received two Golden Globe nominations for Best Motion Picture (Drama) and Best Director.
4. The books of both series have been made into profitable and popular movie franchises.

5. Winner of the 1994 Newbury Medal.
6. Ranked on the IMDb website as one of "Top 100 Best TV Shows."
7. To such an extent that more possible admonishing regarding religious injunctions concerning the conduct of the war were eclipsed.
8. In so doing they are therefore challenging "land for peace" initiatives.

REFERENCES

Altheide, D. L. (2002). *Creating fear: News and the construction of crisis.* Hawthorne, NY: Aldine de Gruyter.
Altheide, D. L. (2006). *Terrorism and the politics of fear.* Lanham, MD: AltaMira Press.
Baudrillard, J. (1994). *Simulacra and simulation.* (S. F. Glaser, Trans.) Ann Arbor: University of Michigan Press.
Best, J. (2012). *Social problems (2nd edition).* New York: W.W. Norton.
Bivins, J. C. (2008). *Religion of fear: The politics of horror in conservative evangelicalism.* New York: Oxford University Press.
Bob, C. (2005). *The marketing of rebellion: Insurgents, media, and international activism.* New York: Cambridge University Press.
Boyle, D. (Director). (2002). *28 Days Later* [Motion Picture].
Collins, S. (2008). *The hunger games.* New York: Scholastic Books.
Conant, J. (2008). *The irregulars: Roald Dahl and the British spy ring in wartime Washington.* New York: Simon and Schuster.
Danner, B. (2012). *Dark futures: A VOYA guide to apocalyptic, post-apocalyptic, and dystopian books and media.* Bowie, MD: VOYA Press, an imprint of E.L. Kurdyla Publishing, LLC.
Darabont, F., Kirkman, R., Moore, T., and Adlard, C. (2010-2017). The Walking Dead. AMC Studios.
De Zengotita, T. (2005). *Mediated: How the media shapes your world and the way you live in it.* New York: Bloomsbury.
Diamond, J. (2012). *The world until yesterday: What can we learn from traditional societies?* New York: Viking.
Doyle, R. (2013-). *Doomsday Castle.*
Fensterman, L. (2007, April 5). Last "Left Behind Book Debuts," National Public Radio, Day to Day (K. G. Bates, Interviewer).
Forster, M. (Director). (2013). *World War Z* [Motion Picture].
Fresnadillo, J. C. (Director). (2007). *28 Weeks Later* [Motion Picture].
Fulkerson, G. M. and Thomas, A. R. (Eds.). 2014. *Studies in urbanormativity: Rural community in urban society.* Lanham, MD: Lexington Books.
Gabler, N. (1998). *Life: The movie. How entertainment conquered reality.* New York: Vintage.
Giddens, A. (1984). *The constitution of society: Outline of the theory of structuration.* Berkeley: University of California Press.
Gilliam, T. (Director). (1995). *Twelve Monkeys* [Motion Picture].
Glassner, B. (1999). *The culture of fear: Why Americans are afraid of the wrong things.* New York: Basic Books.
Griffin, R. S. (2001). *The fame of a dead man's deeds: An up-close portrait of white nationalist William Pierce.* 1st Books Library.
Gross, M. B., and Gilles, M. (2012). *The last myth: What the rise of apocalyptic thinking tells us about America.* Amherst, NY: Prometheus Books.
Hoffman, D. E. (2009, October 8). "Dead Hand" reexamines the Cold War Arms Race. National Public Radio, Fresh Air (T. Gross, Interviewer).
Huxley, A. (1932/1998). *Brave new world.* New York: Perennial.
Ishiro, H. (Director). (1954). *Godzilla* [Motion Picture].
Kirkman, R., and Erickson, D. (2015). Fear the Walking Dead.
Kripke, E. (2012-14). Revolution.

LaHaye, T., and Jenkins, J. B. (1995). *Left behind.* Carol Stream, IL: Tyndale House Publishing.

Larson, G. A., Moore, R. D., and Eick, D. (2004-2009). Battlestar Galactica.

Lepucki, E. (2014). *California: A novel.* New York: Little, Brown and Company.

Lowry, L. (1993). *The giver.* Boston: Houghton Mifflin.

Madison, A. (2011-). Doomsday Preppers. National Geographic Channel.

Mandel, E. S. (2014). *Station eleven: A novel.* New York: Alfred A. Knopf.

Manjoo, F. (2008). *True enough: Learning to live in a post-fact society.* New York: Wiley.

Menzies, W. C. (Director). (1936). *Things to Come* [Motion Picture].

Miller, G. (Director). (1979). *Mad Max* [Motion Picture].

Miller, G. (Director). (1981). *Mad Max 2: The Road Warrior* [Motion Picture].

Miller, G. (Director). (2015). *Mad Max: Fury Road* [Motion Picture].

Miller, G., and Ogilvie, G. (Directors). (1985). *Mad Max: Beyond Thunderdome* [Motion Picture].

O'Bannon, R. S., Murphy, K., and Taylor, M. (2013-2015). *Defiance.*

Polletta, F. (2006). *It was like a fever: Storytelling in protest and politics.* Chicago: University of Chicago Press.

Post, T. (Director). (1970). *Beneath the Planet of the Apes* [Motion Picture].

Reeves, M. (Director). (2014). *Dawn of the Planet of the Apes* [Motion Picture].

Rodgers, D. T. (2011). *Age of fracture.* Cambridge: The Belknap Press of Harvard University Press.

Roth, V. (2011). *Divergent.* New York: Katherine Tegen Books.

Schaffner, F. J. (Director). (1968). *Planet of the Apes* [Motion Picture].

Schaffner, F. J. (2015, May 15). "Mad Max: Fury Road," Still Angry After All These Years. *The New York Times.*

Sheridan, S. (2013). *The disaster diaries: How I learned to stop worrying and love the apocalypse.* New York: Penguin.

Stirling, S. (2004). *Dies the Fire.* New York: Roc Books.

Stout, H. S. (2006). *Upon the altar of the nation: A moral history of the American civil war.* New York: Viking.

Taleb, N. 2007. *The black swan: The impact of the highly improbable fragility.* Random House Publishing Group.

Taylor, C. (2004). *Modern social imaginaries.* Durham, NC: Duke University Press.

Wells, H. (1933). *The shape of things to come.* New York: Macmillan.

Williams, E. C. (2011). *Combined and uneven apocalypse: Luciferian Marxism.* Washington, DC: Zero Books.

Wyatt, R. (Director). (2011). *Rise of the Planet of the Apes* [Motion Picture].

Chapter Six

Urbanormativity in News Coverage of Rural Life

Pilar Erin McKay

News archives offer one of the most valuable places that historical researchers can visit to collect data, peruse publications, and amass a collection of articles about past events or local stories. Methodologically, researchers may choose to study the content of the stories, or alternatively focus on the tone. Knowledgeable of their archival role—or else proceeding along unwittingly—a news press will effectively serve to create and maintain an historical record of different places across the country that can ultimately be used for constructing narratives and ideas that inform rural community identity.

While there are still rural-based newspapers covering local news, the drive towards consolidation and regionalism in the United States is having an impact on the scope of coverage. Borders drawn by the government for counties and municipalities do not necessarily prevent media markets from spreading into places that are not technically part of the same region. In some cases, a trip two hours one way could end in the same media market, while a thirty-minute trip in another direction would land in an entirely different region. Within an urbanormative society, the topics urban-based news organizations are covering in their region's rural areas do influence the recording of the public stories and history of local communities. Local rural newspapers may have access to stories based on their proximity, but the urban-based regional newspaper has an ability to reach more people than the rural news organization. In a hunt for impact and legitimacy from a historical point of view, the channel with the larger circulation and reach may come to be viewed as "the paper of record." As a result, the unique stories and perspectives of rural localities may come to be eclipsed in favor of a more regional and urban perspective.

This chapter focuses on the potential implications of urbanormativity in news coverage and how this may impact a particular rural area's ownership of their public story and history. The discussion will focus primarily on the rural area's coverage by urban-based regional newspapers. This study helps to highlight first-level agenda setting implications as well as ground the discussion with an empirical case study on rural news coverage.

NEWS MEDIA'S ROLE IN AGENDA SETTING

In an ideal situation, a news organization could cover all significant events in its region at all times. However, in reality, there are only a limited number of resources available to cover the news. Reporters, page and word limits, and newsroom budgets may each conspire to limit coverage. Given these constraints, people within the various news media ultimately bear the burdensome responsibility of deciding on where, what, and who they can and will report. There is no scientific standard for identifying what is to be deemed "newsworthy." Choosing a news story could depend on the type of media on which the news is broadcast, such as TV, radio, print, online, or mobile. It could also depend on the news organization's mission and commitment to report on areas outside of their core urban area. When resources are ample, organizations may have bureaus reporting from the suburbs or rural areas. When resources are scarce, reports may have to contract back to the urban area. Each news organization has its own process for determining where to report and what constitutes appropriate coverage. Events themselves can be seen as newsworthy, but there is no scientific or objective basis to make this call.

While the assumption may be that similar urban-based newspapers will uniformly decide against reporting on rural areas, this may not always be the case. In Menifield et al. (2001) it was found that some urban-based, national newspapers reported rural-based school violence at a higher rate. This study observed that the *New York Times* and *Louisville Courier-Journal* both reported rural school shooting events at a higher rate than their urban counterparts (Menifield et al., 2001). However, the same article found that the *Wall Street Journal* and *Los Angeles Times* did not find rural school shootings newsworthy and therefore did not write about the same events covered by the *New York Times* and the *Louisville Courier-Journal* (Menifield et al., 2001).

Corbett (1992) also found differences in coverage on wildlife stories between rural and urban newspapers. The environment can be a topic of regional interest, and Corbett (1992) noticed, "environmental issues—including wildlife issues—are often the focus of conflict, especially when community self-interest is involved." She found that urban-based papers picked up stories that the local, rural news organizations did not (Corbett, 1992).

Both studies, by Menifield et al. (2001) and Corbett (1992), highlight the news media's role in agenda setting. To summarize agenda setting theory: "the media not only can be successful in telling us *what to think about*, they also can be successful in telling us *how to think about it*" (McCombs, 2005). In this statement, McCombs (2005) is talking about first-level (*"what to think about"*) and second-level (*"how to think about it"*) agenda setting. The first-level refers to which particular topic the news organization chooses to report, while the second level is related to how the issue will be framed and thus how the public will be influenced on how to think about these topics (McCombs, 2005; Weaver, 2007). In other words, for second-level agenda setting, how the news is reported can affect the ultimate public opinion on the topic (McCombs, 2005; Weaver, 2007).

Agenda setting at its first level is what this chapter is primarily documenting. McCombs (2005) describes this first-level agenda setting as the news media determining the "salience of objects, usually public issues, but sometimes other objects." Weaver (2007) notes that the "relative salience" is "usually operationally defined as perceived importance." In this theory, journalists are the first people who perceive the importance of these objects or public issues. In fact, McCombs (2005) reports that agenda setting will "involve the transfer of salience" from the news media to the public. The topics that the public encounters are the result of what the news organization chooses as the story. This demonstrates the immense influence that is exercised by the news media.

There are many ways that news organizations contribute to a society. Outside of merely providing a broadsheet record of the day, they assign perceived importance of issues in a community. Local media are useful in fostering and supporting a vibrant social society, as demonstrated in Nicodemus (2004) in reference to creating a "viable political community." When communities have conflict, the news media may record and also illuminate issues—as in the discussion of "large-scale swine facilities" in Reisner's (2005) study of a controversy in rural Illinois, or Corbett's (1992) study on wildlife stories. Creating this dialogue is a very important function of news media—and in some ways establishing the value of the fourth estate in rural areas.

However, before news media can build dialogue within a community or region, the channel has to cover relevant events and issues. If there is no coverage of a particular area, rural or urban, there can be no dialogue. Within the American urbanormative society, the areas that lose the most are rural. Not only are they constrained by urban-based coverage of their news and events, but they are also controlled by whether or not the media consider their event or issues to be newsworthy. In other words, the salience of rural issues may be altogether missed and thereby rendered invisible or unimportant.

The idea that rural areas have to prove their newsworthiness may not be evident to people working and living in these regions. For an urban-based newspaper, they may see their city as their most immediate community and focal point for the region. This is not a dereliction of duty, as this may make sense to their media channel and institutional mission. Unless this mission's geographical radius clearly defines the distance to report on stories, and helps flag the newsworthiness of a story from an outside area, it may not always be noticed and captured by the news organization. Theories of regionalism and regional development that inform these decisions have tended to group rural areas in with their urbancore (Katz, 2000).

Understanding the outcome of first-level agenda setting is useful for rural areas. This can help determine the extent of urbanormativity that frames the public story of a rural areas within the media market. Understanding what current events are perceived as important gives us clues as to what future historical researchers will see in the archives of the past. The challenge is this: will rural areas be able to effectively communicate in the historical record that which the urban core did not have the responsibility to cover with regard locally relevant events or issues?

JOURNALISM'S ROLE IN RECORDING HISTORY

When studying people or places in history, one of the first places research is conducted is in the archives. Archives offer a trove of materials, and are one of the richest areas for historical data. The content reported in local and regional newspapers is often taken as the primary source document for historical researchers, and this is why it is important to ensure that local histories are being successfully captured and recorded.

The connections between journalism and historical research include similar methodologies and objectives. Feldstein (2004) discusses the relations between "journalism and oral history," and to highlight the two, he outlines a personal narrative of his experience as a journalist interviewing former slaves and reflecting on what made him different from an oral historian. Feldstein (2004) brings up important contrasting points in how the two are alike and dissimilar, finding that "But the differences between the two are more than a matter of time. Ultimately, the two have different purposes, different standards and norms, different techniques. Yet at the same time, similarities abound; both must grapple with parallel issues of empathy, ethics, and evidence" (Feldstein, 2004).

This tension between historical data collection and news reporting that Feldstein (2004) references affects how present events will be viewed in the future. Importantly, we must ask, was the framing of an event caused by a deadline or by a larger more significant social phenomenon? Would the journalist have the ability to comment on his or her mindset when filing the story (Feldstein, 2004)? With reflection, as would happen with an oral history interview, would the participant have the ability to add context (Feldstein, 2004)?

The reality is that historical data from news sources, especially in the case of newspapers, is not the same as research compiled by an oral historian (Feldstein, 2004). However, these are the only data that we are left with for some events. If an event has escaped the agenda of historians, then the newspaper will shed light on what happened and give most of the facts: who, when, where, what, and why. This information is extremely valuable for defining what happened to or between various people and places.

The key issue for an urbanormative society is this: do urban-based news organizations adequately report on rural areas? And, secondarily, what topics do they choose to report? Events can happen anywhere regardless of population density. Within a given archive, there is no fixed quotient that can be assigned that would highlight the level of urbanormativity of a particular news source. As a result, historians may not receive the full context on how a news organization chose topics or how they decided to frame them. Accessing the local news sources may include a visit to the area, but would there be a news archive in the rural community to access? Following this a step further, the question then becomes to what extent will the history of rural areas be shaped by urbanormative influences?

REGIONALISM AND ITS IMPACT ON NEWS MEDIA

Regions have vague and ill-defined borders, especially for the rural areas that surround them. In fact, when defining regions, there is an urbanormative focus: "the term *region* is certainly ill-defined in popular usage. It is sometimes used to describe a large city, the surrounding suburbs, and perhaps the farms, forest or open space just beyond the suburban fringe" (Katz, 2000). Rural areas are thus an afterthought when constructing regions. In Katz's (2000) edited volume, *Reflections on Regionalism*, the index reveals ten entries for "rural areas" whereas "suburban" has thirty-seven.

Regions are becoming increasingly important for the purposes of governance and economic development, in addition to organizing media markets. For rural areas, it often means that there may be a strong urbanormative bias in institutions that have a regional scope with an urban headquarters. Media is not immune to regionalism, as media markets are derived geographically with each having an urban core of varying sizes. These are called Designated Market Areas® (DMAs) (Nielsen, 2013). DMAs are primarily television areas defined and measured by the Nielsen Company (Nielsen, 2013). The

Nielsen Company owns these maps, but the FCC also maintains broadcast mapping resources (Mazumdar, 2011; FCC, 2009).

There is overlap between regions, even if they have been carefully drawn up with borders, but news organizations operating from the urban core tend to be those with the largest circulation and influence. While large circulation may not always equate with the quality of reporting, it does indicate that this news organization has the largest reach or number of people that it can potentially influence. As such, the historical researcher may ask why not gravitate to the newspaper with the largest circulation? It would indicate greater resources, influence, and quality of reporting.

A historical researcher may have time to travel directly to a locality of an event's coverage. In that case, there may be local news sources available, particularly if the rural area has a regular local press, as would ideally be the case. Currently, there is less variety of news organizations because of a lack of resources to report, coupled with a pressure to consolidate. It is rare, for instance, for a rural area to have a television station with a daily broadcast. While news may be reported from a rural area through the urban core, is that news going to necessarily reach back to the rural area of origin? Circulation or reach of some media sources, like print newspapers or radio, could therefore be constrained. More than ever before, owing partly to increased online circulation, rural areas are gaining more access to urban-based newspapers with regularity, while local print newspapers are becoming increasingly rare.

As online journalistic outlets continue to develop, news emanating from the urban core grows even more distant from the localities once covered by traditional media sources, like television, radio, and print. Although there are some regional boundaries from a media context, news can move faster and farther than ever before, thus becoming somewhat disembodied from physical contexts and places. Studying what issues urban newspapers cover about rural areas may offer insights into their potential urbanormative biases. Applying a case study approach will allow for an exploration into the selection of topics chosen to be reported and deemed newsworthy.

CASE STUDY

What Topics are Published about Rural Areas from the Urban Core?

The rush towards regionalism has a profound impact on rural communities and the many facets of their public stories. With respect to the recording of history, an analysis of urban-based newspaper coverage of rural areas can help to understand what topics are of interest and deemed newsworthy enough to be published. Revealing first-level agenda setting—what the news is saying about rural areas—can help illuminate whether an urbanormative point of view permeates reporting on rural areas.

The objective of this case study is to explore the topics covered by urban-based newspapers reporting on the rurals outlying area of their media markets. It is important to note that there is no clearly defined responsibility for any given urban-based newspaper to cover all the areas that surround it, even if the area is within its media market. Though important and relevant, the political economy and regional cultural influence of news organizations is not the focus of this case study. This study is not meant to indict the urban newspaper in its abdication of rural areas because the analysis does not have an understanding of what is going on in newsrooms. Instead, the goal is to understand which rural topics the urban-based newspaper selects to report and publish. The research question for the case study is: what news topics do urban-based newspapers publish and record about rural areas in their media market?

This study encompasses three regions. Each media market contains whole or parts of counties, so an efficient way of defining place in this context is by studying rural counties. FCC maps were used to determine the rural areas under analysis. These maps do refer specifically to television markets, but it is an easy way to determine a media market more generally. In this study, media market will refer to areas within a region to which the urban core may broadcast. Obviously, there will be some spill-over in all media channels, including television, radio, and newspapers, the most traditional of our media channels.

The rural counties chosen had no municipality designated as a city and had populations of fewer than 50,000 residents. Media markets analyzed were: Buffalo, New York; Las Vegas, Nevada; and Denver, Colorado (FCC, 2009; FCC, 2009; FCC, 2009). The rural counties had at least some (Nye County) if not all (Wyoming County and Elbert County) coverage coming from the urban core, according to their respective FCC maps (FCC, 2009; FCC, 2009; FCC, 2009). The media markets under study represented three different time zones, and each region offers a different environment and context, leading to potential differences in news events and stories.

A content analysis was conducted in order to measure the frequency of topics covered by each news organization. Newspapers with the largest circulation in the center city of their media market (Buffalo, Las Vegas, and Denver) comprised the set analyzed. Newspapers offered easily accessed archives as well as a text data as a basis of analysis. The archives of the *Buffalo News*, *Las Vegas Review-Journal*, and the *Denver Post* are all included in NewsBank's Access World News database (NewsBank, 2016). The databases varied on how far back in time they collected the archives, but for all newspapers, the database included the time period analyzed (2013–2015).

NewsBank's Access World News (2016) offers the following data in its search: article title, page it appeared on, number of words, reading level, and a brief summary of the search term in context (anywhere from a few words to

Table 6.1.   Media Market, Publication, and Counties Studied

Media Market	Publication	Circulation** S/Su(wkdy) Report date	Rural County (population*)	Urban County (population*)
Buffalo	*Buffalo News*	192,172 (136,962) 06/2015	Wyoming (42,155)	Erie (919,040)
Las Vegas	*Las Vegas Review-Journal*	190,572 (125,669) 06/2015	Nye (43,946)	Clark (1,951,269)
Denver	*Denver Post*	515,483 (331,223) 03/2015	Elbert (23,086)	Denver (600,158)

several sentences). Some newspapers in the database also included the edition or section of the newspaper. Search terms for the database were used to access the publications' archives, and paired with a search for "the name of the county" (for instance, "Wyoming County," "Nye County," or "Elbert County"). Although this left out municipality level news (reporting a town without saying the county it was located in), this offered the most consistent way to operationalize coverage in a rural area. In many cases, the topic of the article was expressed in the title and/or the summary of where the search term appeared in the article. In the cases where the article's topic was unclear from the title, the article was accessed to learn more about the topic of the article and then coded.

Codes were developed organically. Each year was treated as a separate unit of analysis from the next: codes were developed annually and not carried over to the following year. Each article was given one code, and after the codes were developed, they were finally collapsed based on commonalities. For topics that are discussed in detail, an example story is cited in the analysis in order to offer additional detail on that code. While many stories may have covered the same story, the highlighted story will provide some further detail on the topic—it is meant to be illustrative and descriptive, but not generalizable.

Wyoming County, New York

Wyoming County is included in the Buffalo, New York, media market. Buffalo is located in Erie County, which had 919,040 residents according to the 2010 U.S. Census. Wyoming County had a population of 41,155 (U.S. Census, 2010). The *Buffalo News* is the major urban-based newspaper in its media market. As of June 2015, the *Buffalo News* had a circulation of 192,172 on the weekend and 136,962 during the week (Alliance for Audited Media, 2016). The *Buffalo News* covered Wyoming County with varying frequency over the archival period (1989 to 2015). As seen in Figure 6.1, the number of articles peaked in 1999 at 547 and dipped to 130 in 2008. The average mentions of Wyoming County per year over 1989 to 2015 are 348.3. The database indicated many duplicate stories, and for this case study, all stories were counted as distinct as it was unclear in what capacity they were similar other than repetition in words.

The *Buffalo News* had the most consistency in the topics they reported on with frequency over all three newspapers analyzed. Table 6.2 outlines the topics of coverage over the case study span of time. When it came to Wyoming County, Police Courts (Local News Section, 2013, November 21) and Crime (Gryta, 2013, October 30) was the most reported on topic by the *Buffalo News*. Auto racing was covered with consistency (Ott, 2014, December 8).

The *Buffalo News* also reported on the economy of the area, news about businesses (Local News Section, 2013, December 12), as well as reporting on grants (Financial Section, 2015, September 2015). In 2014, a severe snowstorm swept through the area causing an increase in weather reporting (Zremski, 2014, December 12). Not only did Buffalo and Wyoming County share a media market, it appears they shared a snowstorm in 2014.

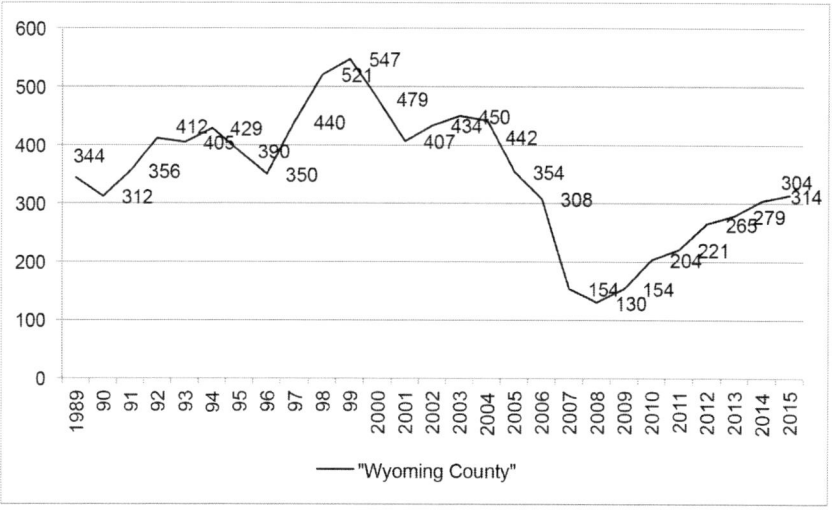

Figure 6.1.

Nye County, Nevada

Outside of Las Vegas, which is located in Clark County, is Nye County. This rural county has a population of 43,946 residents (U.S. Census, 2010). Clark County, in contrast, has a population of 1,951,269 (U.S. Census, 2010). The urban-core newspaper, the *Las Vegas Review-Journal*, has a circulation of 190,572 during the weekend and 125,669 during the weekdays (Alliance for Audited Media, 2016). The peak of "Nye County" reporting was in 2010 when 175 articles were published about it and the lowest amount was thirteen in 1996 (Figure 6.2). The average number of articles is 97.3 between 1996 and 2015.

Table 6.3 outlines the most reported topics in Nye County by the *Las Vegas Review-Journal*. Crime was the major topic reported on in Nye County by the *Las Vegas Review-Journal*. Crimes could include coverage on court cases, as in 2014, or high-profile events as in 2015. That year, celebrity Lamar Odom was found unconscious in a brothel in Nye County (Laux, 2015, October 13). Since that event included alleged illegal activity, the news story was included under the code for crime.

Yucca Mountain, a potential hazardous waste site, is located in Nye County (Sokolova, 2015, September 18). Driven by Yucca Mountain news, land use and natural resources of Nye County are considered very newsworthy (Tetreault and Brean, 2015, July 10).

In addition to crime and land-use issues, in 2014 and 2015, Nye County accidents were part of the news landscape, including highway accidents (Taloma, 2014, November 20). Although environmental disasters like fires may not happen every year, when they do, such as in 2015, the newspaper devoted coverage to them (Rogers, K., 2015, October 21). Although crime is a consistently covered topic in Nye County, each year the *Las Vegas Review-Journal* introduced new topics. The inconsistency in what constituted newsworthy events indicates temporal flexibility by the year they happened. While Yucca

Table 6.2.   Topic Coverage about Wyoming County 2013–2015

	2015	2014	2013
First Topic	Police & Courts/Crime (48%)	Police & Courts/Crime (39%)	Police & Courts/Crime (41%)
Second Topic	Auto Racing (10%)	Auto Racing (12%)	Auto Racing (14%)
Third Topic	Financial (13%)	Weather (9%)	Financial (9%)
Total Number of Articles	314	304	279

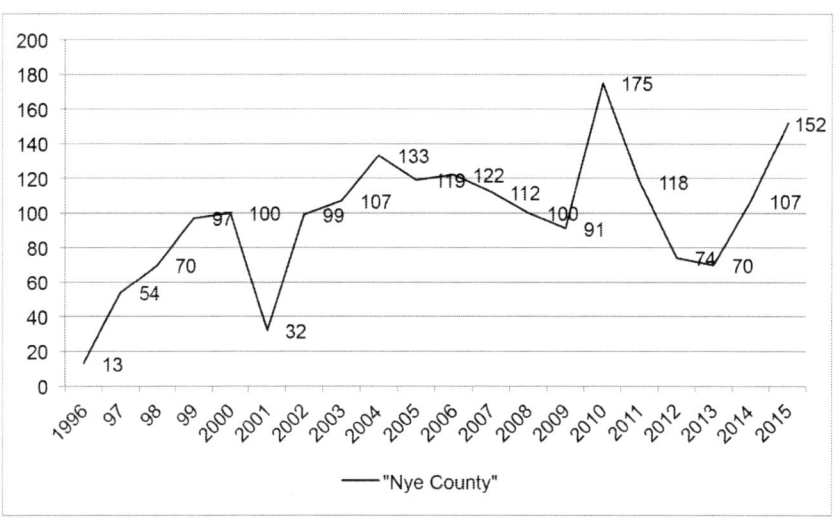

Figure 6.2.

Mountain and various criminal acts continue to be perennial issues, events like Lamar Odom's incident are not expected to happen continually each year.

Elbert County, Colorado

Elbert County, Colorado, is the smallest rural county by population covered in this study. The county has a population of 23,086 and is located in the Denver media market. The NewBank Access World News (2016) database revealed that between 1989 and 2015, the most the *Denver Post* published about the county was sixty-one stories in 2004 and the least was seven in 1993 as shown in figure 6.3. The average number of stories over the archived years (1989 to 2015) was 31.4.

Denver is located in Denver County, with a population of 600,158 according to the 2010 U.S. Census. The *Denver Post* is the urban-based newspaper for the media market, and it has a circulation of 515,483 during the weekend and 331,223 during the week as of March 2015 (Alliance for Audited Media, 2016). This newspaper had the largest circulation of the three analyzed in this study.

The *Denver Post* covered a variety of stories about Elbert County as shown in table 6.4. In fact, the only topics that were repeated in any of the years were crime, that at times included animal cruelty as in 2014 (Hobbs, 2014, September 27) and issues around elections (Bartels, 2014, November

Table 6.3.   Topic Coverage about Nye County 2013–2015

	2015	2014	2013
First Topic	Crime (36%)	Crime and Court Cases (28%)	Crime (27%)
Second Topic	Land Use (including Yucca Mountain and BLM issues) (11%) and Accidents (11%) * Tie	Land Use (including Yucca Mountain and mining) (15%)	Yucca Mountain/Nuclear Waste 19%
Third Topic	Environment/Fires Weather (7%)	Accidents (11%)	Natural Resources/ Natural History (7%)
Total Number of Articles	152	107	70

2). Like Nye County, land use issues and nature resources were issues that urban-based newspapers covered (Jaffe, 2013, June 16). Much like the other case study counties, inclement weather was considered newsworthy in Elbert County (Hernandez and Nicholson, 2015, August 17).

What is notable is that although the *Denver Post* has the largest circulation of all three newspapers, it also covered Elbert County with dramatically low frequency. Unlike Wyoming County and Nye County, Elbert does not share a border with its urban core county. It also has the least number of residents of any rural county in this analysis. Interestingly, stories that did not involve people—weather, nature, natural disaster, and land use—all dominated the topics covered in Elbert County by the *Denver Post*, with the exception of the memorials in 2014 (Section Z, 2014, January 8).

DISCUSSION

The case studies of each of these rural areas reveal which topics urban-based newspapers consider newsworthy. This helps to measure first-level agenda setting, the idea that the media can influence the saliency of *what* the public thinks about by selectively covering particular topics (McCombs, 2005; Weaver, 2007). Each urban-based newspaper covered the rural area under investigation at differing rates and each covered differing topics. The findings here can contribute to ways to begin to measure the urbanormative bias of urban-based newspapers.

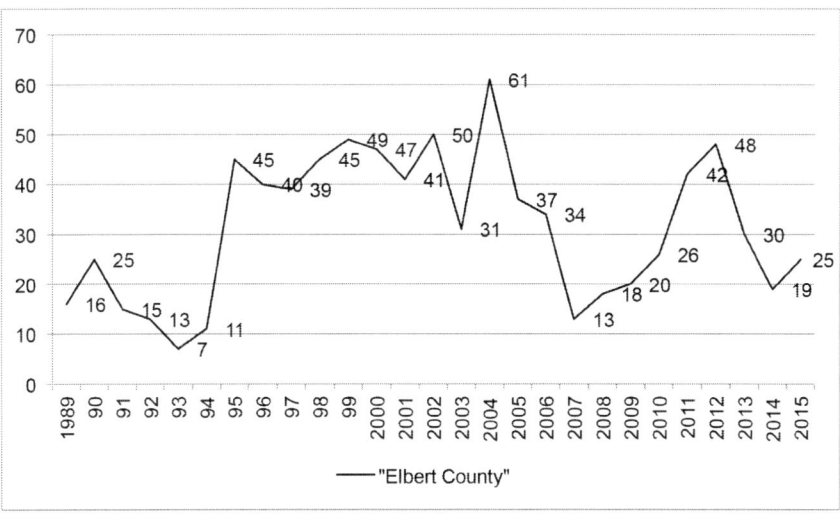

Figure 6.3.

Despite commonalities over several papers, this content analysis did not create a predictive formula of what type of topic would be seen as objectively "newsworthy" for urban-based newspapers to cover rural areas. Crime appeared most frequently over all three areas. The implications of crime reporting on a certain place could influence the public's perception on the safety of the area. Also a potential red flag to safety is the frequency of natural disasters in an area. As observed, natural disasters over this period were reported on in all three case study regions. Whether it was snow in Wyoming County or fires in Nye County and Elbert, these events were covered. Not all stories had serious implications as in the case of crime or natural disasters although these uplifting stories were sometimes not as frequently reported on as were the latter topics. However, that wasn't always the case: for Wyoming County, New York, the *Buffalo News* covered auto-racing news with high frequency.

While this study only focused on topics covered, there are implications to what future historical researchers will see about rural areas in the archives. Mainly severe events like disasters or stories focused on social problems like crime may dominate the historical record. If the urban-based newspaper in a rural area's media market does not cover a particular event that occurs there, how will the event be found and studied in the absence of a vibrant local press?

Another insight in this case study lies in starting to understand the amount of control that rural areas are demonstrating in constructing their public

Table 6.4.   Topic Coverage about Elbert County 2013–2015

	2015	2014	2013
First Topic	Weather (40%)	Crime (26%)*	Election/Governance/ Dysfunction (30%)
Second Topic	Crime (28%)	Personal Memorial (21%)	Natural Disaster: Fire (23%)
Third Topic	Nature, Accident, Fire (16%)	Election (11%)	Mining/Extraction/Wells (10%)
Total Number of Articles	25	19 *Includes animal cruelty stories	30

story. The data exist on what topics urban-based newspapers are covering and the frequency of these stories. What is not included or addressed is whether rural residents find this regional news to be important or newsworthy to themselves or their community. The regional focus may find land-use issues particularly interesting, but does that mean the rural point of view will be the prevailing one or will it be at odds with the urban one? This study provides insight on what topics are covered, but as seen in previous studies the content and frequency of this coverage varies (Corbett, 1992; Menifield et al., 2010; Reisner, 2005).

Urbanormativity (Fulkerson and Thomas, 2014) creates challenges in many areas of a civil society. Covering the impact of urban-based newspapers on the recording of the rural stories in the historical record is one way of understanding the importance of urbanormativity in the media. The news media plays a very important role in creating a vibrant democracy and a "viable political community" (Nicodemus, 2004). Measuring the kinds of topics that are being discussed is one important step towards understanding if there is an urbanormative bias in the news media. If rural areas are covered with low frequency by urban-based regional newspapers, how do members of society know that these rural areas still exist during times of low criminality and disasters? This representation of rural areas may create the impression that there is a constant state of emergency. By regaining control over their public story and image, rural places may be able to steer the tide against this trend. The issue is largely tied to whether or not news resources will continue to exist to tell the stories of rural areas? The ability for rural residents to control their public story will continue to be important as news organizations transition from print to online, and from television to mobile. In this way, rural news topics may be able to reach more people than ever before—but will important topics to rural residents even be covered by news organizations in the future as in the past?

REFERENCES

Alliance for Audited Media. (2016). Media Intelligence Center [media database]. Arlington Heights, IL: AAM. http://abcas3.auditedmedia.com/MICenter/.

Bartels, L. (2014). Colorado candidates chase ballots as Tuesday's election approaches. *The Denver Post*, November 2, Retrieved 02/14/2016 from http://infoweb.newsbank.com/resources/doc/nb/news/151697C0D8867910?p=AWNB.

Corbett, J. B. (1992) Rural and urban newspaper coverage of wildlife: Conflict, community, and bureaucracy. *Journalism Quarterly, 69*(4), 929-937.

FCC (Federal Communications Commission). (2009). Buffalo, NY, Retrieved 02/14/2016 from: https://transition.fcc.gov/dtv/markets/maps_current/ Buffalo_NY.pdf.

_____. (2009). Denver, CO, Retrieved 02/14/2016 from: https://transition.fcc.gov/ dtv/markets/maps_current/Denver_CO.pdf.

_____. (2009). Las Vegas, NV, Retrieved 02/14/2016 from: https://transition.fcc.gov/ dtv/markets/maps_current/Las_Vegas_NV.pdf.

Feldstein, M. (2004). Kissing cousins: Journalism and oral history. *The Oral History Review 31*(1), 1-22.

Financial Section. (2015). On the Record/September 8, 2015. *The Buffalo News*, Retrieved 02/14/2016 from http://infoweb.newsbank.com/resources/doc/nb/news/157BAEA7A2898D80?p=AWNB.

Fulkerson, G. M., and Thomas, A. R. (Eds.). (2014). *Studies in urbanormativity: Rural community in urban society.* Lanham, MD: Lexington Books.

Gryta, M. (2013). Cattaraugus County Court—5 years' probation, restitution ordered for larceny and forgery in Olean. *The Buffalo News*, October 30, Retrieved 02/14/2016 from http://infoweb.newsbank.com/resources/doc/ nb/news/149C39C60B1AF4E0?p=AWNB.

Hernandez, E., and Nicholson, K. (2015). Winds damage barns, silos, other structures east of Denver; no injuries. *The Denver Post*, August 17, Retrieved 02/14/2016 from http://infoweb.newsbank.com/resources/doc/nb/news/157563CC24E217C8?p=AWNB.

Hobbs, S. (2014). 10 seized horses slowly improving: the animals were moved from a Black Forest property and are getting basic care. *The Denver Post*, September 27, Retrieved 02/14/2016 from http://infoweb.newsbank.com/ resources/doc/nb/news/150A997974FC06A0?p=AWNB.

Jaffe. M. (2013). Wells spark local outcry: Oil and gas drilling—local jurisdiction push up against state regulation of industry. *The Denver Post*, June 16, Retrieved 02/14/2016 from http://infoweb.newsbank.com/resources/ doc/nb/news/146FD79E88EE58B0?p=AWNB.

Katz, B. and Lang, R. E. (Eds.). 2003. *Redefining urban and suburban America: Evidence from Census 2000, Volume I.* Washington, DC: Brookings Institution Press.

Laux, K. (2015). Lamar Odom found unconscious in Nye County brothel. *Las Vegas Review-Journal*, October 13, Retrieved 02/14/2016 from http://infoweb.newsbank.com/resources/doc/nb/news/159099D0C9CADDD0?p=AWNB.

Local News Section (2013). 'Suboptimal outcome' carries uncertain impact on WNY. *The Buffalo News*, December 12. Retrieved 02/14/2016 from http://infoweb.newsbank.com/resources/doc/nb/news/14AA68D9E9488EC8?p=AWNB.

Local News Section. (2013). Police courts. *The Buffalo News,* November 21. Retrieved 02/14/2016 from http://infoweb.newsbank.com/resources/doc/nb/news/14A37EAE1492A5B8?p=AWNB.

Mazumdar, A. (2011). Nielsen's designated market area maps protectable as creative, original, elements. *Bloomberg BNA*, September 13. Retrieved 02/14/2016 from http://www.bna.com/nielsens-designated-market-n12884903463.

McCombs, M. (2005). A look at agenda-setting: past, present and future. *Journalism Studies, 6*(4), p. 543-557.

Menifield, C. E., Rose, W. H., Homa, J., and Cunningham, A. B. (2010). The media's portrayal of urban and rural school violence: a preliminary analysis. *Deviant Behavior, 22*(5), p. 447-464.

NewsBank. (2016). Access World News [media database]. Naples, FL: NewsBank. http://infoweb.newsbank.com/.

Nicodemus, D.M. (2004). Mobilizing information: Local news and the formation of a viable political community. *Political Communication 21*(2), p. 161-176.

Nielsen (2013). DMA® Regions. Retrieved 02/14/2016 from http://www.nielsen.com/intl-campaigns/us/dma-maps.html.

Ott, L. (2014). WNY Auto Racing By Larry Ott—Layfield, Packman to Hall honorees. *The Buffalo News*, December 8. Retrieved 02/14/2016 from http://infoweb.newsbank.com/resources/doc/nb/news/152164DAB5B5B9B0?p=AWNB.

Reisner, A. E. (2005) Newspaper coverage of controversies about large-scale swine facilities in rural communities in Illinois. *Journal of Animal Science, 83*(11), p. 2705-2712.

Rogers, K. (2015). Nye County officials sorry for fire information lag time. *Las Vegas Review-Journal*, October 21. Retrieved 02/14/2016 from http://infoweb.newsbank.com/resources/doc/nb/news/159099E447E911F8?p=AWNB

Section Z. (2014). Obituaries and Memorials. *The Denver Post*, January 8. Retrieved 02/14/2016 from http://infoweb.newsbank.com/resources/doc/nb/news/14FF8A6C331F2498?p=AWNB.

Sokolova, D. (2015). Nye County residents split over Yucca's potential impacts. *Las Vegas Review-Journal*, September 18. Retrieved 02/14/2016 from http://infoweb.newsbank.com/resources/doc/nb/news/1590EEEB45A8E9E0?p=AWNB.

Taloma, C. (2014). NHP: Woman killed in Nye County crash with semi. *Las Vegas Review-Journal*, November 20. Retrieved 02/14/2016 from http://infoweb.newsbank.com/resources/doc/nb/news/151B47970C3434E0?p=AWNB.

Tetreault, S., and Brean, H. (2015). A done deal, Obama to create Basin and Range monument. *Las Vegas Review-Journal*, July 10. Retrieved 02/14/2016 from http://infoweb.newsbank.com/resources/doc/nb/news/1567D201CB19A8D8?p=AWNB.

United States Census Bureau. (2010). *Profile of General Population and Housing Characteristics: 2010. 2010 Census Summary File 1.* Retrieved 02/14/2016 from http://factfinder.census.gov/faces/tableservices/jsf/pages/productview.xhtml?pid=DEC_10_SF1_SF1DP1prodType=table.

Weaver, D. H. (2007). Thoughts on agenda setting, framing, and priming. *Journal of Communication, 57*, p. 142-147.

Zremski, J. (2014). Upstate's storm damage estimate tops $49 million—Governor earlier asked Obama to declare disaster in nine upstate counties. *The Buffalo News*, December 12. Retrieved 02/14/2016 from: http://infoweb.newsbank.com/ resources/doc/nb/news/1522B6D1ECFC5F68?p=AWNB.

Chapter Seven

The Cow College and Critical Rural Knowledge

Barbara Ching

In this essay, I analyze narratives and discourse surrounding land grant institutions in order to explore their role in both shaping and disrupting a social hierarchy based on rusticity and topped by urbanity. These institutions become visible in mainstream discourse mostly through sports rivalries. The framing of these rivalries often takes place through jokes which simultaneously ignore and undermine the land grant ideal of teaching practical knowledge *alongside* the traditional liberal arts to students who would otherwise lack access to higher education.[1] The punchlines (re)introduce social stratification by placing the land grant graduate in a subservient, simple-minded position. "What does the Clemson graduate call the University of South Carolina graduate? Boss." "What does the Iowa State grad say to the Iowa grad? Do you want fries with that?" Other jokes, usually less fit to print, center on the bestiality of land grant students, indistinguishable from the livestock they supposedly tend: "Why did MSU change their field from grass to artificial turf? To keep their cheerleaders from grazing." What is the difference between a heifer and an Auburn cheerleader? About twenty pounds." The short story told in these jokes casts students at "Cow Colleges" as rustic others perceived to be receiving no education at all in the *higher* sense even as their practical training may render them more useful to their betters.[2]

WHAT DOES A COW SAY?

Land grant students' and graduates' accounts of their own experiences would supply an important perspective on this dynamic, but significantly, no interest calls it forth. Memoirs about the college experience focus almost exclu-

111

sively on elite institutions; a WORLDCAT search on the subject of "College Students—United States—Biography" brings up titles such as or Walter Kirn's (2009) *Lost in the Meritocracy* (Princeton), Nathan Harden's (2012) *Sex and God at Yale: Porn, Political Correctness, and a Good Education Gone Bad*, and Regina Barreca's (2005) *Babes in Boyland: A Personal History of Co-Education in the Ivy League*. Academic novels, usually set on recognizable or archetypal college campuses reinforce this selective attention. In his comprehensive study of recent American academic novels published in the definitively titled *American Literary History*, Williams (2012) notes the plethora of major novelists who have published in this genre in order to conclude that:

> [T]he academic novel has grafted with the mid-life crisis novel, the marriage novel, and the professional-work novel to become a prime theater of middle-class experience. Rather than a coterie audience, this new wave aims at the grail of a general, educated audience, most of whom have some college, and many of whom have professional-managerial jobs, worry about colleagues, and juggle job with family and life. It is also directed toward an adult audience, as opposed to the 12–25 demographic of campus films.

The mainstreamed academic novel, in other words, has an audience of the urban ruling class—not the 1 percent, perhaps, but certainly the 5 or 10 percent. Its generic name also smothers any other college experiences; in other words, it's not academic if it's not written for affluent city dwellers—in spite of Williams's use of the term "middle class."[3] (Consequently, movies with academic settings also avoid the land grant.)

Thus, I focus on Jane Smiley's (1995) novel *Moo* to explore both an exception that proves the rule as well as how sense is made of the land grant experience and its role in shaping educational and social hierarchy. The novel's title subtly underscores its connection to the land grant system while the place names make the connection explicit. The streets and buildings around the university, such as Ames Road or Red Stick [English for Baton Rouge] Avenue, Stillwater Hall, home of the English department, all point toward real land grant universities. "Old Meats" plays a significant role in *Moo* and is a disused building on the Iowa State campus. The conflicts in *Moo* make no reference to sports rivalries. They lodge in the rifts between the public interest in an educated citizenry, the liberal arts component of the university, and the private interests at work in the corporatization of the university's real estate and research agenda, especially in the agriculture school. Three symbolic sites encapsulate these competing forces in the university: a pig named Earl Butz hidden in Old Meats, an unused abattoir, being secretly fed as much as he will eat at the behest of a Bo Jones, a grant-happy professor wanting to learn just how much consumption and pork production is porcinely possible, Chairman X's Edenic campus garden, surrounding Old Meats, bringing lovingly selected and theoretically forbidden fruits to the harsh climate of the Midwestern setting, and finally the supposedly secret plans created by economist Lionel Gift, one of Moo's most distinguished professors, to dig a gold mine under a Costa Rican Cloud Forest (named Tierra del Madre) and cover it with a cattle ranch. This "consulting work" has been paid for by the expansive Trans America Corporation, a band of villains poised to assume world domination on a scale that exceeds the petty powers that Alabama and Michigan grads assume. Gift, whose name in German means "poison," sees himself as "the personal savior-consultant" to the students who throng to his classroom to learn the secrets of wealth and power and whom he thinks of as "customers" (Smiley, 1995, p. 145). He teaches them that to do well in economics, they must "maximize one's own profits at the expense of the group" (Smiley, 1995, p. 142). Keri, a farm girl and former Pork Queen of Warren County, feels that Gift is selling them a fantasy, a "Bizarro Planet" completely at odds with her family's dispiriting experience with "practical economics" during the 1980s farm crisis (Smiley, 1995, p. 144).

This fiction is stranger than truth because Smiley's imaginative visions build on elements of memoir, a necessary blend since there is little other cultural knowledge to reframe the hierarchical structure that urbanizes Tuscaloosa over Auburn or Ann Arbor over Lansing. Smiley experienced both sides of the joke/story in her academic career. She earned her Ph.D. in English at the University of Iowa as well as an MFA at the university's renowned Writers Workshop. In 1981, when she accepted a job in the English department at Iowa State, Jack Leggett, then director of the Iowa workshop, reports that "people kind of looked down on Iowa State as the cow college. We thought it pretty amusing that she'd be teaching creative writing to all these experts in piggery and grain."[4] Nevertheless, Smiley earned tenure, a Pulitzer Prize, and served a two-year term on the faculty senate during her fifteen years at Iowa State, leaving one year after the publication of *Moo*.[5] Throughout her career, she has maintained an openly professed political radicalism including an early stint in a Maoist commune that reappears in the youthful years of Chairman X and his consort Lady X. Capitalist excess is a theme of several of her novels including *A Thousand Acres* (1991) about the 1980s farm crisis, and *Good Faith* (2003) about real estate bubbles.

The novel keeps the "land" in land grant by taking literally the Latin term "campus" and plotting one of the novel's central conflicts around the feud between Chairman X, leader of the horticulture department, and Nils Harstad, dean of the College of Agriculture. A feisty and philandering Maoist, Chairman X leads his student gardeners in the tending of an amazing garden along the southern exposure of "Old Meats." (Its former resident, the Ag. College, has moved on to far better facilities.) Delicious peaches and apricots grow there in spite of the frigid winters of the upper Midwest. This tending of gardens echoes the book of Genesis and Voltaire's *Candide* where the gardens represent, respectively, a life of blissful ignorance and the culmination of the pursuit of knowledge and happiness. If the campus is a field, horticulture is where you learn to tend it. If the campus is an alma mater, the mother of one's soul, horticulture is where you learn to tend it, too, a sort of Tierra del Madre in a benignly formative sense. The gestational nine month rhythm of the residential campus already evokes a precapitalist dream, where time isn't money, it's just learning; when that campus has horticulture's garden, it also has a place where money deliberately doesn't grow on trees because a self-reproducing, non-patented wealth of fruits and nuts, a pre-capitalistic cornucopia, does.

In contrast, agriculture, done the Moo U way, corrupts and marauds. Opening in fall semester 1989, the crumbling of the Berlin Wall and the unraveling of the Iron Curtain unleashes global capitalism even at Moo U. The novel portrays most faculty members and administrators as foolish, failed neo-liberal graspers writing grant proposals to develop corn by-products and meat production techniques that will be transferred back to the corporations who funded the research. These events plunge X into a deep depression. He stops being the young man he thought he was—"hopeful and well meaning, always expecting people to come to their senses and devote their means and their lives selflessly to the common good" (Smiley, 1995, p. 365). Now, he says "communism is collapsing all over Europe and . . . *I can't figure out an alternative* and my whole life is a failure" (Smiley, 1995, p. 150). Naturally, rebirth comes in the spring semester. Then, word of Lionel Gift's plan to commercialize Tierra del Madre leaks out and reinvigorates X. While the protest he organizes does not go as planned, the outcome still brings a turn for the better, an eruption of critical rural knowledge (Thomas et al., 2011). Old Meats get destroyed in the aftermath. As the building collapse ruins the garden, Earl Butz escapes, revealing the true nature of pig: an animal who longs to enjoy life outside of confinement, in the fresh air. This Earl Butz managed to get big *and* get out. The run to freedom, though, kills him, since his legs and lungs have never been exercised.

Crucially, a farmer-inventor, Loren Stroop, funds whatever hope the future holds by creating a self-propelling piece of farm equipment that replaces nearly every other machine on a farm. While not a graduate of Moo U, Stroop guilelessly believes that the university's agricultural extension office exists to serve the state's small farmers. (On his frequent visits to campus, he helps himself to the horticulture department's peaches and apricots and saves the pits to seed his own orchard.) He naively assumes that the venal dean of agriculture, Nils Harstad, is equally committed to the land grant ideal and will help market his invention, "the fruit of his brain" (Smiley 1995, p. 290). Cobbled from odd parts and hidden in Stroop's barn, this contraption will make the family farm competitive with corporate holdings at the same time that it minimizes the environmental impact of farming. It creates fertilizer as it harvests and ploughs. Because of this multitasking efficiency, Stroop is convinced that government agents and/or the big agricultural corporations want to kill him. Yet, as he tells Dean Harstad, "this has got to get out . . . and a secret is not good to anybody, especially if it's this kind of secret" (Smiley, 1995, p. 89). Stroop suffers a debilitating stroke just after taking the plans to be photocopied and the resulting brain damage makes him incapable of any sounds but what a cow says, or of saying anything but the title of the novel. The chapter when his plans resurface and save the university from massive budget cuts implicitly deifies this cow/human in its title: "Deus ex machina." Perhaps it's also safe to say that in the beginning was Stroop's word—and in the end.

While Stroop may be the presiding deity of the piece, Earl Butz also acts as a savior. His namesake, dean of agriculture at Purdue then Richard Nixon's secretary of agriculture (1971–1976), told American farmers to "get big or get out." Stroop's invention undoes that threat of failure, and Butz the pig manages to do both. Underscoring the pig's powerful role, the chapter depicting Earl's Christmas is named "Away in the Manger." While the Christmas carol elevates the humble birth of Christ, the chapter title points to Earl's location: he's away in a manger, too, even if we'd be more likely to say hidden with the trough or concealed in a CAFO (concentrated animal feeding operation—although the "C" could just as logically, albeit less euphemistically, stand for "confined" or "concealed"). On Christmas, memories of his early days on the farm where he was born return to him: "All the piglets gambolled and frolicked in the yard, and the farmer sat nearby . . . remarking to his wife that the grandkids should see this. . . .The farm dogs wandered over and barked in their official capacity, the farm cats looked on from a distance, and the days, five or six of them, passed in a rare dream of mammalian amity" (Smiley, 1995, p. 270). Keri, the former pork queen, has similar memories of life on her family's farm before the 1980s collapse (Smiley, 1995, p. 144).

The secrets of American agricultural industry have withered thanks to literary exposes such as Michael Pollan's *The Omnivore's Dilemma* (2006) and Jonathan Safran Foer's *Eating Animals* (2009). Films like *Food Inc.* (2009) and *Fed Up* (2014) expose these secrets to even larger audiences. Foer, in his account of sneaking into Iowa CAFOs most obviously casts himself as an enlightener in the dark realms of agriculture. But when Smiley wrote *Moo* in the early 1990s, concentrated animal feeding operations were enjoying the invisibility that they were designed for and the term "corn-fed" exuded a specifically American wholesomeness. Still, the novel offers something that these non-fiction narratives do not: a vision of agency for the students at the land grant and for the farmers who rely on the knowledge produced there. For example, Earl Butz's captivity and death hints at the end of farm animal confinements, an end brought about by student actions. Near-ly everyone on campus witnesses the pig's escape and collapse; indeed the memory of it troubles them for weeks afterward and eventually changes them. Two students take immediate action: Keri and Bob, Earl's devoted caretakers, rush to comfort the dying hog. Their humaneness brings them together and distinguishes them from the onlookers. In the happily-ever-after coupling that closes the novel, to be discussed further below, they represent a perspective on rural life and livelihood that allows for change, preservation, and visibility along the lines of that recently postulated by philosopher and urban theorist Peter Sloterdijk. He envisions "an internationalized animal rights movement [in the coming century], almost already fully developed, that will emphasize the unbreakable connection between human rights and animal suffering. This movement could transpire as the vanguard of a development that assigns a new meaning to non-urban ways of life" (Sloterdijk, 2013, p. 230).

CRITICAL RURAL KNOWLEDGE AND CAMPUS WRITERS AND DESIGNERS

Smiley imagines such an assignment of "new meaning" through ancient traditions of sense making. She writes with strong consciousness of genre and an ambition to write novels in every fictional genre. Thus, she deliberate-ly cast her novel, *The Greenlanders* (Smiley, 2005), as an Icelandic epic, and she followed her Midwestern tragedy, *A Thousand Acres* (Smiley, 2003), with a comedy/academic novel, *Moo.* For the characters who won't live in Gift's poisoned "Bizarro World," Smiley's story shows the creation and acquisition of "critical rural knowledge"[6]—ways to intervene and expose the social structures that exploit them and the planet. Their knowledge comes with the disruptive power to choose, demonstrated, as comedies do, by the choice of a partner and a wedding party in the end. These choices, though, shape a community. The "I dos" entail "I don'ts." Provost Harstad marries his longtime lover, Helen Levy, a professor of French. X and Lady X, to the delight of their four children, and to the surprise of everyone else, who had always assumed the two *were* married, finally forsake all others. Helen's explanation of this delay links the political and personal: "Because . . . not only do you have to act once in a while, it's also so exhilarating to choose" (Smiley, 1995, p. 411). The reject[ion]s, in the theory of comedy, are "scape-goats"—the evil forces uninvited to the party and exiled from the renewed community—Bo Jones, the CAFO experimenter, disappears into the tumult of barely post-communist eastern Russia where he seeks to learn more about pigs. Lionel Gift, the theorist of globalization, deliberately chooses not to act on his desire for a female colleague in order to remain a "homo economicus" who refuses to "indulg[e] in an unproven, never to be proven, faith in the common good" (Smiley, 1995, p. 403). Their self-interested, uncritical knowledge of "piggery," literal and figurative, leads to their expulsion from Moo: the chapter that tells of Gift's decision is titled "Off-off-off Campus." Butted out, the jokes are on them and the happy endings belong to those left behind.

Writing itself creates critical knowledge, rural or urban, and in *Moo* we see an aspiring writer and his teacher both struggle to know their places. Tim Monahan, striving for tenure even as he longs to be elsewhere, especially in New York City, with the (male) movers and shakers of literary prestige, muddles around in the literary novel firmament until his happy ending when he embraces the stories that surround him at Moo U. His student, Gary, writes misogynistic fantasies of affluence and destruction, projecting his surroundings into the future and onto the other. His drafts all feature a fatly disguised student who has rejected him in favor of Bob Carlson, a farm boy and student hired to surreptitiously feed Earl. In these unpolished glosses on *Moo*, Gary's heroine appears either as a rapacious Wall Street executive or a gluttonous housewife too fat to care for her children. While we never see Gary succeed as a writer, he doesn't abandon hope, noting that Monaghan's agricultural dictum "Cultivate your memory" is the best lesson he learned. That field, in other words, may yet yield a harvest. Gary has time to build skills and make sense from his lust and greed, time to transform it into a story about the urban hegemony that now leads him to see everything in terms of getting and expanding.

Smiley creates more effective plot shapers in the administration (of all places!). Mrs. Lorraine Walker, the provost's secretary, constantly critiques, transforms, and plots to bring about happy endings. A Native American and lesbian, she makes crucial choices according to her principles. She makes sure the library has money for books (and for her own research) by surreptitiously transferring funds from the athletic department as needed. Thanks to her research, she consciously knows things that the upper administration does not want to know—about the interlocking directorates and collusion amongst the university's corporate donors. With this knowledge, she warns her cousin on the Menominee reservation when the university, at the behest of corporate donors, develops mining plans that threaten to disrupt water quality on the reservation. She copies Lionel Gift's plans for the Tierra del Madre mine and leaks them where she knows they will do damage. She signs the permit for X's protest. And in the end, she surprises herself with her sympathy for even the most repellent of Moo U's herd; she learns to nuance her view of these characters, concluding "that sometimes it was necessary to suspend two or more contradictory thoughts in your mind at the same time (Smiley, 1995, p. 367). She chooses to do this when she leaves her office to witness the demolition of Old Meats and the garden. More momentously, she does this when she makes the choice that saves the university from drastic budget cuts: she decides to share the building specifications of Loren Stroop's machine with the provost rather than hide them, knowing that her superiors don't deserve this windfall but others may use it for good. In fact, her boss, Provost Ivar Harstad, Nils's less evil twin, embraces a similar novelistic philosophy at the novel's end. Although he trained as a physicist, the laws of the universe don't interest him nearly so much as managing the plots and characters in a university: as he tells his wife-to-be, "my only real interest was how Oppenheimer got all those warring personalities to live together in the desert. Didn't know a single other physicist who wasn't bored by just the idea of personality. I think that I've loved being an administrator after all" (Smiley, 1995, p. 336). His vision of the university at its best puts students and their teachers in a similar position of authorship: "The university could teach a kid, male or female, to do anything from reading a poem to turning protein molecules into digital memory, from brewing beer to reinterpreting his or her entire past" (Smiley, 1995, p. 386). By eliding the hierarchical gulf between practical knowledge and the liberal arts and instead seeing the two forms of knowledge as a sort of marriage the provost articulates why, and how, the land grant creates critical knowledge—and why and how he works to hold it all together. In the Provost's best vision, Moo U's students don't always have to take, or be, the jokes that others tell—thanks to their time at Moo. But in the novel, there are characters forced to ask "do you want fries with that?", characters who can only respond to others' choices: the cafeteria workers who don't have higher education. For them, "the choice was pretty stark: after McDonald's put a franchise in the commons, everybody who worked there could either quit or go to work for McDonald's" (Smiley, 1995, p. 360).

Like Provost Harstad, Chairman X gets a moment of reinterpretation and rehabilitation. His eden of horticulture didn't die nor, after all, did his hopes for the future. X and his students simply replant the garden; the seeds were theirs to begin with, reproducible cultivars rather than patented hybrids, and they have no need for a New Meats to replace Old Meats. Their moral victory flourishes as a campus landmark. Likewise, on real world land grant campuses, these spaces for practical experience and critical contemplation persist. Mary Burgan (2006) goes so far as to argue that the intent of the Morrill Act includes a (traditional) residential campus that represent[s] our "sanction of a substantial learning interlude for young adults" (p. 79).[7] Campus design, a form of place making akin to the sense making of novels, publicly proclaims it. Cornell University's language about its intentional design strikes an especially formal note as it emphasizes the feats of engineering and imagination that created the campus: "this landscape is designed. It has been crafted carefully and lovingly— indeed artistically—to produce the picturesque quadrangles that define the individual precincts of the arts, agriculture, and engineering colleges. It is tethered audaciously to its surrounding environs with bridges that span two gorges and provide a platform and frame for viewing 400 million years of earthwork below. It has been leveled into terraces and graded into slopes that yield the grand vistas and secluded nooks that generations of Cornellians discover anew each fall semester. . . . Cornell is an ensemble of artfully sculpted open space . . . measured promenades and meandering pathways, mighty oaks sited decades ago with great care to appear as if they were always thus. All this makes Cornell . . . a most fitting canvas for a community of wildly creative students and scholars."[8] The University of Illinois consciously builds its campus around a cornfield, the Morrow Plots. The department of Crop Sciences explains their centrality: They are "the oldest agronomic experiment fields in the United States. . . . In 1968, the Morrow Plots became a National Historic Landmark. . . . They are a living reminder of the purpose for which this university and the land-grant system were established."[9] While the signs that mark the plots announce that the "use of science and technology has increased crop productivity over four-fold," longitudinal findings of the experiment show that soil quality practices (such as crop rotation) rather than chemical fertilizers best sustain productivity—and another sign suspends this (somewhat) contradictory conclusion. Public art, a feature of many campuses, also invites and incites a critical perspective on the campus mission. Iowa State University's WPA mural "Breaking the Prairie Sod" (1934), designed by Grant Wood, illuminates the main library, forcing students and other spectators to evaluate the urbanormative perspective. The painted prairie, an expanse of American earth being tilled for the first time, looks like a carpet, a comfort of refined home, even a luxury. A farmer cuts it away to reveal the soil, a sustaining richness more valuable than a warm and pretty floor. Still, the aesthetic impulse that the carpet expresses can also emerge from the soil: underlining the full scene, you see an array of beautiful flowers, arranged for beauty rather than botany. In its ordered complexity, this mural pulls the rug out from under the urbanormative gaze.

The rug can always be rolled back, and thus the land grant experience feels imperiled by the ever lurking vagaries of capitalism. In 1989, the year of Moo U's travails and triumph, Iowa State University's students gave their yearbook (*The Bomb*) the theme of metamorphosis, not only because the sudden end of communism promised dramatic change for Eastern Europe but also because cuts in state support for the university threatened to narrow the land grant's scope. The editors worried about (then) University president Gordon Eaton's claim that the liberal arts were an "erosion" of the university's mission. The 2008 financial meltdown brought similar attempts to create "efficiency" and avoid "duplication" with offerings at other state supported institutions such as the University of Iowa. Decreased state support nationwide also creates concerns about continuing accessibility and future-eating levels of student debt.

NEXT STEPS

Student concerns about the fate of the land grant mission and interest in maintaining both the practical and traditional components of higher education indicate that their stories can broaden our view of American higher education and its social purposes. While the campuses materially create opportunities for critical knowledge, and Smiley's *Moo* patterns a complex performance of such opportunities, the effects and efficacies of land grant education need qualitative research to fully document its impact and ultimately magnify its visibility. CAFOs and proprietary hybrid seeds, outgrowths of agricultural research, are known quantities and to the extent that they *are* visible, contribute to the ideological devaluation of rural lives in spite of urban dependency on the food supply and relatively low prices enabled by these innovations. Earl Butz's demise, a sort of eruption of visibility, brings about actions and choices that have impact in the telling. The characters, teachers and students, reinterpret and reshape the rural not only for themselves, but also for the people who will eat the food and burn the fuel they produce. Those urban dependents care about the expense and value of college education; they care about what they eat. They need to know what's really at stake when the cow college is in the game. Not everyone who studies and teaches at a land grant can bring attention to what happens at these institutions, but some have precisely that knowledge, and the audience, when their own needs are at play, can develop a thirst for that knowledge.

NOTES

1. The Morrill Act of 1862 allowed states to sell parcels of land given to them by the federal government and use the proceeds for the "endowment, support, and maintenance of at least one college where the leading object shall be, without excluding other scientific and classical studies, and including military tactics, to teach such branches of learning as are related to agriculture and the mechanical arts, in such manner as the legislatures of the States may respectively prescribe, in order to promote the liberal and practical education of the industrial classes in the several pursuits and professions in life." Morrill later emphasized that students at land grants should be free to focus entirely on liberal arts if they preferred.

2. Summarizing a few academic studies about collegiate sports rivalries, Mathis-Lilley (2015) concludes that "ingroup/outgroup relationships were created between groups of students who had a lot in common except for the fact that some of them were liberal arts scholars and the others went to what was originally a farm school. . . . If you're watching a Rivalry Week football game, there's a good chance you are thinking—maybe consciously, maybe not—about your class status." I'd argue, however, that while social class may play a role, the rural associations are what matter here. It's not that land grant universities started as farm schools—they still *are* farm schools, and the rivalry jokes perpetuate the association between the rural and the

backward, the rural and the vanquished. "Why Florida Fans Think FSU Fans Are Dumb: How in-state college football rivalries became a form of class warfare."

3. See Williams (2012). Community college students, except perhaps in the long running sitcom *Community*, are similarly invisible. It's worth noting that City College of New York, also established to educate and advance less affluent students, does not suffer from obscurity.

4. See Wroe (2002).

5. See Nakadate (2010) on Smiley's careful avoidance of interview questions about Moo U's resemblance to Iowa State University.

6. See Thomas et al. (2011).

7. See Burgan (2006).

8. See Kleinman (2016).

9. See University of Illinois (2016).

REFERENCES

Barreca, R. (2005). *Babes in Boyland: A personal history of co-education in the Ivy League*. Hanover, NH: UPNE.

Burgan, M. (2006). Whatever happened to the faculty?: Drift and decision in higher education. Baltimore: Johns Hopkins University Press.

Foer, J. S. (2009). *Eating Animals*. New York: Back Bay Books.

Harden, R. (2012). *Sex and God at Yale: Porn, political correctness, and a good education gone bad.* New York: Thomas Dunne Books.

Kenner, R. (Producer, Director), and Pearlstein, E. (2008). *Food Inc.* [Motion Picture]. United States: Magnolia Pictures.

Kirn, W. (2009). *Lost in the meritocracy: The undereducation of an overachiever. New York:* Anchor Books.

Kleinman, K. (2016). *The arts at Cornell University.* Retrieved 2/14/2016 from http://dos.cornell.edu/voices/arts-cornell-university.

Marson, E. (Producer), Olson, S. (Producer), and Soechtig, S. (Producer, Director). (2008). *Fed Up* [Motion Picture]. United States: Atlas Films.

Mathis-Lilley, B. (2015). Why Florida fans think FSU fans are dumb: How in-state college football rivalries became a form of class warfare. *Slate.* Retrieved 11/27/2015 from http://www.slate.com/articles/sports/sports_nut/2015/11/why_florida_state_and_florida_fans_hate_each_other_so_much.html.

Nakadate, N. (2010). *Understanding Jane Smiley (Revised Edition)*. Columbia: University of South Carolina Press.

Pollan, M. (2006). *The omnivore's dilemma: A natural history of four meals.* Penguin Books.

Sloterdijk, P. (2013). *In the world interior of capital: For a philosophical theory of globalization.* Trans. Wieland Hoban. Cambridge, UK: Polity

Smiley, J. (1991). *A thousand acres: A novel.* New York: Anchor Books.

_____. (2003). *Good faith.* New York: Anchor Books.

_____. (1988). *The Greenlanders.* New York: Anchor Books.

_____. (1995). *Moo.* New York: Anchor Books.

Thomas, A. R., Lowe, B. M., Smith, P., and Fulkerson, G. M. (2011). *Critical Rural Theory: Structure* Space* Culture.* Lanham, MD: Lexington.

Transcript of Morrill Act. (1862). Chapter CXXX, Section 1-8. Retrieved 02/14/2016 from http://www.ourdocuments.gov/doc.php?flash=trueanddoc=33andpage=transcript.

University of Illinois. (2016). "The Morrow Plots: A Century of Learning." Department of Crop Sciences, University of Illinois. Retrieved 02/15/2016 from http://cropsci.illinois.edu/research/morrow.

Williams, J. J. (2012). The rise of the academic novel. *American Literary History 24*, 3, p. 561-589.

Wroe, N. (2002). Smiley's people. *The Guardian, 23* (Aug). Retrieved 02/09/2016 from http://www.theguardian.com/books/2003/aug/02/featuresreviews.guardianreview8.

Chapter Eight

Common Core, STEM, and Rural Schools

Views from Students and States

Leanne M. Avery and John W. Sipple

The National Center for Education Statistics (NCES) defines rural as residual space, "as those areas that do not lie inside an urbanized area or urban cluster" (Strange et al., 2012, p. 1). Based on this definition, we observe that growth in rural school enrollments outpaces that of urban areas (Johnson, Showalter, and Klein, 2014), while there are slightly more (3.2 million) students growing up in urban rather than in rural settings (Strange et al., 2012). Just under 33 percent of American public schools are rural, and 25 percent of students attend a rural school (Williams, 2010). Despite these facts and trends, attention to rural schools, educators, and communities is dwarfed by the—presumably deserved—attention bestowed upon more urban settings.

Rural schools consistently exhibit lower school funding levels than their urban and suburban counterparts (Sipple and Brent, 2015), though typically have smaller student to teacher ratios, even after the great recession of 2008 (Sipple and Yao, 2015). In addition, exposure and access to educational opportunities offered by science organizations, museums, colleges, and corporations are limited in rural areas. The number and types of STEM (Science, Technology, Engineering, and Mathematics)-related professional and vocational jobs are proportionally low in less populated and technologically disconnected areas. Thus, many rural children are not exposed to the diverse ways in which STEM is practiced in the world and they may not envision STEM-related educational or career pathways (Avery, 2013).

Historically, rural communities have been perceived as "ill equipped to run their own schools and prepare students to be economically competitive and productive in a modernizing world" (Schafft and Jackson, 2011, p. 1). Numerous national policies have presumed that rural poverty and educational inequity can be resolved by outsiders who believe all rural communities are fundamentally alike (Boyer, 2006; Schafft and Jackson, 2011) and will benefit from programs designed for urban areas. However, as rural sociologist Gene Theodori (2003) states, "When you've seen one rural community, *you've seen one rural community*. Every rural community has certain social, economic, and/or environmental issues that are unique to that particular community and contribute to its diversity" (p. 1, italics added).

According to Boyer (2006, p. 104), reform should not be built on mandates but rather, on "a philosophy of education that respects the integrity of rural communities" (see also, Casto et al. in press). In fact, rural schools are often epicenters of community activities and function to maintain that community's unique identity and culture. Unfortunately, rural schools also fall victim to national agenda pressures that may disconnect them from their communities:

> The face of rural communities [is being transformed] by a variety of broad sweeping actions that include: the economic effects of multinational free trade agreements [pervasive and invasive energy extraction movements], proliferation of mass media and information technology, and educational policies that privilege standardized curricula and "high-stakes" accountability for test scores over accountability to contexts of local people and places. (Schafft and Jackson, 2011, p. 2)

Many of these actions have extremely metrocentric underpinnings and agendas that encourage and support urbanormative perspectives and worldviews. Policies such as *No Child Left Behind* and the more recent *Every Student Succeeds Act*, have for the most part, targeted schools located in urban centers (e.g., the New York State "Big Five" districts that include Buffalo, New York City, Rochester, Syracuse, and Yonkers) deemed as the most in need of reform. Elements of these policies lack relevant application to school districts outside urban centers as the policy initiatives often require larger numbers of students, teachers, and schools to calculate gains or deficiencies, choice alternatives, greater numbers of available community groups, and close proximity of parents to schools. However, the pressures loom for standardized implementation across all district types. These urbanormative views have become so pervasive that several books have recently focused on illustrating the importance of rural place (e.g., Tieken, 2014; Williams and Grooms, 2015). Science education journals have elected to take on this issue of inequity and metrocentricity by calling for special issues on rural science education with the goal of changing the predominant urbanormative conversation (Long and Avery, forthcoming). In addition, some have gone as far as to redefine rural—disputing the metrocentric definition touted by organizations like NCES. Brown and Schafft (2011) conceptualize rural in less residual terms, as "places that are spatially delimited natural environments that include demographic and ecological, economic, institutional and sociocultural dimensions where people live, work, and visit" (Brown and Schafft, 2011).

Furthermore, other rural education researchers (Johnson et al., 2014) have fervently echoed:

> Rural education is frustrating to those who wish it would conform to the oversimplifications that have long held sway in the discourse of policymakers and the public in general. Those oversimplifications do not stand in the face of the mounting evidence that rural education is becoming a bigger and even more complex part of our national educational landscape. (p. 28).

It is not uncommon for rural schools to signal to children that important knowledge is non-local, found in standardized curricula and tests, and communicate that the only way to succeed is to leave (Carr and Kefelas, 2009; Casto et al., in press): "Implicitly, we can discern a tension between life in the community and an education enterprise that operates principally as a "link" to elsewhere, particularly when that link seems to function as a one-way street" (Corbett, 2007, p. 12). This outmigration coupled with declining in-migration (Brown and Schafft, 2011; Deitz, 2007) reduces cognitive diversity vital to rural communities (Carr and Kefelas, 2009; Kassam, Avery, and Ruelle, forthcoming).

BIG PICTURE PERSPECTIVE:
A VIEW LOOKING DOWN

It is in this context that we make our argument and illustrations about the tensions between the top-down press for standardization and the value of local agency and locally derived variation. Let's start by stepping back to view why public schools exist, to what ends, and how rural schools fit in the larger picture.

Historical Push for Standardization

The public school system in the United States is immersed in balancing public and private benefit, and in confronting the idealized notions of the roles played by its public schools (Kaestle, 1983). We see substantial investment each year ($600 billion of federal, state, and local dollars) in the public schools to achieve these public and private goods (NCES, 2015; Sipple and

Yao, 2015). The public accrues benefit from this investment through a more productive workforce and democratically engaged citizens while the private benefit is accrued through enhanced opportunity and income for individuals (Labaree, 1997). While at times the public debate has taken on a tenor of private *versus* public benefit (Rose, 2014), generally these goods need not be in conflict. For instance, a quality, skills-based education provides individual economic opportunity while also enhancing a community (or state and nation) with rich human capital, a vibrant economy, and increased tax revenues (Friedman and Friedman, 1982). This generation of a more vibrant and accessible economy and democracy is intertwined in our public schools. These tensions were described by Labaree nearly two decades ago: "Schools . . . occupy an awkward position at the intersection between what we hope society will become and what we think it really is, between political ideals and economic realities" (Labaree, 1997, p. 41).

This intersection of public and private goods occurs in small and large communities alike—though it is most visible in small rural communities. This also helps to explain state and federal investment in local educational systems. In design and reform (historical and contemporary), basic tensions surrounding schools exist across the many layers of American society. Amongst them are the rights and well-being of individuals, the autonomy of local publicly elected boards, the knowledge and autonomy of professional educators, and the responsibilities and oversight by state and federal government. These tensions are especially salient in rural communities and the schools that serve them. Most specifically, the teachers are nested within the needs and interests of the local community but are also instruments of the state and profession serving non-local interests and needs.

Central amongst the decisions debated in rural areas across these levels are classroom curricula, student assessment, teacher quality, district size, and parent choice. Each of these can be illustrated by the value of local determination: Who determines the local elementary science curriculum? Who is in the best position to assess student learning and school performance. Who determines how to best prepare teachers? Who decides whether a two-hundred-student school district should be supported or consolidated? Should each of these decisions be made at the local level, in each of the 100,000 school buildings in the country, by professional associations, by individual states, or nationally?

Prior to the reauthorization of the *Elementary and Secondary Act of 1994* (Under the Clinton administration), states had no systematic federal pressure to create statewide curriculum standards. So, not only was there no attempt to standardize curriculum across states, there was little widespread effort to standardize within states or schools either. As a result of this reauthorization, however, the Federal government incentivized the creation of state curriculum standards with additional federal dollars for state departments of education. This set the stage for the next reauthorization of the ESEA by President Bush in 2001 (i.e., NCLB) that required the creation of state examinations to assess the state curriculum standards. In the years following the implementation of the NCLB, it became obvious that states had established very different levels of learning standards and measures for proficiency, leaving some rigorous (e.g., Massachusetts, New York) while others weak (e.g., Alabama, Louisiana).[1]

The National Governors' Association (NGA) and the Council of Chief State School Officers (CSSO) discussed the need for more rigorous standards and the limitations of each state creating their own standards. Together they pushed for a process to generate a national, though voluntary, set of standards. It is from this that the Common Core Learning Standards (CCLS) were born (see http://ccsr.org). The U.S. has been entangled in this movement toward CCLS since 2010. The simple arguments for the Common Core and a national coordination of curriculum standards are these: 1) A broad, common set of learning standards is more efficient to create and implement, 2) provides more equal educational opportunity and outcomes (e.g., no matter your zip code, you will learn the same standards), 3) does not penalize students from more mobile families as changing locations will not result in a fractured and disconnected set of educational experiences, and 4) the standards reflect the heightened demands of college and career readiness including the development of "critical-thinking, problem-solving, and analytical skills students will need to be successful" (http://www.corestandards.org/what-parents-should-know/). Given this march toward standardization, and the subsequent vociferous debates throughout the nation about the merits and pitfalls of such a trend, how do we understand the idea, the controversy, and the future?

It is in this context that we tackle our main questions for this paper. Do schools and society benefit from standardization of school curricula and instruction? Is the benefit of standardization a myth or reality? Alternatively, is the benefit of true local control in rural schools and hence local variation a myth or reality? From a conceptual standpoint of better understanding rural education, we debate the merits of mandated implementation of various accountability measures (such as the Common Core, APPR, edTPA) and the need for employing a critical lens to challenge and unpack these particular taken-for-granted (and often black-boxed) metrocentric policies and procedures. We first offer a theoretical view of the big picture, top-down perspective. In particular, we pay special attention to rural science education as it is one of our areas of expertise, and it is also one of the subject areas in schools that has taken a big hit in terms of being taught in elementary schools with the onset of the Common Core Learning Standards (CCLS) implementation movement, which focuses heavily on literacy and mathematics.

Theoretical Conceptualization—Big Picture

Conceptually, we present Institutional Theory as a useful tool to help illustrate the pressures and incentives to standardize practice versus market incentives of local community variation (whether state-by-state or community-by-community; Sipple, 2004). Institutional theory is premised on the idea that there exist socially defined macro-level rules, norms, and taken-for-granted views that provide incentives to match the "institutionalized" patterns of organization and practice (Meyer and Rowan, 1977; Selznick, 1957; DiMaggio and Powell, 1991). These incentives to adhere to externally established patterns are most salient when the core technology (or practice) is too expensive or complicated to assess on technical merits. This results in a black-box of core practice left uninspected. The organization and community, given the challenge to inspect, then rely on matching established and valued patterns to secure their legitimacy (Meyer and Rowan, 1977). Long used to explain common patterns in organizational form (Scott, 2014), Institutional Theory has also been used to explain the high value of a label, practice, or form "beyond the technical task at hand" (Selznick, 1957). In other words, adhering to a well-established (i.e., culturally accepted) practice or organization, provides value to an organization (and serves as a proxy to true inspection), increases the flow of resources, and increases chances of survival. Scott (2014) describes formal rules (i.e., coercive in nature), socially defined norms (i.e., professional best-practice, values, and norms), and deeply embedded cultural-cognitive beliefs (e.g., frames through which meaning is made) that guide organizational practice and individuals within organizations. The institutional legitimacy earned by adhering to these dictated or embedded practices outweighs the promise of increased technical efficiency (DiMaggio and Powell, 1983; Meyer and Rowan, 1977).

How does this advance our discussion here? We, and others, argue there are multiple and sometimes competing pressures motivating and constraining, and rural schools must:

1. Serve their local communities, and their uniquely rural needs and qualities.
2. Prepare their students for the global economy and higher order skills.
3. Face pressure to consolidate schools and districts to gain efficiency.
4. Hire teachers with local knowledge that are embedded within the community.
5. Hire teachers with extensive subject matter knowledge.

These pressures capture the essence of the tension between standardization and variation. Issues 2, 3, and 5 represent the value in standardization and include access to global knowledge and skills not present in many local rural communities, and enhanced efficiency. Issues 1 and 4 represent the value in local knowledge and variability across schools and communities.

Institutional theory would lead us to believe that by following the growing status in international competitiveness and twenty-first-century skills and knowledge (ideas dominating the current discussion of schooling in the primary, secondary, and post-secondary levels), legitimacy and resources will follow. Anyone who stands up to discount the importance of being competitive with schools around the world, or denigrate twenty-first-century knowledge and skills in favor of traditional learning would likely face criticism and questions about their motives. Conforming to these new norms enhances the legitimacy of school leaders, politicians, and business leaders alike and serves as a powerful force for standardization and homogenization (Meyer and Rowan, 1978). Running counter to the prevailing norms is organizationally risky and heightens the chance of organizational failure (Kondra and Hinings, 1998). However, Kondra and Hinings also point out that those who break away from the pack and show sustained success, whom they term Renegades, do create new pathways to real innovation across organizational fields and establish the new norm as others follow and mimic.

This pressure to conform leads to the enhanced value of standardization and reduced variability amongst schools whether they be urban, suburban, or rural. Learning skills and knowledge that are recognized as college and career ready seems logical and strategic no matter the location of the school. Operating schools and districts that achieve scale economies, offering the designated set of courses and curricular options recognized and demanded by universities and businesses (e.g., extensive STEM preparation, multiple AP courses) are privileged by society when compared to small, locally oriented, limited curriculum schools in rural areas. Schools of fifty children, districts of 250 children, and classrooms focused on local knowledge fly in the face of these growing expectations of international competitiveness and efficiency.

Hence, our theoretical perspective both explains and predicts that rural schools will face pressures of standardization, and by adhering to the prescribed rules, norms, and taken-for-granteds, will be more stable and supported. Bucking the trends is grounds for challenge, uncertainty, and diminished state and federal resources. But, significantly, running counter to the mainstream narrative is also the path to innovation by the Renegades. Following the leader leads to security but not innovation. Innovation is risky but potentially quite fruitful.

Note how this discussion of homogenization and the chase for legitimacy ignores the concept of quality of instructional practice or actual student learning. The phenomenon rewards conformity and not necessarily proficiency or creativity. It serves the broader narrative (statewide or nationally) and not necessarily the local need as the pressures which we are describing are inherently non-local. Moreover, as Labaree (1997, p. 73) states in his sobering conclusion nearly twenty years ago, "We find credentialism triumphing over learning in our schools, with a commodified form of education winning an edge over useful substance." Labaree's (and Collins, 1979) credentialism is a nice example of how we latch on to indicators of success and learning as opposed to being able to truly measure success and learning.

STUDENT-LEVEL BOTTOM-UP APPROACH: A VIEW LOOKING UP

So given this macro-perspective, we have a lens with which to examine and understand the siren call of standardization. We now turn to a significantly more fine-grained examination and analysis of the micro-level perspective on what is taught in rural schools, why, and to what benefit.

Rural Science Education

Although rural students score significantly higher than, and consistently out-perform urban students on the National Assessment of Educational Progress reading, mathematics, and science assessments (NAEP, 2009, 2011), and although rural students have higher graduation rates, rural student college enrollment still lags behind urban students (Schafft and Jackson, 2011). Issues such as a lack of funding, isolation, and small student populations make it difficult for rural schools to attract and keep highly qualified STEM teachers and administrators (Sipple and Brent, 2015). State and federal incentives often lure professionals to urban schools where they may receive monetary bonuses or graduate tuition. Rural teachers with backgrounds in chemistry, physics, or calculus may be unable to teach these courses because the student body is too small to support advanced courses—or one teacher may require much preparation to teach multiple small classes. One strategy that small rural school districts are now undertaking includes sharing various resources including partnering in ways to offer distance-learning or other web-based programming to provide upper level/AP courses to their students. Another strategy involves small rural schools partnering with regional universities to provide STEM programming for their students as a means to provide rural children with opportunities to enter and pursue the STEM higher education and career pipeline (Hine, Podsiedlik, Avery, and Herman, 2015).

Rural students may also feel a disconnect between their local and academic knowledge and a perception of lower expectations (Boyer, 2006). Their cultural, socioeconomic, or indigenous perspectives might result in feelings of disenfranchisement (Semali and Kincheloe, 1999). Although rural students may possess deep understandings of STEM concepts learned outside of school (Avery and Kassam, 2011), their knowledge does not fit the mold of traditional school science and the view of science advanced nationally through the Common Core. Standardization often leads to the implementation of curricula that are disembodied from local contexts (Schafft and Jackson, 2011). Rural students need to see the relevance of science in their daily lives. Students in courses that connect STEM to their everyday lives are able to connect the STEM they learn inside and outside school—enhancing student success in science (Avery and Kassam, 2011).

STEM in the United States

As pressures mount to increase the number of scientists and engineers cultivated in the United States, the nation is ramping up its focus on science, technology, engineering, and mathematics (STEM) education in K–12 school settings. Organizations like the National Research Council (NRC, 2000) and the National Academy of Engineering (NAE, 2008) are calling on colleges and universities and on professional and technical societies to rethink how science and engineering have been portrayed in society and to create new and better methods to teach and learn science—and particularly engineering—in elementary and secondary school classrooms. In so doing, we see this new focus as a unique opportunity to build on the science and engineering foundations children have developed in their local environments by bridging the gap between what children already know and the required science curricula. In fact, Avery and Hains (forthcoming) suggest a more robust and nuanced approach that positions rural families' funds of knowledge (intergenerational knowledge) at the epicenter of their science education.

STEM and Educational Standards

With the advent of the Common Core Learning Standards (CCLS), now more than ever before, students, teachers, and administrators in the public education system are being held under a lens of intense scrutiny, subjected to a series of high-stakes tests and performance evaluations under the auspices of accountability. The content and evaluation focus of the CCLS is Literacy and Mathematics. Thus, other disciplines, such as science for example, are for the most part becoming extinct in many elementary school classrooms (Hine et al., 2015). Furthermore, although some of the CCLS and Common Core Modules mention science, the limited science content is often overshadowed by the demands and expectations to focus teaching on literacy exclusively. Not all science education programs subscribe to this practice. Hine et al. (2015) demonstrate in their rural science programmatic model, that higher order thinking skills and twenty-first century problem-solving skills, valuing what learners bring to the classroom (local knowledge), capitalizing on student motivation in science, and implementing teaching and learning strategies that include differentiated instruction and differentiated assessments found in the CCLS and the Next Generation Science Standards (NGSS), can be attended to in parallel with place-based strategies to enhance teaching and learning for more learners. This synergistic approach addresses what teachers are required to do while simultaneously harnessing and enhancing the science and engineering local knowledge and motivation rural children possess.

Collectively in our work within a variety of rural school districts in New York State, we have observed the spectrum of CCLS implementation that ranges from complete adoption, some adaptation or modification, to complete rejection. School districts that adopt the CCLS typically use them as the school curriculum. Districts that adapt the CCLS may use this curriculum along with other curricula selected by the school districts and individual schools or programs. Districts that reject the CCLS use a variety of curricula other than the CCLS. Therefore, we find it important to differentiate between policy intention, implementation, and operationalization with reference to CCLS. In so doing, to illuminate the often taken-for-granted nuances and/or behind the scenes work in the CCLS policy development, implementation, operationalization, and reconfiguration, we offer what we believe to be a productive and interesting lens by which to explore how the CCLS have been assimilated by rural school districts. This perspective, when viewed from the ground, illuminates three particular modes of operationalization: 1) discriminate implementation, 2) indiscriminate implementation, and 3) complete rejection.

Our unique methodological perspective is rooted in understandings from Science and Technology Studies (SandTS). By putting the light on the social construction and social interactions with human and nonhuman agents surrounding the CCLS, more interesting and helpful conversations are likely to arise. We apply methodologies from engineering studies in the Social Construction of Technology (SCOT) to the educational context. We view curricula as technologies (Shapin and Schaffer, 1985; Mulcahy, 1998; Avery, 2003) and teachers as "users" of those technologies (Bardini andHovarth, 1995; Kline and Pinch, 1996; Lindsey, 1999; Avery, 2003).

Operationalization of the CCLS

Before launching into our discussion on the three forms of implementation via the SCOT lens, it is extremely important to note (and we will revisit this again later in the chapter) that educational policy creation, implementation, and reconfiguration are extraordinarily complex for a variety of reasons that we outline here, especially with regard to rural school settings, as most policy is designed for more urban contexts (Sipple and Brent, 2015).

First and foremost, there are numerous variables in play that are constantly in flux: the policy, policy makers, politics and politicians, rules, norms and expectations, rationalities, contexts, humans (teachers, students, administrators, communities, school boards, families), and society in general (Cooper, Cibulka, and Fusarelli, 2008). This speaks to the nature of this highly complex system. Unfortunately, almost immediately, the societal discourse seemingly strives to oversimplify this very dynamic and complex system. In so doing, the result becomes a standardization of outcomes that measure a lowest common denominator—and values compliance more than excellence. Second, as history also demonstrates, the rhetoric and subsequent actions around this particular system (again, the policy arena in general) that becomes standardized, devolves into the all-too-common dichotomous argument that standardization is "good" or standardization is "bad." Thus, the battle between the myths and realities—the myths of standardization versus the realities of variation—quickly ensues. And third, as the domino chain collapses, we are left with an unproductive and unhealthy conversation that in the end serves no one.

Consequently, one of our goals, which we discuss next is to offer a way out of this moor of "chasing our tails" by providing a different lens by which to investigate the nuances of interactions within the complex system. In particular, this lens sheds light on the variation that takes place locally when the policy (technology) gets in the hands of the users (school districts): indiscriminate implementation, discriminate implementation, or complete rejection.

THE LENS OF SCOT[2]

The Social Construction of Technology (SCOT; Bijker, Hughes, and Pinch, 1987) is an approach that provides a vehicle for attending to notions otherwise taken for granted in human practice and the details of everyday life. It also provides a structure of analysis of inherently complex and nuanced sociological situations. Distinct from the previously reviewed institutionalism which privileges the macro-perspective, this perspective aims to delve inside the black-box left by institutionalism. SCOT is used to analyze socially significant groups, the users of various technological artifacts, as agents of technological change (Bijker, Hughes, and Pinch, 1987). Pinch and Bijker's conception of technology is purposefully broad: That "'technology' comprises more than machines . . ." "Technology" can include social arrangements as diverse as the postal system, transportation, refuse collection, voting mechanisms, education, and so on (Woolgar, 1991, p. 94).

Distinctly opposite to the common interest in the ways technology affects society, SCOT looks at the evolution of technology and highlights the role that relevant social groups play in the negotiation of technology's structure and function. This genealogy often reveals the existence of alternative possibilities prior to reaching consensus about what becomes the standard design and implementation of a technology. Determination of the prevailing design is a product of the interaction of different relevant social groups. Both in the technology design phase and after assumed closure (stabilization of an artifact), users' interactions with technological artifacts can effectively result in their reconfiguring the technology (Kline and Pinch, 1996; Bijker, Hughes, and Pinch, 1987). The SCOT framework views the developmental process of technology as an alternation of variation and selection. This results in a multidirectional model of analysis. A major tenet of this model claims that the design, technical content, and use of technological artifacts are all open to sociological analysis. It incorporates three components for examination in user analyses: (a) the role of relevant social groups and interpretive flexibility of an artifact; (b) closure or artifact stabilization; and (c) a detailed description of the case studies of users and their technologies for communication to the larger context.

An additional important concept that applies here is the notion of a black box. A black box is an entity (such as a law, relationship, text, procedure, protocol, technology, device, instrument, etc.) whose validity and internal nature is not in question (cf. Latour, 1987, p. 2). It is this metaphorical black box, that when unexamined or viewed to be too expensive or complex to assess, leads organizations to adhere to the socially prescribed rules, norms, and taken-for-granteds of the institutional analysis. Thus, in our case, curricula (CCLS) is viewed as a black box. Central to our argument for the application of SandTS to education is the notion that teachers' practices and "school" in general, are filled with black boxes and hence are difficult to examine and assess, leading local communities and school leaders to rely on adherence to non-local standards (e.g., teacher licensure for qualification, years' experience for pay increase). Other examples of black boxes might include a state mandated exam, a textbook definition, or a course sequence. From a research standpoint, however, examination of these black boxes, and their use by teachers (and students as well as districts, administrators, boards of education, and the like), is absolutely necessary for a full accounting of curricular implementation and school science teacher practice. For example, one can examine the interaction between the science teacher and an object such as a state-mandated test. In this instance, the focus becomes the negotiation between the teacher and the test including the language and use of or reference to the test in the context of this teacher's science. Thus, the black box—the state test—can be opened for the sociological analysis of its design, content, and use (Bijker, Hughes, and Pinch, 1987). Using these tools forces the researcher not to 'privilege' (Bijker, Hughes, and Pinch, 1987) the teacher but allows for equal observational treatment of all human and nonhuman entities. It allows the researcher to explore taken-for-granted notions, such as the state test, without taking it for granted themselves. The concept of black boxes assists the researcher in avoiding privileging established institutions and authorities (e.g., the role the 4th grade science test plays in ensuring science minimally gets taught in 4th grade if nowhere else in grades K–3. It's a mandate, a leverage tool, and typically remains un-opened).

Adopting the practice of following technology users from SCOT—viewing school districts as users—provides an interesting way to investigate the ways they implement curricula (CCLS). For the purposes of this chapter, we will focus on two out of the three forms of implementation: indiscriminate and discriminate. The third, outright rejection, although most exciting, powerful, and impactful in its own right in terms of influencing New York State CCLS educational policy as well as exemplifying what happens when a technology is railed against by its potential (mythical users discussed below) users (the renegade or "bad-ass" teacher), is discussed in great detail elsewhere (VanSlyke-Briggs, Bloom, and Boudet, 2015). Thus, we explore the two forms of implementation from the SCOT lens: the CCLS is the curriculum as technology (and black-boxed) and school districts (with a primary focus on the unit of analysis of the teacher) are the users of that technology/curriculum. We begin with a broad description of implementation and then narrow the focus to rural science teachers in particular. This focus was selected as a specific representation of what happens when a metrocentric policy created with mythical users in mind does not incorporate the actual users including rural science teachers, whom many of do not fit the predetermined urbanormative model of the prescribed teacher-user.

Indiscriminate Implementation

Indiscriminate implementation (indiscriminate standardization for that matter) is a linear and direct implementation of a policy or in this case, CCLS, without changing any of its attributes in any way, shape, or form. It does not entail opening the black box—simply put—it remains closed. This form of implementation can be disconcerting for a variety of reasons. First, some argue, in its most dangerous form, an "indiscriminate nationwide adoption and implementation of the CCLS may amount to an assimilationist education policy not unlike the historical treatment of Indigenous communities in North America" (Kassam, Avery, and Ruelle, forthcoming, p. 15). Furthermore, as Karen Eppley has noted elsewhere, indiscriminate implementation can lead to *a pedagogy of erasure* for rural school children (Eppley, 2011). Second, without the illumination offered by lenses such as SCOT, a robotic implementation might be misconstrued solely as a rational conformist behavior in response to fear, weakness, and/or obligation/mandate; when in actuality, it is more about (mis)perception than intention (Avery, 2003), and not at all about uniformity (as imagined and scripted by the original designers). Third, a form of indiscriminate implementation can indeed include a robotic implementation. In New York State, this is tantamount to the verbatim implementation of literacy and mathematics lesson plan scripts available via Engage-NY (https://www.engageny.org/). This too, was not necessarily the intention of the designers (EngageNY), however, once in the hands of some users, it is a very real form of implementation taken. Finally, there are also others who would again warn against indiscriminate implementation. Dr. Michael Fortunato eloquently reflects,

> An influential mentor and close friend, Ted Alter, would often say in his lectures, "There is power in the rules, but the real power lies in who makes the rules for making rules." These are the meta-rules, the constitutional architecture, the stuff that educational standards are made of. When values are inculcated at a meta-level, they can not only constrain what can occur within the system, they can also constrain what is considered possible, desirable, and deemed respectable. It may be a throwback to Peter Berger and Thomas Luckmann (1966), but standards can, in very meaningful ways, construct a reality for students that is highly homogeneous in terms of basic values, and limit the realm of the possible (Fortunato, forthcoming).

Discriminate Implementation

Discriminate implementation entails implementing a modified version of a policy or in this case, the CCLS curriculum, in some shape or form. It entails opening the black box for inspection. This type of implementation also takes numerous forms and these too are often *not* what the original designers intended (part of the myth we describe later). It indeed is a case-and-point of the variation observed and practiced on the ground—quite different from the policy intentions described earlier. Before embarking on this line of discussion, distinguishing between the different types of users is paramount.

Germane to our conversation here, are the ways in which teachers adopt, integrate, and reconfigure technologies (NGSS and CCLS) in their portrayal of science (and/or other content areas for that matter). Focusing on users and their interactions with technologies throughout the technology's life cycle offers provocative insights into teachers' identities as practitioners of science and as members of the science education community. Teachers' interactions with technologies—in the process of making or using—are explored and analyzed by the ways in which teachers represent themselves when teaching science in a sociologically useful way. We distinguish between two categories of users: the curriculum "maker" and the curriculum "user" (Avery and Carlsen, 2001) and we discuss these next.

Users

As a technology, a curriculum is open to interpretation and reconfiguration by its users (Kline and Pinch, 1996), teachers. As has been used in SCOT studies, it is useful to conceptualize two categories of teacher curriculum users—the " innovator " or technology maker and the "would-be user" or technology user. The maker represents the teacher who has been involved in a curriculum evolution process: its design, development, implementation, and reconfiguration in the classroom. Like the computer designers of the 1960s and 1970s, teacher makers are the first to develop and implement a technology (Bardini and Hovarth, 1995). The user is the individual for whom the technology is designed and by whom it will be used (Lindsey, 1999). In terms of curriculum development, the teacher who has not been part of a curriculum development project but who chooses to implement the curriculum or technology in the classroom is the "user."

Conceptualizing curricula as technologies illuminates the importance of considering teachers' identities as a part of those technologies. Curricula are designed with an end user in mind, thereby constructing widely varying identities of the teacher. Some curricula conceptualize the teacher as a near robotic implementer of the technological artifact, intending for the teacher to follow a formulaic procedure. Others conceptualize the teacher as an active participant, inviting him or her to play a part in shaping the learning process. However, just as with other technologies, the end users often take the initiative to reconfigure both their identity and the technology as a whole. Some teachers make significant alterations to formulaic technologies. Other teachers adopt the mantle of a straightforward implementer, thereby altering a technology that originally intended a more diverse implementation. The type and level of interaction seems to be related to teacher identity (including teacher history, such as experience with science and scientific research), the role they have in interacting with a particular technology during its creation and development (including whether they have had a hand in making it or not), and their particular relationship with the content (including their beliefs about the role of classroom science, how they black box the content in the classroom and ownership of the content) (Avery, 2003). For example, Mulcahy (1998) has studied the ways in which teachers interacted with and reconfigured a standardized curriculum. Her work exemplifies how teachers can have alternate perceptions about and interpretations of the same technology.

Example Cases of (Science) Teachers and their Indiscriminate Implementation

Very relevant to this thread and worthy of merit up front, is the observation that in classrooms where teachers tend towards a robotic implementation of the CCLS (likely motivated by such things as pressures of accountability, administrative mandates, and/or limited STEM content knowledge for some examples), classroom science is overshadowed by literacy such that science is *read about within literacy lessons, not practiced as a process.* In more extreme cases, science is simply not taught at all. This phenomenon is so strong that even the state-mandated grade 4 test is not enough to dissuade teachers from committing the majority of their classroom instructional time to literacy and mathematics instruction. In fact, on a related note, in preservice teacher education, the edTPA, a high-stakes exam in which licensure is dependent, overtly addresses only literacy and mathematics instruction—thus telegraphing early on to developing teachers which content areas are important and which are not.

The CCLS tend to remain black-boxed with indiscriminate implementation. Their history, meaning, decisions around what content and how the content is portrayed (and potentially delivered), is not unpacked nor opened up for examination and discussion.

A quite different example of indiscriminate implementation is exemplified by a teacher who perceives that it is his or her duty to implement curricula in their full integrity to honor what the designers originally intended (Avery, 2003), rather than be the result of a particular weakness or incentive (e.g., accountability, administrative mandate, insufficient content knowledge).

Example cases of (Science) Teachers and their Discriminate Implementation

At a glance, discriminate implementation is nuanced in somewhat similar ways but upon closer inspection, plays out differently within each classroom context for a variety of reasons. Avery and Carlsen (2001) found that teachers who choose to teach science in a sociologically useful way have strong subject matter knowledge, research experience with science, and tend to draw upon their memberships in communities of practice for support, ideas, and curricular innovations. Specifically, they found that teachers (makers) who are involved in, and have ownership in, a curriculum development project—over time—tend to implement and reconfigure the curricula when given a medium (such as a curriculum development community of practice) for collegial support, interaction, and resources to practice authentic science in their classrooms (Avery, 2003).

Others have explored the ways in which teachers' backgrounds or histories with scientific research impact how they represent the nature and process of science in the classroom context. These teachers have what Cunningham described as a sociological understanding of science (Cunningham, 1995). Science teacher identity also factors into this form of implementation (Helms, 1998; Avery, 2003).

Allegiance to certain pedagogical strategies also seems to play a role in discriminate implementation. Teachers who engage in a place-based approach to education (PBE)—that is interdisciplinary in nature and utilizing the local environment to teach science—focus on structuring learning around local history, culture, language, environment, and economy. In so doing, they emphasize hands-on and real-world learning experiences. This approach increases academic achievement, strengthens students' ties to their community, enhances students' appreciation for the natural world, and creates a heightened commitment to serving as contributing citizens (Sobel, 2005, p. 7). For example, Avery and Kassam (2011) found that teachers who value anchoring their teaching and their students' learning of science and engineering in children's experiential habitat often are more successful at bridging the gap between children's local knowledge and global science. More recently, research has demonstrated that rural contexts can be rich environments for learning science (Avery, 2013). The unique knowledge base and learning needs of rural children, and effective strategies focused on valuing and using local knowledge across students, teachers, and communities can increase rural students' access to, engagement in, and achievement in science (Hine et al., 2015). Additional research with rural children also suggests that when describing science and engineering in their community, children illustrate a complex connectivity with their environment. Their sense of being emerges from their engagement with their environment, revealing an understanding of complex, diverse, and co-existing relationships to their habitat (Kassam and Avery, 2013).

Place-based science education is very much in alignment with the Next Generation Science Standards (NGSS), which, for example, emphasize engineering design and the use of cross-cutting ideas in the teaching and learning of content overall. In addition, specific concepts such as the central focus; community, cultural, and individual assets; purposeful alignment of objectives and assessments; attention to differentiated instruction and assessment; use of higher levels of Bloom's Taxonomy (via a broad buffet of language functions, not exclusive) are all elements of CCLS and the preservice teacher educator edTPA that can be interwoven within a PBE approach. Thus, teachers who choose this pedagogical approach often "cherry-pick" the best parts of many curricula to reconfigure their own classroom curriculum. This technology maker would very likely employ many of these aforementioned components of the CCLS in concert with the cross-cutting ideas contained in the NGSS because she would view a subset of them as meshing well with PBE strategies, critical thinking, problem-solving, and making real world connections. So, in a sense, this form of technology maker creates the best of both worlds, as she values and utilizes the local simultaneously with using elements of the CCLS and NGSS to bridge the gap to global which represents a more diverse implementation (Kassam, Avery, and Ruelle, forthcoming). This occurrence, we would argue, being similar to what Lindsey described in her SandTS user studies, in many ways far surpasses what the designers originally intended (Lindsey, 1999). Clearly, this particular discriminate implementer is in sharp contrast to the robotic indiscriminate implementer described earlier. The PBE teacher, as a technology maker, does not at all bear resemblance to the urbanormative teacher would-be-user originally envisioned by the CCLS designers.

Discriminate implementation, unlike indiscriminate, often leads to users exploring the black-boxed CCLS. This exploration might entail questioning the integrity of its design in content akin to the ways that echo Dr. Fortunato's earlier cautionary tale to us regarding the rule-makers and those that make the rules for the rule-makers. Others open the black-boxed CCLS and adapt it by choosing to use some of the standards within and interweaving the selected standards within other existing curricula such that a new curriculum is reconfigured and packaged as the user's own hybridized model (similar to what Lindsey [1999] observed with Radio Shack TRS 80 computer users over thirty years ago!) (Avery, 2013).

MOVING FORWARD!

Within both modes of implementation presented here, we have observed unintentional and varied results. SCOT's multidirectional analysis reveals that like technology and/or engineering design, the process is not linear and technologies can be continually reconfigured, even when they were thought to be stabilized or closed. Thus, there appear to be both myths and realities in play in the educational arena. Things are often not what they seem.

Theoretical and Research Implications

Employing a SCOT lens and thereby shining light on the interactions between human and non-human entities illuminates the myth of standardization. Hence, the reality of the on-the-ground variation is undraped. Consequently, what was originally envisioned by the CCLS designers and the policy makers (rule-makers), the implementation of the predetermined standardized curriculum for the mythical would-be-users, never quite plays out fully in its intended capacity. What happens when the technology (CCLS curriculum) gets into the hands of the user is something quite different. Whether it be the engineering studies of technology users and innovators, or teachers interacting with curricula, black boxes can be and are opened, technologies/curricula are reconfigured once they get in the hands of the users, and the would-be-users are not always robotic. On the contrary, they are often very multifaceted both in nature and in action. In fact, as several of the cases here illuminate, complexities are at work on both macro and micro levels in diverse contexts. The nuances and variables that comprise the playing field on the ground enhance the system. All of these, which factor into the educational equation are seen and valued as unique and worthy of consideration. There is genetic strength in variation. Furthermore, these variables are very real and ultimately not easily corralled by standardization. The SCOT lens does not aim to "solve" our educational policy dilemmas, but it does provide the fervor and traction needed to replace the historically stale and vacant conversations. In so doing, all participating actors—human and non-human (Callon, 1996) are recognized so that we might better appreciate and understand the diverse nature of this increasingly complex system.

The pervasive and stubborn attachment to dichotomous conversations (or heated arguments as oft the case seems to be), is fruitless, and consistently causes the public discourse to get stuck in the mud of rhetoric in the name of simplification. Rather, when diverse nuances are unveiled via looking through the lens of alternative methodologies/perspectives such as offered by SandTS, and SCOT in particular, opportunities for new and engaging conversational niches emerge. Thus, a more pluralistic dialogue can evolve that better reflects our increasingly diverse educational landscape, and the inherent complexities of learning, schooling, and leading. Viewing diversity as perception (Kassam, 2009), and thus expanding the concept of diversity beyond conventional measures can help accomplish this. Promoting and engaging in pluralistic conversations and employing alternative research methodologies that focus on exploring both micro and macro spaces/contexts of learning are powerful tools to utilize to begin a new dialogue.

Practitioner-Based Strategies and Implications

Programmatic structures geared at linking community to school and school to community such as those offered by several science educators (Avery, 2013; Chinn, 2011) prepare educators to teach engaging, place-based instruction and design-based experiences focused on STEM curriculum in the school setting. In an institutional sense, this practice may be risky and a potential loss of long-standing legitimacy, but also the path to true innovation. Using a place-based, team approach allows for collaboration and partnerships for lesson planning and preparation. These programs provide teachers with the opportunity to try out curriculum units and engagement lessons to get authentic feedback from learners as well as collaborate with fellow educators and professionals in the field (Hine et al., 2015).

Rural teacher leaders have implemented engineering design lessons in their classrooms and extending the learning into their surrounding community, they have leveraged local resources, affirmed students' knowledge and value of place, and earned the support of rural families, administrators, and community members (Hine et al., 2015). Each of these "gains" is not from conformity but rather from innovation.

Furthermore, partnerships can play a critical role in supporting rural communities as they identify and use contextual resources to foster interest and relevance in learning for their youth. The greatest asset of any community is the character of its people, and the future of any community lies in the attitudes and aspirations of their children. The youth of today will need to respond to the global needs of tomorrow. Programs like the Summer Snapshot Series (Hine et al., 2015) provide students with an accessible toolkit of STEM knowledge, skills, and self-assurance to make the difference both in their own rural community and abroad. Rural contexts can be rich environments for learning science. Place-based pedagogies that focus on the unique knowledge base and learning needs of rural children (Shamah and MacTavish, 2009; Bartsch, 2008), and effective strategies focused on valuing and using local knowledge in science education across students, teachers, and communities (White and Reid, 2008) can increase rural students' access to, engagement in, and achievement in science (Avery, 2013; Smith, 2002). In sum, breaking open the black box of instructional practice in an informed, thoughtful way is not necessarily a path to risk and loss of resources, but rather a path to reform and enhancement of local educational opportunity and outcomes.

NOTES

1. This assessment was highlighted by the difference between state-calculated proficiency levels and NAEP proficiency levels—our nation's only means of commonly assessing students and schools across the country (US Department of Education, 2014-2015).

2. Much of the information presented in this section builds on and extends the work published in Daniel Z. Meyer and Leanne M. Avery (2010). A third use of sociology of scientific knowledge: a lens for studying teacher practice, *Studies in Science Education*, 46:2, 153-178, DOI:10.1080/03057267.2010.504546.

REFERENCES

Avery, L. M. (2003). *Knowledge, Identity, and Teachers' Communities of Practice*. Ithaca, NY: Cornell University Press.
Avery, L. M. (2013) Valuing local knowledge in rural science education. *Theory into Practice*, 2: 28–35.
Avery, L. M., and Carlsen, W. S. (2001). *Knowledge, identity, and teachers' multiple communities of practice*. Paper presented at the Annual Meeting of the National Association for Research in Science Teaching, St. Louis, MO.
Avery, L. M., and Kassam, K-A. (2011). Phronesis: Children's local rural knowledge of science and engineering. *Journal of Research in Rural Education, 26* (2), 1-18.
Avery, L. M., and Hains, B. J. (Forthcoming). Oral traditions: A contextual framework for complex science concepts. *Cultural Studies of Science Education* (CSSE) Special Issue on Rural Science Education.
Bardini, T., and Hovarth, A. (1995). The social construction of the personal computer user. *Journal of Communication, 45*(3): 40–65.
Bartsch, J. (2008). Youth as resources in revitalizing communities. In D. A. Gruenewald and G. A. Smith (Eds.), *Place-Based Education in the Global Age* (pp. 65–84). New York: Routledge.
Berger, P. L., and Luckmann, T. (1966). *The Social Construction of Reality: A Treatise in the Sociology of Knowledge*. New York: Anchor Books.

Bijker, W. E., Hughes, T. P., and Pinch, T. J. (Eds.). (1987). *The social construction of technological systems*. Cambridge, MA: MIT Press.

Boyer, P. (2006). *Building community: Reforming math and science education in rural schools*. Retrieved June 11, 2011, from www.ankn.uaf.edu/publications/building_community.pdf.

Brown, D., and Schafft, K. A. (2011). *Rural People and Communities in the 21st Century: Resilience and Transformation*. Malden, MA: Polity Press.

Carr, P., and Kefalas, M. J. (2009). The rural brain drain. Retrieved November 28, 2013, from http://chronicle.com/article/The-Rural-Brain-Drain/48425/.

Casto, H., McGrath, B, Sipple, J. W., Todd, L. (in press). "Community Aware" education policy: Enhancing individual and community vitality. *Educational Policy Analysis Archives*.

Chinn, P. (2011). Developing a sense of place and an environmental ethic: A transformative role for Hawaiian/Indigenous science in teacher education? Retrieved July 10, 2010, from jan.ucc.nau.edu/~jar/HOH/HOH-5.pdf.

Collins, R. (1979). *The Credential Society: An Historical Sociology of Education and Stratification*. New York: Academic.

Cooper, B. S., Cibulka, J. G., and Fusarelli, L. D. (2008). *Handbook of Education Politics and Policy*. New York: Routledge.

Corbett, M. (2007). *Learning to Leave: The Irony of Schooling in a Coastal Community*. Black Point, NS: Fernwood Publishing.

Cunningham, C. M. (1995). *The Effect of Teachers' Sociological Understanding of Science on Classroom Practice and Curriculum Innovation*. Ithaca, NY: Cornell University.

DiMaggio, P., & Powell, W. (1983). The Iron Cage Revisited: Institutional Isomorphism and Collective Rationality in Organizational Fields. *American Sociological Review, 48*(2), 147–160.

DiMaggio, P. J., and Powell, W. W. (1991). The iron cage revisited: Institutional isomorphism and collective rationality in organizational fields. In W. W. Powell and P. J. DiMaggio (Eds.), *The New Institutionalism in Organizational Analysis* (p. 63-82). Chicago: University of Chicago Press.

Eppley, K. (2011). Reading mastery as pedagogy of erasure. *Journal of Research in Rural Education, 26*(13), 1–5.

Fortunato, W-P, M., (Forthcoming). Advancing educational diversity: Antifragility, standardization, democracy, and a multitude of education options. *Cultural Studies of Education* (CSSE) Issue on Rural Science Education.

Friedman, M., and Friedman, R. D. (1982). *Capitalism and freedom*. Chicago: University of Chicago Press.

Helms, J. (1998). Science and me: Subject matter and identity in secondary school science teachers. *Journal of Research in Science Teaching, 35*(7), 811–834.

Hine, L. K., Podsiedlik, M., Avery, L. M., and Herman, E. (2015). Summer Science Snapshot: A developing partnership model to spark interest in STEM among rural learners. *Excelsior*, Fall/Winter 2015.

Johnson, J., Showalter, D., and Klein, R. (2014). *Why Rural Matters 2013-14*. Retrieved January 11, 2014, from http://www.ruraledu.org/user_uploads/file/2013-14-Why-Rural-Matters.pdf.

Kaestle, C. F. (1983). *Pillars of the Republic*. New York: Hill and Wang.

Kassam, K-A. S. (2009). *Biocultural Diversity and Indigenous Ways of Knowing: Human Ecology in the Arctic*. Calgary: University of Calgary Press.

Kassam, K-A. S., and Avery, L. M. (2013). The oikos of rural children: A lesson for the adults in experiential education. *Journal of Sustainability Education*. Available at: http://www.jsedimensions.org/wordpress/content/the-oikos-of-rural-children-a-lesson-for-the-adults-in-experiential-education_2013_05/.

Kassam, K-A. S., Avery, L. M., and Ruelle, M. L. (Forthcoming). The cognitive relevance of rural: Why is it critical to survival? *Cultural Studies in Science Education* (CSSE) Special Issue on Rural Science Education.

Kline, R., and Pinch, T. (1996). Users as agents of technological change: The social construction of the automobile in rural America. *Technology and Culture*, October 1996, 763–795.

Kondra, A. Z., and Hinings, C. R. (1998). *Organizational Diversity and Change in Institutional Theory. Organization Studies, 19* (5), 743.

Labaree, D. (1997). Public Goods, Private Goods: The American Struggle over Educational Goals. *American Educational Research Journal, 34*(1), 39-81.

Latour, B. (1987). *Science in Action.* Cambridge, MA: Harvard University Press.

Lindsey, C. (1999, April). Invisible computers and constructed users: The TRS-80 computer 20 years on. Paper presented at the Technology and Identity, Cornell University, Ithaca NY.

Long, D., and Avery, L. M. (Forthcoming). Guest Co-Editors, *Cultural Studies in Science Education* (CSSE) Special Issue on Rural Science Education.

Mulcahy, M. D. (1998). Designing the user/using the design. *Social Studies of Science,* 28(1), 5-37.

Meyer, J. W., and Rowan, B. (1977). Institutionalized organizations: Formal structure as myth and ceremony. *American Journal of Sociology, 83*(2), 340-363.

Meyer, J., and Rowan, B. (1978). The structure of educational organizations. In M. W. Meyer (Ed.), *Environments and Organizations.* San Francisco, CA: Jossey-Bass.

NAE (Committee on Public Understanding of Engineering Messages, National Academy of Engineering). (2008). *Changing the Conversation: Messages for Improving Public Understanding of Engineering.* Washington, DC: National Academy Press.

NAEP. (2009, 2011). Grades 4 & 8 Mathematics, Reading and Science Scores. Author's calculations. Retrieved May 24, 2012 from http://nces.ed.gov/nationsreportcard/naepdata/

NCES (2015). "The Digest of Education Statistics." National Center for Educational Statistics, USDOE: Washington, DC. https://nces.ed.gov/programs/digest/2015menu_tables.asp

NRC (Center for Science, Mathematics, and Engineering Education, National Research Council). (2000). *Inquiry and the National Science Education Standards: A guide for teaching and learning.* Washington, DC: National Academy Press.

Rose, M. (2014). *Why School?: Reclaiming Education for all of Us* (revised and expanded edition). New York: The New Press.

Schafft, K. A., and Jackson, A. (2011). (Eds.) *Rural Education for the Twenty-First Century: Identity, Place, and Community in a Globalizing World.* University Park: Penn State University Press.

Scott, W. R. (2014). *Institutions and Organizations.* (2nd ed.). Thousand Oaks, CA: Sage Publications.

Selznick, P. (1966). *TVA and the grass roots: a study in the sociology of formal organization.* New York: Harper & Row.

Semali, L. M., and Kincheloe, J. L. (Eds). (1999) *What is indigenous knowledge? Voices from the academy.* New York: Taylor and Francis.

Shamah, D., and MacTavish, K. A. (2009). Rural research brief: Making room for place-based knowledge in rural classrooms. *The Rural Educator, 30,* 1–4.

Shapin, S., and Shaffer, S. (1985). *Leviathan and the air pump.* Princeton, NJ: Princeton University Press.

Sipple, J. W. (2004). Local anchors versus state levers in state-led school reform: Identifying the community around public schools. In W. K. Hoy and C. G. Miskel (Eds.), *Educational administration, policy, and reform: Research and measurement* (pp. 25–57). Charlotte, NC: Information Age Publishing.

Sipple, J. W., and Brent, B. O. (2015). Challenges and opportunities associated with rural school settings. In H. F. Ladd and E. B. Fiske (Eds.), *Handbook of Research in Education Finance and Policy,* 2nd ed. (pp. 612–629). New York: Routledge.

Sipple, J. W., and Yao, Y. (2015). The unequal impact of the Great Recession on the instructional capacity of rural schools. In Williams, S. M., and Grooms, A. A. (Eds). *Educational Opportunity in Rural Contexts: The Politics of Place.* Charlotte, NC: Information Age Publishing.

Smith, G. (2002). Place-based education: Learning to be where we are. *Phi Delta Kappan, 83,* 584–594.

Sobel, D. (2005). *Place-based education: Connecting classrooms and communities.* Great Barrington, MA: Orion Society.

Strange, M., Johnson, J., Showalter, D., and Klein, R. (2012). *Why rural matters 2011-12*. Retrieved February 12, 2012 from http://www.ruraledu.org/articles.php?id=2820.

Theodori, G. (2003). The community activeness – Consciousness Matrix. *Journal of Extension*, 41(5).

Tieken, M. C. (2014). *Why rural schools matter*. Chapel Hill: University of North Carolina Press.

U.S. Department of Education (2015-2016). Mapping state proficiency standards onto NAEP scales. Retrieved January 26, 2016, from http://nces.ed.gov/nationsreportcard/subject/publications/studies/pdf/2015046.pdf.

VanSlyke-Briggs, K., Bloom, E., and Boudet, D. (2015). *Resisting reform. Reclaiming public education through grassroots activism*. Charlotte, NC: Information Age Publishing.

White, S. and Reid, J. (2008). Placing teachers? Sustaining rural schooling through place-consciousness in teacher education. *Journal of Research in Rural Education, 23*, 1–11.

Williams, D. T. (2010). *The rural solution: How community schools can reinvigorate rural education*. Retrieved December 13, 2011 from www.americanprogress.org/issues/2010/09/pdf/ruralschools.pdf

Williams, S. M. and Grooms, A. A. (2015). *Educational Opportunity in Rural Contexts: The Politics of Place*. Charlotte, NC: Information Age Publishing.

Woolgar, S. (1991). Configuring the user. In J. Law (Ed.), *A Sociology of Monsters* (pp. 57–102). London: Routledge.

Chapter Nine

Conclusion

Reimagining Rural

Gregory M. Fulkerson and Alexander R. Thomas

There is no rural without urban, and there is no rural culture without the interdependencies of city and country. It is thus not truly accurate to talk of "rural culture," and the essays of this volume are best understood as examining the artifacts of a dominant culture that sees rural people, values, and landscapes as something "other" than normal. Whether the stereotypes are negative, as the slack-jawed rural rapists of *Deliverance* victimizing "normal" suburbanites are portrayed, or ostensibly positive *Mayberry* types, urbanormativity is at the service of a dominant urban order. From deep in prehistory when complex networks of trade allowed the populations of individual settlements to grow beyond the carrying capacity of their respective environments, the dependency of urban areas upon the network connecting the city to the distant countryside continues to foster an ideological bulwark of urbanormativity and perceived urban superiority.

This volume has attempted to contribute to the expanding research program devoted to the analysis of rural media and rural knowledge production with the hopes of dispelling myths, debunking stereotypes, and ultimately advocating new ways of thinking—indeed, of reimagining rural. As the contributions in this volume make clear, popular culture is filled with images of the rural that, while contradictory at times, generally promote the urbanormative standards of superior urban life and backward, degenerate, deviant rural life. At best, the rural is shown in an idyllic light, or held to be attractive only in the wake of a collapsed urban society, as in the post-apocalyptic media examined by Lowe in this volume. As observed by Hayden, the horrendous rural stereotypes of the inbred horror genre, as emphasized in the *Wrong Turn* film franchise, have become so familiar that we are starting to see spoofs that poke fun at the ridiculousness of rural stereotypes and iconic figures. According to Hayden, this is the premise of the 2012 film, *Tucker and Dale vs. Evil*. Fulkerson and Lowe, in their chapter, highlight that rural and urban themes are prominently featured, not only in obscure niche genres, but also for the prime time mainstream viewership, although this has waned in recent decades. They note that the most highly watched television programs of all time offer an evolving representation of the rural, from the untamed, wild, and dangerous rural West of the mid-twentieth century, to the comedic, naïve, and unintelligent rural simpletons of the 1960s, through the contemporary supernatural and hyper-real dangers of zombies, vampires, werewolves, faeries, and the Headless Horseman. The entire genre of rural reality shows, as studied by Jicha, not only plays a role in reinforcing rural stereotypes, but has the power to reify these stereotypes by virtue of the fact that what is being viewed is in some way "reality." Jicha discovers that the rural reality genre is so popular that there are over one hundred such series in existence. While conceding that some of the shows portray rural people and places in a positive or heroic light, they still contribute to the oversimplification of rural. A theme that runs through the volume turns on the idea that many misrepresentations of rural depend on the assumption that rural places are all alike, and are generally homogenous, white, patriarchal places, where livelihoods are always derived from the primary sector—farming, mining, fishing, timber, and so on. Jicha notes how baseless these ideas are by offering some empirically grounded observations, as we also attempt later in this concluding chapter. Avery and Sipple quote Theodori who proclaimed, "if you have seen one rural place, you have seen *one* rural place." It is thus a common mistake to assume that all rural places are alike.

In the effort to examine popular cultural views of urban and rural, it is important not only that we engage in media studies, but also examine the wider process of knowledge production. In this light, the analysis by McKay offers important insights into how the nation's news media operate. She notes the growing regional focus of news agencies, and particularly newspapers, whereby the experiences of smaller rural communities may be underemphasized or altogether ignored. This has the effect of minimizing or erasing the local narratives that give form and content to the identity of rural communities. McKay points out that the historical researcher of the future may find it very difficult to piece together local histories in the absence of local news outlets, effectively marginalizing rural community narratives and relegating them to secondary importance to the larger urban-based region.

Noting similar patterns with regard to education, Avery and Sipple provide a compelling piece of evidence to support the idea that contemporary educational policy and discourse is imbued with urbanormative standards. Indeed, education policy directs attention and resources almost exclusively to urban areas, relegating and marginalizing the educational needs of the countryside. Avery and Sipple point out that the increasingly homogenous uniformity endemic to education policy—epitomized by standardized testing—denies alternative approaches that are place-based, where teachers may integrate general knowledge with locally unique problems or experiences. Each rural community has a unique set of political, economic, social, cultural, and environmental conditions, and it may be more beneficial for students if teachers emphasize locally unique conditions, rather than act on the premise that they are irrelevant or unimportant.

These themes of urban superiority and rural irrelevance are notable in higher education as well, as noted by Ching in her discussion of the Cow College, about land grant institutions—once viewed as a beacon of hope devoted to providing the public with a well-rounded education—that has literally become the butt of jokes and is tacitly understood to be tasked with the impossible: making the rural public educationally enlightened. Through her analysis of socially conscious literary works, Ching reveals a highly developed sense of urbanormativity in higher education.

At this stage we briefly reflect on the value of this research and offer a few observations that will hopefully put the existing rural stereotypes and generalizations to rest. Of course, urbanormativity as a phenomenon existed from the beginning of cities themselves—Gilgamesh of Mesopotamian lore waxes poetic on the superiority of urban life—even though it is only a recent phenomenon that the majority of humans actually live in cities! And so while we are hopeful that such stereotypes can be confronted, we are also realistic that such work will be ongoing and require persistent vigilance.

RURAL IMAGINARY AND INEQUALITY

An important and fair question to ask about this project is "why does it matter?" On the one hand, it seems like harmless and trivial fun to play with the existing cultural ideas of rural people as objects of admiration and ridicule. We would point out that this was exactly the attitude taken with regard to racial stereotypes found in various media through the twentieth century, as I am reminded when my kids happen upon an old episode of *Looney Tunes* or *Casper the Friendly Ghost*—both routinely featuring gross characterizations of Native and African Americans. As social norms have shifted, tolerance of such media has all but vanished. With regard to rural stereotypes, we cannot say the same. Existing social norms can be characterized, as we have noted in other publications (Thomas, Lowe, Fulkerson, and Smith, 2011; Fulkerson and Thomas 2014), as urbanormative. This means that the benchmark standards drawn upon for evaluating normalcy are predicated on urban life, rendering rural life as the exception, or as itself a deviant condition.

Another argument against the worthiness of validating rural experiences would be that most rural representations feature white people, many of whom are male characters, and therefore do not qualify as members of a protected minority group. We would argue that this is an unfair and inaccurate claim, as rural is itself a minority group characteristic, as numerically fewer people are living in rural areas globally than ever before, but more importantly, rural communities occupy structurally disadvantaged locations in wider political, economic, and social networks. Leaving these facts aside, we would also highlight that the residents of rural communities are not always white. There is considerable regional variation on this issue, as for instance, a significant percentage of the rural population in the Southeastern United States is African American—a region poetically dubbed the "Black Belt" by Booker T. Washington for the color of the soil as well as the color of the skin of the people who have historically worked the soil and resided in this region. It is interesting that the term "urban" has become a code word for "Black," as this denies the rich and historically significant experiences of rural African Americans. Moreover, as the non-metro white population has been shrinking, the non-metro Latino population has been growing at a rate of two percent (USDA, 2014). Native Americans have not been ignored by media, but their inclusion has been highly informed by racial stereotypes. By continually reinforcing the idea that rural is white, various media are effectively erasing diverse rural populations from the social imaginary. This marginalization could itself be taken as a subtle act of racism.

When it comes to issues of social class, we would maintain that to a large degree, rural stereotypes are actually mostly derogations of the poor, the working poor, and the working class populations. It is not coincidental that most occupations considered "rural"—for example, farming, forestry, energy extraction—are also working class jobs. Less common are images of the well-to-do rural population, perhaps with the exception of the *Dallas* television series, featuring the wealthy and genteel Ewing family. As noted by Fulkerson and Lowe's chapter, the rural is more of a background variable for the *Dallas* series, where the focus is on personal relationships and there are fewer possibilities for negative rural stereotypes. In contrast, the gross characterizations of the inbred rural featured in horror films and reality TV series alike, emphasize the exceptionally low intelligence of the rural poor. They also suggest unpredictability, impulsiveness, erratic qualities, and generally wild behavior. For males this manifests in uncontrollable violence, while for females it manifests as hyper-sexuality, introducing layers of gender stereotype that intersect with rural identity.

From the above we hope we have made it clear that any understanding of social inequality is incomplete so long as it neglects to include rural and urban dynamics, and the ways by which they interact and intersect with other dimensions of identity. Intersectional studies should therefore identify ways

of integrating place-based identities, as it is in some cases a master identity—
that is when people identify primarily as urban or rustic (Ching and Creed,
1996).

SOME FACT CHECKING

As this volume has explored, the current imagination of rural is prone to
distortion, stereotypes, and gross characterizations, so we believe that it is
worth considering a few of the actual trends and facts that exist for rural
communities in the United States. To begin with, one of the longest running
misunderstandings of rural is that it is synonymous with agriculture, or the
related idea that most rural people are somehow involved in farming. While
it is true that rural people are more likely to be employed in agriculture than
their urban counterparts, agriculture is overall a small part of the rural economy. In the United States, 1.9 percent of the overall population is employed in
agriculture (USDA, 2015), while for rural areas it is only slightly higher.
Yes, that does mean rural people are more likely to farm, but if you examine
the overall picture, the rural economy is dominated—much like the urban
economy—by the service sector. That is to say that most rural people are
employed working in health care, education, retail, other specialty services
including finance, accounting, sales, marketing, as well as the numerous
occupations found within the criminal justice system, as rural areas are often
home to prisons, jails, treatment centers, halfway houses, and other related
institutions or organizations defined as LULUs (locally unwanted land uses).
Most affluent suburban communities are resistant to the idea of there being a
prison or waste dump in the vicinity, while rural areas often accept such
LULUs in exchange for the limited economic benefits they bring, in terms of
higher employment and an improved tax base. Overall, the economic profile
of the rural U.S. is similar to that of the country as a whole, and it is thus a
mistake to equate rural with agriculture and farming, or even to view the
contemporary rural economy as vastly different in structure from the rest of
the economy.

Another rash of rural stereotypes revolve around the ideas of violence and
sexual aggression among rural people. The image set forth portrays rural men
as being more prone to violent outbursts, while rural women are more likely
to invite sexually aggressive behavior. Most national crime data, such as the
FBI's Uniform Crime Report, suggests that rural areas have a lower violent
crime rate. For example, in 2015, the National Crime Victimization Survey
(NCVS) found that in 2012 the highest rates of violent victimization were
urban areas (3,240 out of 100,000 residents), followed by suburban areas
(2,380 out of 100,000), while in last were rural areas (2,090 out of 100,000).
Rates of aggravated assaults fall in the same order, with urban areas leading

(470 per 100,000 residents), followed by suburban areas (360 per 100,000), and last are rural areas (260 per 100,000). According to the NCVS (2015), in 2012, rates of forcible rape followed a similar pattern with the highest rate being in urban areas (180 out of 100,000 residents), followed by suburban areas (120 out of 100,000), and last are rural areas (6 per 100,000). It is important to note that crime data are inherently flawed due to uneven record-keeping and underreporting, as is particularly true of sexual crimes that are known to be underreported. Even considering these shortcomings of crime and victimization data, the patterns are strikingly consistent and suggest that overall, rural areas are the safest places to live. We therefore find that images of such media as the *Wrong Turn* movie franchise or of *Deliverance* (known for its gruesome rape scene) are baseless.

Beyond criminality, there are some other forms of danger that plague rural areas. According to the USDHHS (2012), rural areas lag behind more urbanized places across a number of health indicators, including the mortality rate for all age groups, from young children to elderly adults, as well as for the number of motor vehicle accidents, and the overall self-reported health status of residents. While rural people are suffering worse health conditions it would be a mistake to attribute this gap to the inherent wild lifestyles of rural people, as stereotypes would suggest. Rather, rural health disparities are largely explained by the fact that rural people have more limited access to health services, due partly to the physical distance required to visit medical facilities, and importantly, due to the fact that those living in rural places are less likely to have health insurance (USDHHS, 2012). With respect to the motor vehicle accident rate, the reasons are less clear, but we would propose that it may be due to the fact that rural people simply spend more time on the road driving, as physical space is a major component of rural life. Living in an urban area without a car is viable, but extremely difficult or impossible for rural populations. The key point is that the reality is always more complicated, so it is worthwhile to overcome the cultural tendency to draw unfair conclusions and commit what psychologists term the fundamental attribution error. Rural people have to live with the realities of vast physical space for all of their benefits and costs—among them, health costs.

This brief tour of some of the actual conditions confronting rural areas in the United States is not meant to be exhaustive or complete. We offer these basic facts as a way to highlight just how distorted the social imaginary has become when it considers rural life. The goal of reimagining rural is therefore more than a critical reflection on the past, it is likewise a challenge for the wider public to examine the present and future conditions of rural areas through a clearer lens, and to raise questions that will challenge the many prevailing distortions.

FUTURE DIRECTIONS

Having completed this collection of studies on cultural dynamics, we would like to briefly consider what we consider to be important next steps for the study of urban-rural dynamics. As noted in the introductory chapter, it is important to bear in mind that the material and cultural dynamics linking urban and rural people and places are inseparable. We may separate them analytically for the sake of scholarship, but they are in actuality closely intertwined. Our next project will be a collection of studies that focus more heavily on the material connections, sending the cultural dynamics into the background. Following this we expect to offer a theoretical contribution that clearly articulates material and cultural interconnections embedded in urban-rural dynamics, based on many of the inductive discoveries of this and other works. We also hope to see the focus of analysis expand upon what we have begun with our focus on dynamics in the United States, by shifting to a comparative or global focus. It will be particularly interesting to study the urban-rural dynamics of less developed nations, where much of the rural population remains employed in traditionally rural occupations.

REFERENCES

Ching, B., and Creed, G. W. (1996). Recognizing rusticity, in Ching, B., and Creed, G. W., *Knowing your place: Rural identity and cultural hierarchy*. New York: Routledge.

Fulkerson, G. M. and Thomas, A. R. (eds.). 2014. *Studies in urbanormativity: Rural community in urban society*. Lanham, MD: Lexington Books.

NCVS (National Crime Victimization Survey). (2015). Urban and rural crime. Retrieved 1/28/2016 from: http://victimsofcrime.org/docs/default-source/ncvrw2015/2015ncvrw_stats_urbanrural.pdf?sfvrsn=2.

Thomas, A. R., Lowe, B. M., Fulkerson, G. M., and Smith, P. J. 2011. *Critical rural theory: Structure, space, culture*. Lanham, MD: Lexington Books.

USDA (U.S. Department of Agriculture). (2014). Rural Hispanic population growth mirrors national trends. Retrieved 1/29/2016 from http://www.ers.usda.gov/data-products/chart-gallery/detail.aspx?chartId=49195. Economic Research Service.

———. (2015). Rural atlas data. Retrieved 1/29/2016 from http://www.ers.usda.gov/data-products/atlas-of-rural-and-small-town-america/download-the-data.aspx. Economic Research Service.

USDHHS (U.S. Department of Health and Human Services). 2012. NCHS Urban-rural classification scheme for counties. Vital and health statistics, series 2, number 154, January. Centers for Disease Control and Prevention, National Center for Health Statistics.

Appendix

*Rural Reality Series and Television Networks
(2005–2015)*

- Billy the Exterminator (2009), A&E
- American Hoggers (2011), A&E
- Cajun Justice (2012), A&E
- Duck Dynasty (2012), A&E
- Lady Hoggers (2013), A&E
- Rodeo Girls (2013), A&E
- Big Smo (2014), A&E
- Country Bucks (2014), A&E
- Duck Commander:Before the Dynasty (2014), A&E
- Alaska Wildlife Troopers (2011), Animal Planet
- Call of the Wildman (2011), Animal Planet
- Finding Bigfoot (2011), Animal Planet
- Hillbilly Handfishin (2011), Animal Planet
- Gator Boys (2012), Animal Planet
- North Woods Law (2012), Animal Planet
- American River Renegades (2014), Animal Planet
- Cold River Cash (2014), Animal Planet
- Ice Lake Rebels (2014), Animal Planet
- Yankee Jungle (2014), Animal Planet
- Alaska: Battle in the Bay (2015), Animal Planet
- Rocky Mountain Bounty Hunters (2015), Animal Planet
- Rugged Justice (2015), Animal Planet
- My Big Redneck Wedding (2008), CMT
- Bayou Billionaires (2011), CMT

- Jenny Garth: A Little Bit Country (2012), CMT
- My Big Redneck Vacation (2012), CMT
- Redneck Island (2012), CMT
- Guntucky (2013), CMT
- Hillbillies for Hire (2013), CMT
- Swamp Pawn (2013), CMT
- My Big Redneck Family (2014), CMT
- Party Down South (2014), CMT
- Party Down South 2 (2014), CMT
- Operation Wild (2010), Destination America
- Buying Alaska (2012), Destination America
- Hillbilly Blood—A Hardscrabble Life (2012), Destination America
- Buying the Bayou (2013), Destination America
- Buying Hawaii (2013), Destination America
- Mountain Monsters (2013), Destination America
- Alaska Monsters (2014), Destination America
- Amish Haunting (2014), Destination America
- Prepper Hillbillies (2014), Destination America
- Buying the Rockies (2015), Destination America
- Deadliest Catch (2005), Discovery
- Gold Rush (2010), Discovery
- Alaska (The Last Frontier) (2011), Discovery
- American Loggers (2011), Discovery
- Flying Wild Alaska (2011), Discovery
- Moonshiners (2011), Discovery
- Swamp Brothers (2011), Discovery
- Amish Mafia (2012), Discovery
- Bering Sea Gold (2012), Discovery
- Jungle Gold (2012), Discovery
- Yukon Men (2012), Discovery
- Backyard Oil (2013), Discovery
- Porter Ridge (2013), Discovery
- Tickle (2013), Discovery
- Weed Country (2013), Discovery
- Alaska Bush People (2014), Discovery
- Billy Bob's Gags to Riches (2014), Discovery
- Boss Hog (2014), Discovery
- Edge of Alaska (2014), Discovery
- Pacific Warriors (2015), Discovery
- Sons of Winter (2015), Discovery
- Building Alaska (2012), DIY
- Amish Renegades (2014), DIY
- Vanilla Ice Goes Amish (2014), DIY

- Farm Kings (2012), GAC
- Frontier House (2012), GAC
- Living Countryfied (2012), GAC
- Barnwood Builders (2013), GAC
- Barn Hunters (2014), GAC
- Farm Queens (2014), GAC
- Growing up Gator (2014), GAC
- Moving Country (2014), GAC
- Ice Road Truckers (2007), History
- Ax Men (2008), History
- Swamp Loggers (2009), History
- Swamp People (2010), History
- Big Shrimpin (2011), History
- Mountain Men (2012), History
- American Jungle (2013), History
- Legend of Shelby the Swampman (2013), History
- Appalachian Outlaws (2014), History
- Down East Dickering (2014), History
- The Hunt (2014), History
- Great Wild North (2015), History
- Mississippi Men (2015), History
- The Woodsmen (2015), History
- Alaska State Troopers (2009), National Geographic
- Border Wars (2010), National Geographic
- Wild Justice (2010), National Geographic
- Rocket City Rednecks (2011), National Geographic
- American Colony: Meet the Hutterites (2012), National Geographic
- Amish: Out of Order (2012), National Geographic
- Mudcats (2012), National Geographic
- Kentucky Justice (2013), National Geographic
- Life Below Zero (2013), National Geographic
- Snake Salvation (2013), National Geographic
- Ultimate Survival Alaska (2013), National Geographic
- Yukon Gold (2013), National Geographic
- Filthy Riches (2014), National Geographic
- Life Free or Die (2014), National Geographic
- Smoky Mountain Money (2014), National Geographic
- Southern Justice (2014), National Geographic
- The Legend of Mick Dodge (2014), National Geographic
- The Pioneers (2014), National Geographic
- Badlands Texas (2015), National Geographic
- Port Protection (2015), National Geographic
- Rocky Mountain Law (2015), National Geographic

- Yukon River Run (2015), National Geographic
- High Tech Rednecks (2015), MAVTV
- Buckwild (2013), MTV
- Hollywood Hillbillies (2014), REELZ Channel
- Rural Heritage (2010), RFD-TV
- Tough Grit—The Rural America Challenge (2012), RFD-TV
- Cowboy Authentic (2013), RFD-TV
- R U Faster than a Redneck (2013), Speed Network
- Coal (2011), Spike
- Breaking Amish (2012), TLC
- Here Comes Honey Boo Boo (2012), TLC
- Escaping Alaska (2014), TLC
- Black Gold (2008), truTV
- Southern Fried Stings (2010), tru TV
- Bear Swamp Recovery (2011), tru TV
- Lizard Lick Towing (2011), tru TV
- Way Out West (2014), tru TV

Index

About the Contributors

Leanne M. Avery is associate professor in science education in the Department of Elementary Education and Reading at SUNY Oneonta. Her research focuses on science and engineering photodocumentation work with rural children. Her research provides key insights into how these children learn, where they learn, and from whom they learn. Via place-based teacher development in collaboration with other university faculty, teachers, students, and families, she also works to promote ways in which to value this knowledge base in the classroom. By anchoring student learning to the local rural context as well as connecting this knowledge to global science and twenty-first-century skills, her work enables rural children to navigate and succeed in a rapidly changing world. She has published broadly in academic journals, practitioner newsletters, and at numerous regional, national, and international conferences. She earned her BS from Cornell University, an MS from SUNY Albany and Cornell University, and a PhD from Cornell University. Dr. Avery's newest project entails exploring the role intergenerational knowledge plays in school science.

Barbara Ching is a professor of English and department chair at Iowa State University She is the author of *Wrong's What I Do Best: Hard Country Music and Contemporary Culture* (2001) and many articles on rural identity, popular music, and film. She edited and introduced *Old Roots, New Routes: The Cultural Politics of Alt. Country Music* with Pamela Fox (2008), *The Scandal of Susan Sontag* (2009) and with ethnographer Gerald Creed, she introduced and edited *Knowing Your Place: Rural Identity and Cultural Hierarchy* (1996).

Gregory M. Fulkerson is associate professor of sociology at the State University of New York at Oneonta. He received his PhD from North Carolina State University, with specializations in global social change and development, as well as rural and community sociology. He earned his MA from Western Michigan University and his BS from Michigan State University. He currently teaches and develops courses related to research methods, data analysis, environment, community, and demography. His current research interests are on global environmental and energy issues as well as urban-rural dynamics. Dr. Fulkerson is co-editing the book series, *Studies in Urban–Rural Dynamics*. He has published in a variety of journals and encyclopedias, is co-author of *Critical Rural Theory: Space*Structure*Culture*, and co-editor of *Studies in Urbanormativity: Rural Community in Urban Society*. He has presented at several regional and national conferences, including the Rural Sociological Society, Eastern Sociological Society, American Sociological Association, and New York State Sociological Association.

Karen Hayden, PhD, is associate professor in the Department of Criminology at Merrimack College in North Andover, Massachusetts. Dr. Hayden earned her PhD from Northeastern University and her MA and BA from the University of New Hampshire. Dr. Hayden's areas of interest within criminology and sociology include girls, women, and crime; rural crime; law and society; and cultural criminology. Her work has appeared in *Studies in Symbolic Interaction*, *Teaching Sociology*, and she wrote two chapters in the 2014 edited volume, *Studies in Urbanormativity: Rural Community in Urban Society*. She is currently working on a book about images of rural people and places for the *Studies in Urban–Rural Dynamics* series for Lexington Books.

Karl A. Jicha, PhD, is a lecturer in the College of Agriculture and Life Science's Agricultural Institute and the Department of Sociology and Anthropology at North Carolina State University. His areas of specialization are rural sociology and place-based inequality, community sociology, global change and development, and social capital. Current research interests include social capital formation in the aftermath of natural disasters and determining the factors that contribute to disparities in access to public recreation and resultant health outcomes at the community level.

Brian M. Lowe, PhD, received his BAH and Master's in sociology from Queen's University at Kingston, Ontario, and his PhD in sociology from the University of Virginia. Dr. Lowe's research and teaching interests include sociological theories, animal and society, cultural and comparative-historical sociology, and spectacular conflicts. He is the author of *Emerging Moral Vocabularies: The Creation and Establishment of New Forms of Moral and Ethical Meanings* (2006), co-author of *Critical Rural Theory: Struc-*

ture*Space*Culture, and several articles and book chapters. In 2008 Lowe became chair of the Animals and Society section of the American Sociological Association.

Pilar Erin McKay, PhD, is a communication professor, rural arts and culture advocate, and active placemaking practitioner. Committed to applying theory in practice, she serves as an accelerator on many rural-based start-up projects. She co-founded Shake on the Lake, a Shakespeare festival based in Perry, New York and is also managing partner of Silver Lake Brewing Project in Perry. Dr. McKay conducts multimedia communication research including producing a film on immigrants' impact on food culture in a post-industrial, northeastern Pennsylvania rural community and conducting academic research on the influence of news media on place identity. She studied rural sociology and applied economics & management at Cornell University (College of Agriculture and Life Sciences), and social research methodology at the University of California, Los Angeles (College of Education & Information Sciences). She currently teaches advertising and research methods at American University.

John W. Sipple, PhD, is associate professor in the Department of Development Sociology at Cornell University. Additionally, he serves as director of the New York State Center for Rural Schools and co-faculty director of Cornell's Community and Regional Development Institute. Professor Sipple's research analyzes the implementation of education and social policies on local communities and their public schools. He is currently studying the impact of state and federal policies (e.g., finance and staffing, shared municipal services, pre-kindergarten, school-based health) on rural communities. He has published broadly in academic journals, for more popular audiences, and at numerous regional, national, and international conferences. He earned his BA from Dartmouth College, an MEd from the University of Virginia, and a PhD from the University of Michigan.

Alexander R. Thomas is professor of sociology at the State University of New York at Oneonta. He received his PhD from Northeastern University with specializations in urban sociology and deviance and criminology. He currently teaches courses related to urban sociology and criminology. His current research focuses on the economic and environmental relationship between cities and their hinterlands, or urban-rural dynamics. He is currently co-editor of the Lexington Books series, *Studies in Urban–Rural Dynamics*. He has authored or co-authored eight books, including *In Gotham's Shadow* (2003), *The Evolution of the Ancient City* (2010), and *Critical Rural Theory* (2011; with Brian Lowe, Gregory Fulkerson, and Polly Smith), as well as scholarly articles and technical reports. He has presented at several regional and national conferences, including the Rural Sociological Society, Eastern Sociological Society, American Sociological Association, and New York State Sociological Association.